BICENTENNIAL

YEAR

The Story of a Rutgers Celebration

By George H. Holsten, Jr.

Rutgers University Press

New Brunswick, New Jersey

Preface

THE more-than-a-yearlong celebration during 1966 and 1967 of the 200th anniversary of Rutgers University—its original charter from New Jersey's Royal Governor, William Franklin, was granted on November 10, 1766—was a fond look at the institution's history and a long and serious look at its future. This book is intended as a fond look at that celebration and a small memorial to the Bicentennial Year.

The Bicentennial was a birthday party. But more than anything else, it was an attempt to recall some of the major events of two centuries of educational and scholarly endeavor as they relate to the present-day problems and opportunities of the institution which has in only very recent times become Rutgers – The State University.

This book does not attempt to recall all the events of the anniversary celebration nor even to report the major occasions in full. In most instances the proceedings of the various academic and scholarly meetings are being published in full or at some length for the benefit particularly of the participants and other scholars interested in the special areas of these conferences. And, secondly, this book is only an attempt to recall some of the highlights of the Bicentennial as a sampler of the atmosphere and character of the Rutgers celebration.

This book attempts no evaluation of Bicentennial activities. It follows the general policy of publishing most or all of the texts of the major birthday events—the Anniversary Commencement, the Bicentennial Convocation, and the dedication of the Law School building—but beyond that the author is content simply to report the highlights of what was said or done. If one or another meeting is given greater attention than another, it is because of the author's belief in the general interest in the subject as compared with some of the more specialized topics. The mathematicians who met at Rutgers in 1966 no doubt heard some very erudite discussions in their field, but for the most part only mathematicians understood and appreciated the presentations.

No doubt this story of Rutgers Bicentennial could have devoted many pages to the preparations and the behind-the-scenes activities which made the principal events possible. Van Wie Ingham, former executive secretary of the Rutgers College of Agriculture, was appointed Bicentennial Coordinator in March of 1963. The account of the effort, the trials, and the frustrations of Mr. Ingham and his co-coordinator, Miss Elizabeth Durham, would furnish a considerable story—but its reading would be of interest mainly to future coordinators of university bicentennial celebrations—a singularly limited clientele.

The preparation and conduct of most of the Bicentennial events involved outlays of varying sums of money and if it had not been for the interest of the Legislature and the Governor in naming and financing the State University Bicentennial Commission, many of the significant and worthwhile aspects of the celebration would have been shelved.

Empowered with State appropriations totaling $150,000 over two years, the Commission carefully considered a large number of proposals for the Rutgers birthday celebration. It underwrote most of the principal events and played a tremendously important role in making the 200th birthday party of New Jersey's State University a memorable event.

The Honorable Walter H. Jones, former State legislator from Bergen County who, while serving as an assemblyman in 1945 introduced the legislation which designated Rutgers as the State University, served as chairman of the Commission. The other members, in either the first or the second year of its existence, were Mrs. Winfield Bonynge, then president of the Associate Alumnae of Douglass College; Hugh N. Boyd, publisher of the New Brunswick *Home News;* State Senator Edward J. Cra-

State University Bicentennial Commission at its organizational meeting on December 27, 1965: from left, standing: Supreme Court Justice Frederick Hall, Senator John A. Lynch, Hugh N. Boyd, Everett Scherer; seated, Mrs. Marion West Higgins, Walter H. Jones, and Mrs. Winfield Bonynge.

biel of Middlesex County; Associate Justice Frederick W. Hall of the State Supreme Court; Mrs. William F. Higgins, former Bergen County assemblywoman; State Senator John A. Lynch of Middlesex; former State Senator William E. Ozzard of Somerset County, since appointed to membership on New Jersey's Public Utilities Commission; Everett M. Scherer, a Newark attorney; Fred R. Sullivan, president of Walter Kidde, Inc.; Assemblyman Norman Tanzman of Middlesex; and Mrs. Douglas G. Wagner, a former University trustee, former president of the Douglass College alumnae, and past president of the State Federation of Women's Clubs.

The Rutgers birthday celebration officially opened on January 4 when Governor Richard J. Hughes came to the campus to proclaim 1966 as the Bicentennial Year in New Jersey. Theoretically it ended with the last day of December of that year, but the fact is that it spilled over into 1967. The Rutgers University-Japan Scholars Conference was held in April of 1967 and the second and third sessions of the Bicentennial Conference entitled "The University and the Challenges of Urban Society," were held during the early months of that year.

Perhaps that is the significant thing about celebrations of this kind. The participants do some looking back and in so doing are inspired to new efforts, new approaches, new ideas.

The Rutgers University Bicentennial is now officially ended and even any informal celebrating is out of date, but the birthday festivities have kicked up enough intellectual dust so that it will not easily be put down. Rutgers and the members of its large and growing family took a fond look at its past and decided that the first two hundred years may have been the hardest but were only the beginning toward ultimate institutional fulfillment.

GEORGE H. HOLSTEN, JR.

New Brunswick, New Jersey
December, 1967

Acknowledgments

CONSCIOUSLY or otherwise, a great many people helped in the writing of this book. Any comprehensive acknowledgment would require several pages and probably leave out someone important anyway. But there are two people whose help has been invaluable and who must be mentioned: George Lukac, editor of the *Rutgers Alumni Monthly*, from whom I borrowed mercilessly, and Miss Mary Merkoski, my secretary, who typed and retyped the manuscript and dug out exact dates, names, and numbers whenever I needed them.

Contents

Preface   v

Acknowledgments   ix

THE BICENTENNIAL BEGINS   3

MUSIC TO CELEBRATE BY   9

THE STUDENTS GET IN ON THE PARTY   21

THE 200th ANNIVERSARY COMMENCEMENT   35

INTELLECTUAL WEIGHT LIFTING   51

GODSPEED IN THE CENTURIES TO COME   93

"SINCERE ESTEEM AND RESPECT"   125

RUTGERS AROUND THE WORLD   143

A STIRRING AND EXCITING VIEW   157

APPENDICES   171

    The Governor's Proclamation   171

    The Glee Club's Bicentennial Tour   172

    The Gonfalons of Rutgers University   176

    President Gross's Commencement Address   178

    Major Special Events of the Bicentennial Year   182

    Article by William Sloane in *Publishers' Weekly*   186

    Article by John K. Hutchens in *Saturday Review*   188

Text of Mr. Justice Warren's Address,
    September 10, 1966   193

Colleges, Universities, Learned Societies, and Foundations
    Who Sent Greetings or Other Tributes to Rutgers   198

Address by Dr. Mason W. Gross to Holland Society,
    November 7, 1966   205

Rutgers Night Around the World Gatherings   213

Address by President Robert F. Goheen of Princeton
    University at New Brunswick Charter Night Dinner,
    November 10, 1966   218

John Lenkey III's letter to Colonel Vincent Kramer
    Describing the Planting of the Rutgers Flag on
    Mt. Fujiyama   222

A Report on the Genovese Case   226

Bicentennial Committees   231

Rutgers Fact Book of 1966   233

INDEX

The Bicentennial Begins

FRANKLIN–RUTGERS–HUGHES

COLONEL Henry Rutgers in 1825 acquired one of the most enduring and lively memorials any man could possibly wish for. Although he was a man of many accomplishments, it is doubtful that he ever believed the struggling little college he aided would grow to its present size and lusty condition. If he had ever entertained such thoughts he must have realized he had made a very good bargain.

Although he was a philanthropist as well as a patriot who had served as an officer in the New York militia, he was, after all, a Dutchman, and he never showered largess on the institution that adopted his name and, in so doing, gave him a living and presumably perpetual memorial.

Colonel Henry arranged for his namesake to receive the income on his bond for $5,000 and paid for a fine bronze bell which was hung in the cupola of Queen's Building. That bell hangs there today and it is rung to signal momentous occasions in the institution's life. At one time it was used for more routine events in the college activities—the changing of classes and daily worship—but nowadays there is no longer daily chapel and the size of the institution makes impractical its use as a signal for the change of classes. Instead, the sounding of that deep bronze voice is reserved for special occasions: the inauguration of a president, an undefeated football season, any signal success or happening, athletic or otherwise.

Thus it was that at midnight on December 31, 1965, a group of dedicated and hearty souls gathered in one of the offices on the

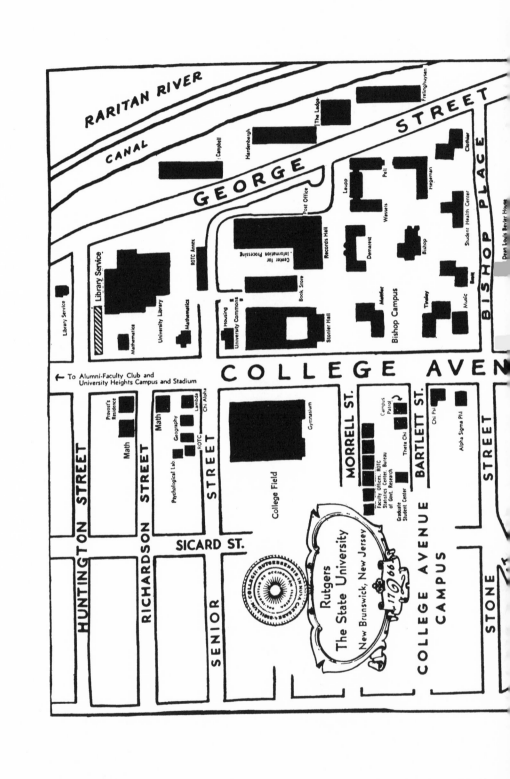

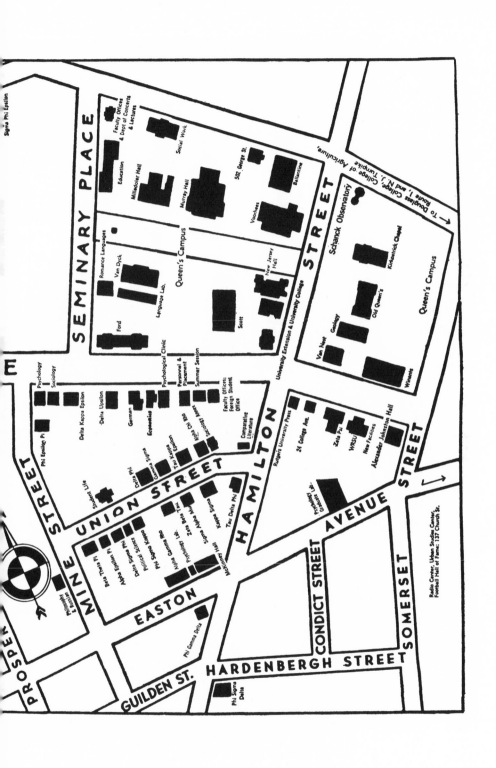

ground floor of Queen's. They grouped around a small wooden cupboard which houses the lower end of the rope attached to the Henry Rutgers bell. One after another they took turns in giving lusty tugs to that rope, and as the bell boomed above them the Rutgers Bicentennial Year had begun.

This was the actual if not the official opening of the University's 200th birthday celebration. The more ceremonious beginning came a few days later on the afternoon of January 4 when New Jersey's Governor Richard J. Hughes gave the State's official blessing to the celebration and proclaimed 1966 as Rutgers Bicentennial Year in New Jersey.

The Bicentennial Begins—Ringing the Henry Rutgers bell in Queen's at midnight on December 31, 1966.

Governor William Franklin   Mary d'Evelin Franklin

He read the proclamation in Kirkpatrick Chapel as Rutgers notables in the flesh and on canvas looked on. Two of the portraits hung in the chapel had particular significance that day for one of them was a likeness of William Franklin, the Royal Governor of New Jersey, who on November 10, 1766, handed down the college charter. The other was a portrait of the Governor's second wife, Mary d'Evelin Franklin.

The portraits of the Franklins had been lent to the University for display during the Bicentennial by Mrs. William Castle of Wilmington, Delaware, a descendant of the Franklins. They were hung on the sides of the chapel platform and, if those painted eyes could have seen or if Governor Hughes had looked up at the right angle, they and he would have been able to see in the window above the front of the chapel a representation of the historic day in 1766 which the Bicentennial was marking. There in a stained-glass window is a representation of Governor Franklin as he presented the charter of Queen's College on November 10, 1766.

In proclaiming the Rutgers Bicentennial Year in New Jersey Governor Hughes took notice of the "invaluable services which Rutgers – The State University has already performed for this State and the nation and the greater service which it will fulfill in the future," and he urged the people of New Jersey to join in the tribute.

Governor Richard J. Hughes signs
the official New Jersey
Bicentennial proclamation.

Governor Hughes proclaims 1966
as the Bicentennial Year in New
Jersey.

The Governor said that "As a colonial college, a land-grant college and a state university, Rutgers uniquely exemplifies the triple traditions of American higher education. Because it has constantly adapted itself to new tasks, it has been able to prepare men and women for a world characterized by rapid change. It has provided the technical knowledge demanded by an age of science. It has grounded its graduates in the enlarging vision of the liberal arts. As a public institution it has fostered democratic approaches to modern problems."*

Governor Hughes had given the Bicentennial the State's official blessing. Dr. Richard P. McCormick, professor of history, University historian, and an alumnus of Rutgers College in the Class of 1938, was to give it historic setting. In a very brief address—little more than six hundred words—he covered the highlights from the early beginnings through the struggles to growth and accomplishment:

---

*See Appendix A—Text of the Proclamation issued by Governor Richard J. Hughes of New Jersey, January 4, 1966.

We are stirred by many feelings as we inaugurate the Bicentennial of Rutgers—gratitude to those who founded and sustained the institution; pride in the achievements of innumerable distinguished alumni; reverence for a long and rich heritage. One of the small company of nine colleges that antedate this nation's independence, Rutgers today shares the additional distinction of being one of America's great state universities.

The circumstances surrounding the origins of the college were anything but auspicious. In 1755 one spirited faction of the discordant Dutch Reformed Church resolved "to plant a university or seminary for young men destined for study in the learned languages and in the liberal arts, and who are to be instructed in the philosophical sciences." Without resources of any kind, and in the face of opposition from the church authorities in the Netherlands as well as from their local adversaries, these zealous men stubbornly pursued their goal.

They sought a charter for their college from successive governors of New Jersey and were rebuffed. Finally, on November 10, 1766, Governor William Franklin—to whom we do honor today—granted their petition. Even now the way was not clear, for, although a board of trustees was constituted, it found difficulties with certain of the charter provisions and could not proceed at once to establish the college. It was necessary to seek a revised charter which, again, was graciously granted by Governor Franklin on March 20, 1770.

Meanwhile, modest funds had been raised, New Brunswick had been selected over rival towns as the site of the college, and in 1771 classes began under a single tutor in a former tavern—the Sign of the Red Lion—on lower Albany Street.

Queen's College had been launched, but its destiny long remained uncertain. Its career was disrupted and all but ended by the dislocations associated with the War for Independence. Later, on three occasions, classes had to be suspended for intervals of several years because of a paucity of funds. When the college assumed the name of Rutgers in 1825 it did so to honor a distinguished benefactor, but also, we suspect, with the hope that a change of name might produce a change of fortune.

Such was indeed the case. The decades that followed were marked by slow but certain progress. Closely associated with one of the smallest Protestant denominations, the college could not look to a large constituency nor anticipate vast resources. Near the end of its first century a new and promising era seemingly dawned when Rutgers was designated the land-grant college of New Jersey. However, nearly forty years were to pass before the State made its first appropriation in support of its state college. Nevertheless, the college faithfully met its public obligations, combining the tradition of service to the State with the older tradition of scholarly integrity.

Excellent though it was in its fine standards, Rutgers still remained small, and its identity—partly private, partly public —remained uncertain. It had yet to encounter its true destiny.

But now, within the past two decades, that destiny has at last become manifest, and the most wondrous era in the history of Rutgers glows with unprecedented achievements. Rutgers has found its mission as the State University of New Jersey, and the State at last has confidently conferred that role on Rutgers.

We celebrate the two centuries of our past with gratitude, pride, reverence, and wonder. We boast not alone of age but of dedicated lives, worthy accomplishments, splendid ideals. The backward look we take on this happy occasion gladdens our hearts, but, equally, it fortifies our faith in our ability to grasp the promise of the future.

The ceremony in the Chapel was followed by a reception in Queen's for the distinguished guests. The 1966 Bicentennial had officially begun.

Music to Celebrate By

MUSIC–SOUND OF THE BICENTENNIAL

WHEN Robert Moevs, professor of music and a composer of considerable reputation, was commissioned in 1964 to write a special choral work to commemorate the Rutgers Bicentennial, it was all a part of the University's intention that, above all else, the Bicentennial was to be celebrated with music.

It was. The 200th anniversary celebration had its meetings of learned societies, the gorgeous pageantry of its Convocation, and the excitement of its Charter Night birthday parties "around the world," but the one steady sound of the Bicentennial was the sound of music—jazz, classical, organ recital, contemporary, vocal, instrumental, and as a crowning touch, the Moevs work for choir and orchestra, "Et Occidentem Illustra."

Vladimir Horowitz, the world's foremost pianist, paid a special tribute to the University and its Bicentennial by performing in New Brunswick in his first concert outside of New York City in fourteen years. He was superb.

There was hardly a week during the Bicentennial Year without one or more music offerings on campus, but Rutgers music went far beyond the campus as the University Choir sang with symphony orchestras in New York, Philadelphia, and Boston, and the Glee Club made a memorable musical tour through Europe, including in its itinerary a concert at the University of Utrecht, Rutgers' academic godfather.

Professor Moevs's "Et Occidentem Illustra" was first performed after the Bicentennial Year. It had its premiere with the Boston Symphony Orchestra in Boston on February 24, 1967, but spiritually it was an important part of the celebration, an instrumental and vocal monument to two hundred years of educational achievement.

The Moevs work was repeated for the Rutgers family audience and area music patrons in a special concert in the University gymnasium on March 2 and then performed again at Carnegie Hall on March 4.

A truly contemporary work, "Et Occidentem Illustra" takes its text partially from Dante's *Divine Comedy* and partially from the commission given to Theodore Frelinghuysen in 1755 "to plant a university or seminary for young men destined for study in the learned languages and in the liberal arts, and who are to be instructed in the philosophical sciences; also that it may be a school of the prophets in which young Levites and Nazarites of God may be prepared to enter upon the ministerial office in the Church of God."

The title of the work is, of course, taken from the Rutgers motto, "Sol iustitiae et occidentem illustra," which indicated the fervent hope of the college's founders that it would help to bring cultural and intellectual activity to the New World.

Preceding and leading directly to the work proper is a Latin Procemium for reciting chorus and percussion, with the opening salutation from the Frelinghuysen Commission. The text from Dante's *Divine Comedy* is found in Canto 26, lines 112-120, of the *Inferno*. There Ulysses urges his followers to continue their search for knowledge and virtue.

For its premiere "Et Occidentem Illustra" had as conductor Erich Leinsdorf, a long time friend of Rutgers and the holder of its honorary Doctor of Music degree awarded in 1952. The Moevs work was performed in a program which included Haydn's "Creation" Mass and Strauss' *Daphne*.

Michael Steinberg, music critic of the Boston *Globe*, wrote of the premiere performance of "Et Occidentem Illustra" at Boston:

"Et Occidentem Illustra" was composed by Robert Moevs for the bicentennial celebrations at Rutgers where he teaches. The title is taken from the university's motto, "Sol iustitiae et occidentem illustra," itself adopted from that of the University of Utrecht; the text uses part of the commission given in 1755 to Theodore Frelinghuysen concerning the establishment of institutions of learning in America, and the nine lines of Ulysses' exhortation to his sailors as found in the 26th Canto of Dante's "Inferno."

The opening salutation, in which "sapientia" and "virtue" are key words as "virtue" and "conoscenza" are in the Dante excerpt, is set apart in the composition. It uses mainly percussion with the chorus, and the chorus itself shouts, murmurs, speaks, rather than sings.

After this dramatic call to attention, an anvil stroke introduces that extraordinary passage in which Dante has Ulysses remind his sailors that they "were not formed to live like unto brutes, but to press on toward virtue and knowledge," urging them to explore even the unpeopled worlds beyond the sun.

Moevs has devised an exciting declamation for these words. They are given in small units that become smaller and more widely separated as the work goes on. Much of the choral writing is sharply, almost percussively, declamatory, but Moevs also makes a grand and expressive effect with long sustained lines, as in the magnificent and visionary expansion on the words, "you have reached the West."

All this is underlined, surrounded, articulated by imaginatively conceived orchestral writing. Its broken texture is characteristically contemporary but the emphasis is on the continuity that binds the rapidly shifting sounds together. Indeed, the sense of continuity, of the ability confidently to bridge large musical spaces, is an impressive achievement on Moevs' part. Even at the end, when the choral interventions occur very far apart, with each, one immediately picks up the thread. Moevs has learned well the lessons in Stravinsky's "Threni."

"Et Occidentem Illustra" is a strong and gripping work, of considerable individuality. It is also entrancing as a piece of virtuoso writing for chorus and orchestra, and that aspect also made itself strongly felt in Friday's (Feb. 24, 1967) performance. F. Austin Walter is obviously a choral conductor of extraordinary ability, and his Rutgers University Chorus is superb. In the Moevs, the singers sang the difficult pitches, which often are not doubled in the orchestra, with assurance and accuracy; they were magnificently confident and precise in the equally difficult rhythms; they sang with a clean, warm, unforced tone. There were a few rough moments in the orchestra, from which Leinsdorf and the players quickly recovered with ready professionalism, but there was much good playing as well, and the performance was altogether an effective one.

Allen Hughes, critic of the *New York Times*, reviewing the performance of the Moevs work at Carnegie Hall on March 4, 1967 wrote:

It might be interesting to know exactly why the Boston Symphony performed the Moevs piece. The work is not so bad as some angry boos at the end of the performance suggested, but it scarcely seemed good enough to merit the attention it got.

Mr. Moevs' musical setting is contemporary with a vengeance. It begins with a speaking chorus and percussion and moves through planned reciting chaos into sparse Webern-like music that contains some nice sound effects. The esoteric texts are rendered incomprehensible. There are no music innovations here and no improvements, refinements or unusually expressive uses of past ones. In the end, the work seems more pretentious than anything else. The performance it got was worthy of a masterpiece.

Mr. Hughes also said that the Rutgers University Choir was "big, well-balanced and smartly trained by F. Austin Walter."

Dr. Walter, who is more affectionately known as "Soup," had been receiving this kind of plaudit for many years, but the Bicentennial brought special attention to this dedicated musician and leader of the Rutgers Choir and the Rutgers Glee Club.

For twenty-six days during the summer of 1966 Soup and his Glee Club performed a specially effective ambassadorial task on behalf of their University. The sixty-five members of that very competent musical organization made a European concert tour which took them to the Netherlands, West Germany, Luxembourg, and France.

One of the highlights of the Glee Club trip was Rutgers' first European "Commencement." The Rutgers singers had had to leave before the 200th Anniversary Commencement in New Brunswick and the eight seniors in the group missed the ceremonies and their diplomas.

But, unknown to them, the diplomas went along in Dr. Walter's suitcase and were presented by Dr. H. M. J. Scheffer, then the Rector Magnificus of the University of Utrecht, in the historic auditorium of that institution on the night of June 3. The "commencement" at Utrecht followed a formal concert in the hall where the Treaty of Utrecht had been signed in 1713.*

The story of the Horowitz concert was told most eloquently by Howard Klein, music writer and critic of the *New York Times*. Mr. Klein wrote in the *Times* of May 9, 1966:

More than 3,000 people jammed into the Rutgers University gymnasium here this afternoon to hear Vladimir Horowitz play. It was the 62-year-old pianist's first recital outside New York since 1953, and there was the usual Horowitz hysteria before, during and after the concert. Mr. Horowitz played at Carnegie Hall last May 9 and again this April 17.

The concert was announced two weeks ago, and the university was immediately deluged with ticket requests. Julius Bloom, who is the executive director of Carnegie Hall and who teaches here, persuaded Mr. Horowitz to give the recital. The pianist wanted to play for students and others who had never heard him.

The price range was $2 to $6. All reserved-seat tickets were

---

*A very lively story of the Rutgers Glee Club's singing tour in 1966 is told in an account written for the *Rutgers Alumni Monthly* of October, 1966, by John A. Vila of the Class of 1967, one of the Club's members. It is found in Appendix B.

gone within two days; students lined up hours before the box office opened two weeks ago. And this afternoon another long line formed for the 900 unreserved seats available.

Mr. Horowitz had arrived at 3:45. He entered the gymnasium, which is decorated with New Jersey State flags and bunting to honor the constitutional convention under way here.

He strode to the large stage that has been put up along the side wall, pulled off his gray gloves and tried out the piano. Roars of chords filled the hall. An usher, who is a member of the university glee club, gasped.

Mr. Horowitz left the stage, the doors opened and the people filed in. When he emerged to begin the recital, a storm broke out, which he quickly quelled by getting right down to business. The program was essentially the same as the April 17 recital at Carnegie Hall, but the opening Scarlatti sonata was dropped and he began right with the Beethoven.

Thirty-two Variations in C minor. It was an exhilarated Horowitz playing; there was much more fire and excitement than there had been in the April recital. There were a few wrong notes, but the control and skill of his playing never flagged. And the electrical fervor that Mr. Horowitz generated was felt throughout.

At the end of the Rachmaninoff Etude Tableau, which was the last of three encores, he was still beaming broadly and waving to the balcony full of students.

The only unusual thing was the ringing of a telephone in Scriabin's Sonata No. 10, which added another trill to the music. Mr. Horowitz was unperturbed.

Another change in the program was the substitution of a Mazurka in F minor for the Chopin E minor Nocturne.

Reaction to the performance was typical—bravos and cheers and sustained applause from beginning to end. Most listeners had never heard the virtuoso before, and they were amazed. One man said, "He looks so human. I expected to see a fire-breathing dragon."

One man drove up this afternoon 400 miles from Virginia Beach. And two students flew down from Canada. On their way to New Brunswick, Mr. and Mrs. Horowitz noticed a car pass them on the New Jersey Turnpike, then slow down and drive alongside. A young woman held up a hastily made sign that read "Bravo." Then she flashed two tickets for the recital.

Mr. Horowitz told his driver to "follow that car—they know where I am going."

Now that the move outside New York has been made—and judging from the smiles on Mr. Horowitz's face after the concert it was a success that he will want to repeat—the pianist may step up his concert activities and plan small tours.

If he does, he will have a ready and willing audience where-ever he chooses to play. As one young woman remarked at the intermission, "This is the best thing that ever happened to Rutgers."

From the standpoint of music lovers it was, indeed, "the best thing that ever happened to Rutgers."

But there were many other exciting musical events during the Bicentennial Year, too many to list, but the outstanding events should be recalled.

The Norwegian Festival Orchestra—officially the Musiksel-skabet Harmonien from the Bergen International Festival—tour-ing the United States for the first time as part of the celebration of its own 200th anniversary, came to the Rutgers concert stage on March 2, 1966, to participate in the Bicentennial.

This outstanding orchestra, under the royal patronage of King Olaf V and directed by Oivin Fjeldstad, venerable music director of the Oslo Philharmonic, in its Rutgers concert featured the works of Edvard Grieg, but also included compositions by Johan Svendsen, Harald Asevered and Klaus Egge. At the conclu-sion of the concert the conductor presented President Gross with a scroll bringing greetings from the University of Bergen and an inscribed book from the orchestra as Bicentennial remembrances to Rutgers.

When the London Symphony Orchestra performed in New Brunswick on April 1, Barry Tuckwell, Order of the British Em-pire, chairman of the board of the self-governing orchestra and its principal horn player, presented Dr. Gross with a scroll of Bicen-tennial greetings from the orchestra.

Hendrik Fasmer, left, chairman of the board of the 200-year-old Musikselskabet "Harmonien" of Bergen, Norway, presents a scroll from the University of Bergen to President Gross.

Greetings from the Master of the Queen's Musick

The scroll had been signed by Sir Arthur Bliss, Master of the Queen's Musick (cq) and honorary president of the orchestra. A composition of Sir Arthur's, Royal Fanfare, opened the program as a salute to the University's Bicentennial.

The greetings from the Master of the Queen's Musick:

I warmly greet Rutgers, The State University on its bicentenary and I am proud that the Orchestra is taking part in the celebration of this important event.

The members of the Orchestra recall with much pleasure their former visit, and both they and I offer the State University congratulations and best wishes on the occasion of this notable milestone in its distinguished history.

The Pittsburgh Symphony Orchestra, celebrating its 40th anniversary in 1966, paid a special tribute to Rutgers on its 200th when it presented its concert in the gymnasium series on October 31, 1966.

William Steinberg, director of the Pittsburgh Symphony Orchestra, presents recordings of Brahms and Beethoven to President Gross.

composers to the Rutgers campuses and to other audiences in New York and on college concert stages around the nation.

In announcing the program President Gross said that the Rockefeller grant was "an emphatic vote of confidence in both our music program and New Jersey's potential for musical development. The ensemble should strengthen our teaching and concert program and make the University a more vital factor in the world of music."

Rutgers' steadily growing musical offerings were also enhanced during the Bicentennial Year by the arrangement which brought Evelyne Crochet, talented young French artist, to campus as pianist in residence. Miss Crochet has played for a number of campus audiences in New Brunswick and at Newark and Camden and she has made top-level instruction in piano available to gifted but developing talent among the student body and faculty.

Organ music also played an important role in the Rutgers musical presentations. David Drinkwater, University organist, played a series of midday concerts in Kirkpatrick Chapel which have appealed to a growing group of music lovers who sacrifice part of their lunch hour to listen to this competent musician on the good chapel organ. The Rutgers organ was completely rebuilt in recent years to an instrument on a level with some of the finest in the nation. The midday concerts were in addition to a Sunday evening series which brought such visiting performers as Maurice and Marie-Madeleine Durufle, Carl Weinrich, and Francis Jackson to Kirkpatrick as guest organists.

Music was the sound to the Rutgers Bicentennial Year. There were more than fifty concerts appealing to a wide variety of musical tastes and demonstrating that, although New Jersey may not yet be aware of what has happened, Rutgers is the musical capital of its State.

As the magazine *Musical America* said recently, Julius Bloom, the University's manager of concerts and lectures, is providing "perhaps the most adventurous collection of programs on the academic circuit."

The Students
Get in on the Party

RUTGERS undergraduates evinced an early and lasting interest in the Bicentennial, carried out their own serious and significant programs, and also produced some light touches which helped brighten up the year. Certainly one of the most exciting aspects of the Bicentennial was the 1966 football season, which should be included in the story of undergraduate participation even though the alumni and the fans may feel that they "own" the game on Saturday afternoon.

The Class of 1966 took special pride in its status as the Bicentennial Class and at least one of its members expressed dismay because he would be graduated before the celebration had ended. He was assured that alumni too could take part in the festivities.

There is probably nothing very noteworthy in the fact that the undergraduates wanted to get in on a party; there is much that is heart-warming in their seriousness of purpose and their unceasing enthusiasm.

While scores of students in all divisions were involved in the planning and arranging for the undergraduate activities, the stories of a few illustrate the effort and the intelligence they all put into their part of the Bicentennial.

Gary L. Falkin, a member of the Class of 1967, who served as chairman of the committee which arranged the intercollegiate student conference on "Ethics in Our Time," held on the New Brunswick campus on March 18, 19, and 20, first became involved with its planning while a sophomore at the end of 1964. Later he had to resign from the Rutgers College Student Council to handle his part of the work. Falkin estimated that from the first of 1966 on he spent ten hours a week on this major student event.

Explaining the student choice of ethics as the theme of their conference, Falkin said: "We didn't want something too scholarly. We wanted a good personal subject that could be applied to current events in the news the very weekend of the conference."

Edward J. Dauber, president of the Student Council, who also worked many hours on the conference and shared with Falkin and others the major responsibility for its functioning, had a different viewpoint:

"Ethics is almost always discussed piecemeal, in the middle of a major public problem. We thought that a conference like this could discuss ethics in a larger, more comprehensive way."

And Rolf Rudestam, a member of the Class of 1966 from California, came into the Public Relations Department one day

Gary Falkin, R'67, was chairman of student arrangements for the Intercollegiate Conference.

sium where some 2,000 students, faculty, and townspeople heard Miss Ayn Rand, author of *The Fountainhead* and *Atlas Shrugged*, and the founder of the Objectivist Movement, speak on education and culture.

The start of Miss Rand's address was delayed by a curious bit of dramatics. While the audience waited, Miss Rand, her husband, Frank O'Connor, and her protégé, Nathaniel Branden, who edits the *Objectivist Newsletter*, made it known that they were upset about the material on the author which had been used in the conference brochure. They particularly objected to what they considered an unfavorable review of one of Miss Rand's novels.

They demanded an apology before Miss Rand would go on. In a gesture which was "above and beyond the call of duty," the apology was given, reluctantly, we can only assume, by Earle W. Clifford, Jr., Dean of Student Affairs. Dean Clifford asked the audience to ignore the portions of the brochure offensive to the Russian-born novelist.

This apparently smoothed Miss Rand's ruffled feelings, and she gave her lecture. In it she dealt with her favorite theme, that the individual should be given full opportunity for freedom of development and the enjoyment of pleasure and not be tied to the needs of others less gifted or less fortunate. She spoke of Romantic Art as a guide to children arguing that they can find in it the moral choices presented in black and white which they need to understand the world.

United States Senator Clifford P. Case, 1925 Rutgers graduate and a former member of its Board of Trustees, spoke the following morning on ethics in government.

Senator Case, who has long been a leader in the campaign to raise ethical standards in all branches of government, discussed the legislation he had proposed to make members of Congress reveal their financial interests as a matter of public information. He noted that corruption in government had been highlighted by the Bobby Baker case, but said that unethical practices are not limited to the national government but are widespread throughout state, county, and municipal levels.

Senator Case said that, while the Congress has the power to police itself, it fails to do so, and noted that the Senate itself is reluctant to act against one of its own members. "It is not popular to raise these uncomfortable questions," he said, "but it must be done because there is a dirtiness and meanness to illicit practices in public offices."

The Saturday afternoon session which presented Walter P. Reuther, president of the United Automobile Workers of America, and Roger M. Blough, chairman of the board of United States Steel Corporation, in a discussion of the ethics of labor and management, proved to be the most lively and interesting session of the conference.

Reuther proposed a review board to hold hearings on all moves for either price or wage increase in the major industries. Such a board, he said, would not arrive at binding levels of agreements but would produce the basis for informed public opinion. Expectedly, Reuther claimed that the percentage of corporation profits has more than doubled that of wage increases since 1960.

U.S. Senator Clifford P. Case, R'25, talks with students at Intercollegiate Bicentennial Conference.

Roger M. Blough, left, chairman of the Board of the United States Steel Corporation, and Walter P. Reuther, president of the United Automobile Workers of America, share the platform at the Intercollegiate Student Conference.

Big Steel's chairman told the audience of more than a thousand that the effect on inflation ascribed to price increases by his company is vastly exaggerated. Blough argued that the real villain in the inflationary spiral is increased government spending. He also said that while the price of labor has increased about 8 percent annually in recent years, the price of steel has increased only about 4 percent annually.

Both Reuther and Blough discussed the role of labor and management in the area of race relations. The labor leader criticized some of those among his own followers who he said had failed to live up to their ideals in the matter of civil rights. He called upon business and labor to join forces for more effective legislation.

On Sunday morning, following a tri-faith religious program, Robert Abernethy of the National Broadcasting Company, a nephew of the Rev. Bradford S. Abernethy, Rutgers chaplain, spoke on ethics in communications.

Abernethy said that, while some reporters may add "a little more color, a little more conflict, a little more significance" to the story of a news event than it warrants, it is also a fact that television coverage of the civil rights movement carried that story "past all the conservative newspapers and the politicians into the shacks of Southern Negroes." He also credited the television coverage of police beatings of civil rights marchers in Selma, Alabama, with being largely responsible for passage of the Voting Rights of 1965.

The concluding address of the conference was given by Archibald Cox, Harvard Law School professor and former United States Solicitor General. Professor Cox began his lecture by posing the question: "How far may a citizen use the weapon of civil disobedience to bring about social and moral reform?"

His own answer is that civil disobedience damages voluntary compliance with law and that there is no alternative to government of laws as an instrument of justice. The rule of law, he said, depends upon voluntary compliance.

"I do not mean to attach value to law just because it is law," Professor Cox said. "Law is important because of what it does.

Robert Abernethy, NBC news, discusses the ethics of communications, a presentation of the Intercollegiate Student Conference.

Archibald Cox, former U.S.
Solicitor General, concluded the
Intercollegiate Student Conference.

Law is a human instrument. Law offers the opportunity for each generation to remake society as it can. Our substitute for power is the rule of law."

The other major event of the student Bicentennial celebration was a week-long party. It was planned and executed by the students with each of the major divisions responsible for one day.

Douglass College held the opening event and can probably claim that it was the most successful. The women's college students arranged an open-air concert for trumpeter Al Hirt and his band on the grounds of the Carpender estate. An overflow crowd from all the campuses in New Brunswick turned out for Mr. Hirt's bright brand of jazz.

Wednesday was Newark-Rutgers Day. The principal event there was a panel discussion of "The Role of the Dissenter." Dr. Walter F. Weiker, associate professor of political science, moderated the program which presented as principal speakers Norman Thomas and Frank S. Meyer, senior editor of the *National Review.*

The College of South Jersey in Camden held a three-night presentation of a play as its part in the Bicentennial Week. The

Newark Student Bicentennial Event—Meyer-Thomas debate

play was *Inherit the Wind* by Jerome Lawrence and Robert E. Lee. It was produced by the Masqueteers, college dramatic group.

Rutgers College took over on Saturday and held an all-day party which included a canoe race on the Raritan, box lunches, a performance by the Trinidad Steel Band, a baseball doubleheader with the University of Pennsylvania, and a lacrosse game with Hofstra. That evening the comedy team of Marty Allen and Steve Rossi appeared with Chad Mitchell and his trio and the Brandy-wine Singers in a concert in the College Avenue gymnasium.

University College sponsored the Sunday event, a concert by the Columbus Boy Choir, in the gymnasium.

Making certain that the light side was not ignored in their Bicentennial celebration, the students held seven dinner dances on Friday night. There were formal dances for Rutgers College and Douglass College students in University Commons, for Newark-Rutgers students at the Robert Treat Hotel, and for Rutgers-Camden students at Cinelli's Country House in Cherry Hill. University College students dined and danced at four locations.

Rutgers undergraduates also helped in the Bicentennial by giving away "birthday presents." These presents were the twenty-seven large replicas of the seals of the colleges and universities of New Jersey which had been created for use in the Rutgers exhibit at the New York World's Fair.

When the exhibit was broken up late in 1965, it was felt that it would be unfortunate to destroy the replicas of the college seals. Hand-carved and painted to simulate weathered bronze, the seals were very attractive and more than one of the colleges represented had expressed a wish to have permanent possession of its own medallion.

When some of the student leaders learned of the availability of the 26-inch replicas, they hit upon the idea of using them as "reverse" birthday presents. With the University's enthusiastic approval, members of the Rutgers Student Council presented them to the student groups of the colleges and universities represented. They will hopefully remain in those hands as permanent mementoes of the Rutgers Bicentennial.

The 1966 football season added its own special excitement to the anniversary celebration. The schedule for the year had been specially constructed to provide a good show and give the Bicentennial wide public exposure. It did all that and for good measure added some exceptional thrills as the Rutgers team gave Princeton and Army a scare, defeated Yale for the first time and pulled a victory out of what seemed certain defeat in alumni homecoming game with Columbia.

The Rutgers football program, officially the Rutgers Athletic News, also took notice of the Bicentennial and won itself a national award. The program covers done in full color by William Canfield, New Jersey artist and cartoonist, highlighted events in the University's history. For the Army game the charter signing of November 10, 1766, was the subject. For the Columbia contest it was Colonel Henry Rutgers not knowing whether to root for his Alma Mater or for the college which took his name. The 1864 land-grant designation was featured for the Boston University game and the rules used in the first intercollegiate football game in 1869 provided the subject for the cover for the Lafayette game, played one day earlier than the historic beginning ninety-seven years earlier. For the finale with Colgate the artist took a look at the future of the University.

The story of the Bicentennial football season is too long to tell here in detail but a few highlights must be recalled as a part of the anniversary story:

Princeton, at Princeton, Sept. 24—Rutgers, after a ragged first half in which it failed to make a first down, came alive in the second and exploded in the fourth quarter to score two touchdowns and put a deep scare into the Tiger. The explosion came too late. Rutgers was unable to overcome the 16-point lead Princeton had rolled up before the Scarlet got going. The final score: Princeton 16 – Rutgers 12.

Yale, at New Haven, Oct. 1—Rutgers bounced back with gusto the following Saturday to beat Yale for the first time in the history of the series with the Blue, which started in 1873. The fired-up Rutgers team, playing against Yale for the first time in thirty years, scored two touchdowns and a field goal in one of the heaviest and most persistent rainstorms the fans will remember. The final score: Rutgers 17 – Yale 14.

Lehigh, at Bethlehem, Oct. 8—The Scarlet got off to a slow start and let the Engineers run up 14 points before going into a football blitzkrieg which netted four touchdowns in the second period alone and wound up with the highest point total amassed by the Knights since 1963. Rutgers total of 522 yards was the biggest offensive punch in more than a decade. The final score: Rutgers 42 – Lehigh 14.

Army, at Rutgers, Oct. 15—Even if this had been one of those "no contest" games, it would have been a thrilling afternoon for the 30,000 spectators who jammed and overflowed the stands and the temporary bleachers. The afternoon's festivities opened with the groundbreaking for the National Football Hall of Fame to be erected on University Heights. Next, the U.S. Military Academy's Corps of Cadets, 3,200 strong, marched on the field with the precision and power that make any but the dullest dullard's spine tingle. And then Rutgers, going into the game definitely the underdog, made a day of it by battling Army right down to the final whistle. As William N. Wallace, sports writer for the *New York Times*, told it in his report of the game: "Army won, 14-9, as it was supposed to, but the cadets had all they wanted from 'the loyal sons of Rutgers battling' as the local song goes."

Columbia, at Rutgers, Oct. 22—Billed as a salute to Colonel Henry Rutgers, the Columbia alumnus whose name the college took in 1825, this was the big Alumni Homecoming Day, and the Columbia football team tried hard to spoil it. The Lions may have read the reports of the tremendous effort Rutgers put on against Army, but they apparently chose to ignore them. They played an all-out game and almost—except for 59 seconds and reserve quarterback Fred Eckert—went home with the victory. Columbia apparently had sewed up the game in the last minutes of the final quarter when a pass from Marty Dombres to Rich Brown gave the Lions a 34 to 30 margin. With less than a minute to go, Rutgers took over and Eckert started a drive which gave the heart specialists of the area full offices for the next week. Eckert tossed passes down the sidelines, used a line play to make a needed first down, and then—14 seconds before the final gun—connected with Jack Emmer in the end zone. Jim Dulin made good the extra point. The final score: Rutgers 37 – Columbia 34.

In addition to this cliff-hanger, the homecomers and their guests that afternoon and evening also enjoyed picnicking on the lawn of the President's House, watched the beautiful and ingenious floats in the annual contest, cheered the customary "queens," saw a crew demonstration with Columbia on the Raritan, and as the sky started to darken, witnessed an exciting fireworks display in Johnson Park.

Boston University, at Rutgers, Oct. 29—Jim Dulin's three field goals—a new Rutgers record eclipsing that of Homer Hazel who kicked two in one game in 1916—gave the Scarlet the margin of victory against the Terriers in a game which featured defensive strategy. Dulin also kicked the extra point after Jack Emmer ran Pete Savino's pass into the end zone in the second period. The final score: Rutgers 16 – Boston University 7.

Lafayette, at Rutgers, Nov. 5—Rutgers had to come from behind to win this game which brought with it the Middle Three title. Gary Marshall, the Leopards' very talented passer, did most of the enemy damage and late in the fourth period the Maroon

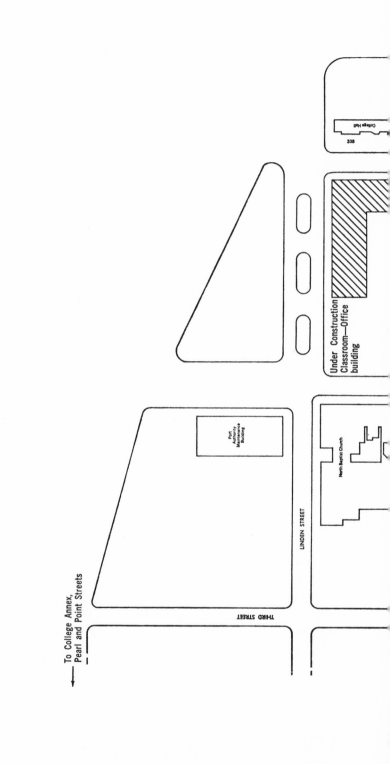

To College Annex,
Pearl and Point Streets

Port
Authority
Maintenance
Building

Under Construction
Classroom—Office
building

College Hall

338

North Baptist Church

LINDEN STREET

THIRD STREET

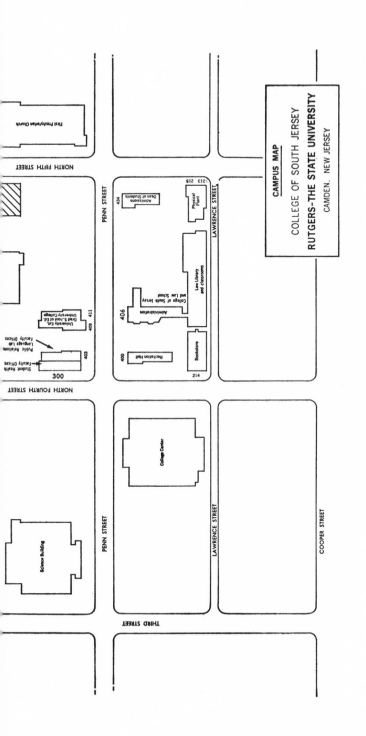

CAMPUS MAP

COLLEGE OF SOUTH JERSEY

RUTGERS-THE STATE UNIVERSITY

CAMDEN, NEW JERSEY

and White was leading 28 to 17. Rewriting some of the Columbia game script, the Knights got down to work during the last eight minutes and scored two touchdowns. The final score: Rutgers 32 – Lafayette 28.

Holy Cross, at Worcester, Nov. 12—Jack Emmer set six new Rutgers records for pass receptions, but it wasn't enough to stop a big, tough Holy Cross team directed by capable quarterback Jack Lentz. The final score: Holy Cross 24 – Rutgers 12.

Colgate, at Rutgers, Nov. 19—Rutgers closed out its Bicentennial football season against a very good Colgate team which came to the Stadium as a favorite and quickly demonstrated the reasons for it. The final score: Colgate 26 – Rutgers 7.

The 200th Anniversary Commencement

A SPECIAL REASON FOR PRIDE

THE graduating class at the first Rutgers Commencement on October 12, 1774, consisted of a single individual—at the Bicentennial Commencement on June 1, 1966, the University awarded nearly 4,000 degrees in course and presented honorary diplomas to an assemblage of twenty notables including nine alumni whose achievements on behalf of the nation and the University brought this high tribute from Alma Mater.

The contrasts between that first graduation, when the lone recipient of a degree was Matthew Leydt, and the Bicentennial Commencement that pleasant June evening were mainly of degree. The business at hand was fundamentally the same and at both there was a reaffirmation of the importance of the educated man to society. But the difference in numbers, in the pageantry, and in the variety and depth of the intellectual achievements demonstrated by the degrees awarded spelled out in dramatic fashion the strengths that Rutgers had slowly and steadily gathered during the intervening years.

The Bicentennial Commencement was a brilliant and exciting show held in the Rutgers Stadium as the only place large enough to hold some 20,000 spectators, but the pageantry and the color were only the setting—the stage properties, if you will—for the principal characters, the thousands of black-gowned and -capped young people who were—as Matthew Leydt was in 1774—the reason for it all.

Leydt, as did most of the early graduates of the college then known as Queen's, entered the ministry.

It was predictable that the thousands of young people who received Rutgers degrees at the 200th Anniversary Commencement were about to start careers which would take them into business, the professions, science, the arts, government, education —wherever a complex and rapidly changing society will have need for them.

The variety of their educational preparation for the careers ahead of them was written in bright symbols that June night. Grouped along the wall of the parapet at the front of the Stadium seating area were colorful banners each with its own special device. These were gonfalons—which Webster says is a name given to any flag which hangs from a crosspiece. The Rutgers gonfalons, making their first official appearance, represented the fifteen colleges taking part in the Bicentennial Commencement.

The gonfalons had first been suggested by the Bicentennial coordinators, Mr. Ingham and Miss Durham. They were to add bright spots of color to the pageantry of the academic events, but they did much more than that. They represented the degree-granting schools of the University, and in so doing demonstrated the variety of academic achievements of the young people who received their degrees that evening.

Each of the gonfalons carries in the upper portion a white field, a device particular to the college represented. The lower portion of the forked streamer is scarlet symbolizing membership in the University, and there is a median strip of the color traditionally used to symbolize the degree the college bestows.

The date of the school's establishment is printed in the lower left-hand corner of the banner. The colleges and schools participating in the Bicentennial Commencement in order of founding were: Rutgers College of Arts and Sciences, 1766; College of Agriculture and Environmental Science, 1864; College of Engineering, 1864; Douglass College, 1918; Newark College of Arts and Sciences, 1946; Graduate School of Education, 1923; The Graduate School, 1952; Graduate School of Social Work, 1954; College of Pharmacy, 1927; School of Law, 1946; College of Nursing, 1956; College of South Jersey, 1950; Graduate School of

Business Administration, 1946; Graduate School of Library Service, 1954; and University College, 1934. The Rutgers Medical School, the newest of the colleges, founded in 1961, was represented by a gonfalon, but was not to admit its first class until the following September. (Appendix C provides a detailed description of the Rutgers gonfalons.)

While the gonfalons represented the diversity of the University, another banner which made its first appearance at the Bicentennial Commencement displayed in the traditional devices of heraldry and unity of the University and the several sources that had given it birth and later nourishment.

This was the new Rutgers coat of arms, which had originated in the Bicentennial Office to remedy a long-standing lack in Rutgers tradition. Most of the other colonial colleges had had coats of arms for many years but, for reasons unknown or obscure, Queen's and then Rutgers had never had one.

It is perhaps just as well, because the changes in the institution down through its history probably would have meant repeated redesigning of any pre-Revolutionary device.

At least that was apparent in the design for the Rutgers coat of arms produced by Liam Dunne of Milford, artist and authority on heraldry.

This coat of arms, which was carried at the head of the academic parade in the Bicentennial Commencement, is quartered to represent in armorial bearings the founding and growth of the University. The upper left quarter of the shield bears the arms of Nassau, House of Orange, in recognition of the contributions of the Dutch settlers who founded the College. The armorial devices in the upper right quarter combine those of George III of England with those of his consort, Charlotte of Mecklenburg, in whose honor the college was named Queen's. The third quarter, lower left, is the emblem from the Great Seal of the State of New Jersey representing status as the State University. Coincidentally, the three plows also symbolize the designation of Rutgers as one of the original land-grant colleges. The fourth quarter, lower right, contains the arms of Colonel Henry Rutgers, Revolutionary War hero and an early benefactor of the college that took his name in 1825.

Adding further color to this colorful ceremony was the first display of the specially designed Rutgers academic gown. The new gown and hat, handsome in full scarlet, had been authorized for the President and Provost, for the Boards of Governors and Trustees, and for holders of Rutgers doctoral degrees, earned or honorary. The scarlet gown faced in black is emblazoned with black chevrons and gold piping on its sleeves and is embroidered with the Rutgers "Q" seal. The Commencement platform truly blazed with color.

The privilege of wearing this new gown was bestowed that day on 160 graduate students who had earned the doctoral degree and upon the 20 recipients of honorary degrees. The honorary degrees had been conferred at separate exercises earlier in the day and the recipients were presented at the evening ceremony.

Those who received honorary degrees made up a distinguished company which included three college presidents, a Pulitzer Prize-winning author, and the chairman of the Board of Directors of the International House of Japan. The last-named's accolade recalled Rutgers' associations with that country extending back a full century to the time when the first Japanese students to study in America had enrolled there. Nine of the group were alumni who were honored for outstanding achievements in finance, music, journalism, science, law, social welfare, education, and business.

The honorary degrees were awarded to:

Dr. Ruth Marie Adams, former dean of Douglass College and now president of Wellesley College, whose citation reads:

> An educator of lively imagination and temperate judgement, you have served this university with distinction. In a period of unprecedented expansion, you have been an outstanding administrator of undergraduate education at Douglass College and a colleague of sound and sensitive discernment in the formulation of policy for the entire University. During these past six years, you have found time to remain a superior teacher and have gained wide recognition as a creative innovator in the classroom. We hate to see you leave, even though you go to preside over that distinguished sister institution of Wellesley,

but since the deed is done, we wish you great happiness there and convey to you our deepest gratitude and warmest affection.

I am pleased to confer upon you, at the direction of the Board of Governors, *honoris causa*, the degree of Doctor of Laws.

Archibald S. Alexander, assistant director, U.S. Arms Control and Disarmament Agency, former Undersecretary of the Army, and a member of the Rutgers Board of Governors since it was organized in 1956. His citation reads:

Generous and modest public servant, wise leader, distinguished citizen of the republic of the mind, and right honorable gentleman in the noble company of men of good will, you have served your nation, your state, and this university long and with distinction. As Undersecretary of the Army, as Treasurer of the State of New Jersey, as Chairman of the New Jersey State Tax Policy Commission, and now as Assistant Director of the United States Arms Control and Disarmament Agency, your public record is illustrious. Ten years a member of the Rutgers Board of Governors, six as Vice Chairman, and four as Chairman, you have given us leadership and wisdom in a momentous period of our development.

I am pleased, by'the enthusiastic direction of your colleagues on the Board of Governors, to confer upon you, *honoris causa*, the degree of Doctor of Laws.

Dr. Frederick L. Bixby, consultant on probation to the Administrative Office of New Jersey Courts and formerly director of the New Jersey Division of Correction and Parole, who was cited as follows:

As educator and administrator you have devoted yourself with distinction to penology and penal administration, disciplines to which you have brought humaneness and intelligence, administrative skill and quiet integrity—qualities that make for true reform. You have been a pioneer. Your work goes on to guide those in this state and nation and abroad who seek to insure the peace of community but not at the cost of compassion.

I am pleased, therefore, at the direction of the Board of Governors, to confer upon you, *honoris causa*, the degree of Doctor of Humane Letters.

Philip M. B. Boocock, a graduate in the Class of 1926, headmaster of the Nichols School. His citation reads:

Descendant of Rutgers' fourth president, nephew of an acting president and beloved Trustee, son of a Rutgers graduate, and brother of two—you have added to the fame and nobility of one of Rutgers' most distinguished families through your own outstanding career as an educator.

During the perilous years of the Great Depression your resourceful and imaginative leadership strengthened the Rutgers Preparatory School, and over the past twenty-nine years, under your able administration, the Nichols School has grown to its high position, accepted and recognized as one of the finest independent schools in the country.

I am pleased, therefore, at the direction of the Board of Governors, to confer upon you, *honoris causa*, the degree of Doctor of Letters.

Charles H. Brower, member of the Class of 1925, chairman of the board of Batten, Barton, Durstine & Osborn, and chairman of the Board of Governors. He was cited as follows:

A leader of the University's governing body, you have given additional wisdom and strength to a group of men and women who have had their full share of difficult and demanding responsibilities. Ever since that day ten years ago when the management of the University was reorganized, an historic change for Rutgers which you did so much to bring about, this institution has moved steadily toward its inevitable position as one of the leading universities of the world. The reasons may be many, but one of them is the distinguished leadership which you have provided, sure and sound in your understanding of what the true university should seek to do.

For this we pay due tribute with gratitude and admiration, but with even stronger feelings we express our appreciation for the depth of your affection for Alma Mater, the keenness of your intellect and wit, and most especially, the enjoyment we have in the warmth of our friendship.

I am pleased, at the enthusiastic direction of your associates on the Board of Governors, to confer upon you, *honoris causa*, the degree of Doctor of Laws.

Katherine F. Coffey, director of the Newark Museum and president of the Northeast Conference of Museums. Her citation reads:

You have been associated with the Newark Museum for many years and have served with distinction as Director.

You are a good and generous neighbor to this University in Newark.

As a wise guide, you have trained more than a generation of museum apprentices in the rare technical skills of your profession. Graduates of your program have carried the name and fame of the Newark Museum throughout the world.

Now President of the Northeast Conference of Museums, you have won a well-deserved reputation in your chosen field.

But beyond the museum world, you and your work are held in the highest esteem by the thousands of individuals who are served by the Newark Museum each year.

Therefore, at the direction of the Board of Governors, I am pleased to confer upon you, *honoris causa*, the degree of Doctor of Fine Arts.

Ralph W. Ellison, author of *The Invisible Man*, winner of many writing awards and a writer-in-residence at Rutgers from 1962 to 1964. His citation reads:

Novelist, teacher, and critic, you have enriched our lives by both your art and your example. As a novelist you have told us a complex truth about ourselves and our times. As a teacher you have shared the full resources of your talent and your craft with those who have come to you for understanding. As a critic you have looked with compassionate intelligence at the problems of our age and discussed them reasonably with us. Your life and your art have been steadfastly and uncompromisingly dedicated to the common humanity which makes all men brothers.

I am pleased, therefore, at the direction of the Board of Governors, to confer upon you, *honoris causa*, the degree of Doctor of Letters.

Clarence Clyde Ferguson, Jr., dean of the Howard University Law School and a professor of law at Rutgers from 1955 to 1962. His citation reads:

As lawyer, Assistant United States Attorney, and former General Counsel to the United States Commission on Civil Rights, you have been a devoted public servant.

As a Professor of Law at Rutgers, as a stimulating Lecturer in its Institute of Continuing Legal Education, and as the present Dean of Howard University's Law School, you have been a resourceful teacher and statesman in the field of legal education.

As an author of books and numerous articles, you have established your reputation as a distinguished scholar of the law.

As an international consultant to governments and foundations, your imagination, intelligence, and energy have provided inspirational leadership toward solution of a number of great problems in the world and in our nation.

Therefore, by direction of the Board of Governors, I am pleased to confer upon you, *honoris causa*, the degree of Doctor of Laws.

Julia Weber Gordon, an alumna of Douglass College in the Class of 1933 who is director of the Office of Child and Youth Study in the New Jersey State Department of Education. Her citation reads:

Dedicated teacher of the young and of other teachers, you have advanced your profession by creative espousal of "the kind of education that will make a difference in the living of people."

This dedication, first applied in rural schools following your graduation from Douglass College, has been characteristic also of your later career as university professor, educational consultant and Director of the Office of Child and Youth Study of the New Jersey State Department of Education.

In recognition of your successful "Adventure in Creative Teaching" and at the direction of the Board of Governors of the University, I am pleased to confer upon you, *honoris causa*, the degree of Doctor of Humane Letters.

George F. Kennan, winner in 1957 of a Pulitzer Prize for his book *Russia Leaves the War*, professor at the Institute for Advanced Study in Princeton, and a former ambassador to the Soviet Union and Yugoslavia. His citation reads:

We pay tribute to you for your eminence in the international scene and for your indefatigable service to your country and mankind.

As a career diplomat of long service, your voice and writings have had profound effect on the formulation of United States foreign policy. You were the author of the Containment Policy toward the Soviet Union during the difficult post-World War II period of Stalin. You have had great influence among members of the foreign service of the United States and represent a phenomenon unusual in both diplomatic and scholarly circles —a diplomat endowed with profound philosophical insight and wisdom, and a scholar with vast diplomatic experience in crucial areas at critical times.

For your significant contribution to international and national affairs and to scholarship in history, for your personal influence on nations and peoples, I am pleased, at the direction of the Board of Governors of the University, to confer upon you, *honoris causa*, the degree of Doctor of Laws.

Willard D. Lewis, president of Lehigh University, whose citation reads:

Distinguished space scientist, research administrator, and advisor to the government, your creative talents in electronic communications and systems analysis have contributed significantly to the Apollo Moon Project.

Your ability to organize complex operations, and your understanding of the broad range of man's problems and his capabilities in our technological culture are reflected in your stimulating leadership as the tenth President of Lehigh University.

In recognition of your success in bringing your scientific competence to bear on the human factors of higher education, I am pleased, at the direction of the Board of Governors, to confer upon you, *honoris causa*, the degree of Doctor of Laws.

Shigeharu Matsumoto, chairman of the Board of Directors of the International House. His citation reads:

Shigeharu Matsumoto, Japanese scholar, journalist, and cultural statesman; distinguished product of Tokyo, Yale, Wisconsin, Geneva, and Vienna universities; officer in your country's National Commission for UNESCO and the United States Educational Commission in Tokyo; President, Japan Association for American Studies; and Chairman of the Board of Directors of The International House of Japan— you have helped design and maintain the "Pacific Bridge" of intellectual interchange between the United States and Japan.

On the occasion of our Bicentennial and celebration of a century of association between Rutgers and Japan, you symbolize for us the lasting values of international education.

By direction of the Board of Governors, I am pleased to confer upon you, *honoris causa*, the degree of Doctor of Laws.

William Christian Miller, a graduate in the Class of 1926, partner in W. E. Hutton & Company, New York brokerage house, and chairman of the Rutgers Board of Trustees. His citation reads:

Rutgers has developed and prospered through the years, aided by thousands of active and devoted alumni, none more so than you. From the day of your graduation you have given freely and gladly to alumni activities, whether, in earlier days, as a player in the annual Alumni-Varsity lacrosse games, or, in later and less physically-strenuous times, as leader in a great variety of alumni advisory groups. As a member of Rutgers' Board of Trustees for the past nineteen years, and now its Chairman, you have been a valued participant in directing the University during its time of most rapid advancement with a sure knowledge of sound financial management and with a deep affection and understanding.

I am pleased, therefore, at the direction of the Board of Governors, to confer upon you, *honoris causa*, the degree of Doctor of Laws.

Caspar Harold Nannes, a member of the Class of 1931, religious news editor of the Washington, D.C., *Star*, whose citation reads:

One of Rutgers' most loyal sons, all-time tennis champion of the University, former member of the Department of English, student of American Drama, and long-time religious editor. You have distinguished yourself and the Washington *Star* by your sensitive, intelligent, and impartial interpretation of the religious news of our generation. Your Alma Mater joins religious and lay leaders of our day in honoring you for your informed and dignified reporting.

By direction of the Board of Governors, I am pleased to confer upon you, *honoris causa*, the degree of Doctor of Letters.

Hilda Christine Reilly, an alumna of Douglass College in 1941 and holder of a doctorate in microbiology from Rutgers, who is now director of experimental chemotherapy at the Sloan-Kettering Institute. Her citation reads:

"Where work comes out from the depth of truth" and truth comes out from the depth of work, there you have found your career and rewards as research scientist.

From the time shortly after your graduation from Douglass College when you assisted in the development of streptomycin and other antibiotics at Rutgers to your present leadership in experimental chemotherapy at Sloan-Kettering Institute for Cancer Research and your professorship in microbiology at

Cornell University's Graduate School of Medical Sciences, you have sought and achieved scientific truth for the preservation of human life.

At the direction of the Board of Governors of the University, I am pleased to confer upon you, *honoris causa*, the degree of Doctor of Science.

Israel Rogosin, president and director of Rogosin Industries of Israel, Ltd., former trustee of Brandeis University and a philanthropist with special interests in medical research and education. His citation reads:

For many years your intensely human enthusiasm and material helpfulness have, by example, taught laymen and reminded scholars that the advance of medicine is a calling of highest excitement. Your philanthropic deeds, performed with a generosity and modesty which have always been characteristic of you, have greatly aided hospitals and universities in areas where you have found that special needs existed.

Rutgers, we gratefully acknowledge, has been a happy beneficiary of your devotion to medical education and research, and, as a result, the wishes and hopes of the people of New Jersey that the State may soon possess the finest medical resources are closer to fulfillment.

I am pleased, therefore, at the direction of the Board of Governors, to confer upon you, *honoris causa*, the degree of Doctor of Humane Letters.

Arthur J. Sills, graduate in the Class of 1938, Attorney General of New Jersey, whose citation reads:

Arthur J. Sills, son of Rutgers, you have brought to the high office of Attorney General of New Jersey the full power of your fertile mind, your unflinching courage, and your warm humanitarianism. You have enforced the laws of this State wisely and fairly, being always sensitive to the rights of individuals and to the injustices suffered by minority groups. Your leadership in the National Association of Attorneys General and particularly in the study of our system of bail and the hardships it inflicts has been of a high order.

I am pleased, therefore, at the direction of the Board of Governors, to confer upon you, *honoris causa*, the degree of Doctor of Laws.

F. Austin Walter, an alumnus in the Class of 1932, who is professor of music and director of the Rutgers Glee Club, whose citation reads:

You have served your University in many ways, always with dedication and enthusiasm. As a teacher, and more recently Professor of Music, you have brought the joys of this noble art to thirty-four years of classes at Rutgers, and have built up the great Rutgers University Choir into one of the pre-eminent organizations of its kind, invited year after year to sing with the major symphony orchestras. For years, too, you have kept the Rutgers Glee Club in the forefront among male ensembles.

As a member of the Class of 1932, you have been a faithful son of this University, serving it with all your heart.

I am pleased, therefore, at the direction of the Board of Governors, to confer upon you, *honoris causa*, the degree of Doctor of Music.

Allan Weisenfeld, an alumnus in the Class of 1933, secretary of the New Jersey State Board of Mediation. His citation reads:

Student of human relations and analyst of industrial organization, you have brought insight and understanding into countless troubled situations.

Beyond such perception, however, you have enhanced the role of all mediators by advocating and practicing the theory that the government mediator's responsibility is to aid the disagreeing parties to solve their own problems on their own terms rather than to impose a settlement. Your philosophy and leadership have helped to make possible the retention of private decision-making at the bargaining table.

For your service to labor, management, and the public, I am pleased, at the direction of the Board of Governors, to confer upon you, *honoris causa*, the degree of Doctor of Humane Letters.

The Rev. Victor Robert Yanitelli, S.J., president of St. Peter's College, whose citation reads:

Yours has been a career of commitment—to your church, to education, and to the community—and in that noble career, which has included service as teacher and administrator, you have demonstrated respect for principle and courage of conviction which we have long admired. In and out of the classroom you have consistently provided excellence in leadership with humility and sense of humor and humanity.

Under your administration the continued progress of Saint Peter's College is assured, and we look forward to the association of our two institutions in joint pursuit of the best in education for the young people of the State and the Nation.

I am pleased, therefore, at the direction of the Board of Governors, to confer upon you, *honoris causa*, the degree of Doctor of Laws.

President Gross's address to the graduating class concluded the 200th Anniversary Commencement program. In it he stressed the interdependence of knowledge, freedom, and happiness, a theme much in harmony with that of Jacob Rutsen Hardenbergh, the first Commencement speaker who had argued 192 years earlier that the welfare of society "is in a great measure embraced in the fate of our seats of learning."*

Calling upon his knowledge of the writings of the English philosopher John Locke, Dr. Gross suggested that in drafting the Declaration of Independence Thomas Jefferson may have been following Locke's thought in his *Essay Concerning Human Understanding:* "As therefore the highest perfection of intellectual nature lies in a careful and constant pursuit of true and solid happiness; so the care of ourselves, that we mistake not imaginary for true happiness, is the necessary foundation of our liberty."

"This really is rather a remarkable statement," Dr. Gross pointed out. "If Jefferson goes along with it, then he is not proclaiming for us three unalienable rights and using for the third a euphemism more palatable than the rather materialistic concept of

*The text of President Gross's Commencement Address of June 1, 1966, is found in Appendix D.

property. If he is following Locke carefully, then in fact he is claiming, first of all, life as a right, which is obviously a necessary condition for any other rights, and then liberty and the pursuit of happiness, which in Locke's language are mutually interdependent. And Locke adds a further thought when he says that the pursuit of happiness is the highest perfection of our intellectual nature, and that the intellectual power to distinguish between true and false happiness is the foundation of liberty.

"What I am trying to say here is that what Jefferson accomplished in 1776 was to lift the whole argument about independence from the British crown to a higher level.

"Independence is in a sense a negative concept, and the mere establishment of independence would have no necessary corollaries so far as self-government was concerned. But liberty is a positive concept as Locke and Jefferson conceived it, and Jefferson's contemporaries seemed to have grasped that point. For you will recall that the most careful of them refused to support ratification of the Constitution until they were sure that there would be a set of amendments which would translate the essential elements of civil liberty into law. It was all very well to believe philosophically in these as natural rights; they wanted civil rights."

Discussing the philosophical outlook of the men who founded Rutgers—Queen's College then—Dr. Gross says that they moved in the right direction "for the road to knowledge must also be the necessary road to freedom and to happiness." This, he says, was a recurring theme in the thinking of Jefferson, Washington, and Lincoln and he concluded:

"At Gettysburg, President Lincoln referred to this country as 'a new nation conceived in liberty.' I believe that the same spirit of liberty presided over the beginnings of this university, the same faith and the same dedication. We have now endured for two hundred years. May the spirit of liberty continue to be our principal source of strength."

Dr. Gross had said that the Bicentennial Commencement was an especially historic occasion. The pageantry and the color, the excellent weather, and the outstanding group of honorary degree recipients all helped to make it one. But there was another important factor which must be recalled. This was the attendance at a University Commencement for the first time of the graduating class of Douglass College. The 550 young women who filled a large block in the North Stands made it the first truly university-wide graduation and added their own special touch when they broke into a spirited cheer as their departing dean, Dr. Adams, received her honorary degree.

And then there were the eight young men who couldn't get to their Commencement. They had left with the Rutgers Glee Club two days before for the Netherlands, where they were to start a four-nation musical tour as a part of the Bicentennial. They left without knowing that their director, F. Austin Walter, who received an honorary degree at Commencement, was bringing their diplomas with him and would present them in a historic setting at the University of Utrecht.

Dr. Walter also carried with him greetings in Latin from Rutgers to the University of Utrecht noting that both were founded in the Dutch educational tradition, that the Rutgers seal is adapted from that of Utrecht and that John Henry Livingston, one of the early presidents of the New Jersey college, was a graduate of the Netherlands university and had been recommended for the position by its officials.

Intellectual Weight Lifting

IN celebrating their birthdays, universities, like individuals, are happiest in the activity they enjoy most in the normal course of their existence. Since universities are regularly busy and happy in the searching for, development of, dissemination and distribution of knowledge, these academic pursuits are always essential to any academic celebration.

They are then generally crystallized in some form of intellectual get-together whether it be called a conference, seminar, symposium, convention, meeting, or congress. It is a kind of intellectual weight-lifting by the scholars in a certain field or possibly several related fields. It provides the opportunity for the display and trial of new discoveries, ideas, theories, and hypotheses.

In keeping with this traditional form of academic celebration, the Rutgers Bicentennial Year was filled with special scholarly and intellectual activity. The University played host to a number of learned societies and to many individual scholars and intellectual leaders during the year. The subject of these meetings and sessions covered a range of subjects from the status of the earth's crust to the most complex mathematical concepts and presented views, arguments, and beliefs on some of the perplexing problems of society in the second half of the twentieth century.

These conferences and meetings or individual lectures brought to the campuses of the University some of the leading scholars in their fields, and in several instances the ideas promulgated at Rutgers during 1966 will almost certainly find a place in man's understanding of his world and himself.

This is not the place to recall every academic or scholarly event of the Bicentennial Year—they are listed chronologically in the Bicentennial Calendar in Appendix E—nor will it attempt to present their content in detail. For one thing, most of the principal papers and talks delivered at these conferences and seminars are being published in full elsewhere for the benefit of their special audiences, and secondly, the intention here is to present only enough of the character and content of these meetings to illustrate the depth and breadth of intellectual excitement at Rutgers during the Bicentennial.

Bicentennial intellectual fare was served up in a wide variety of forms from the single independent lecture to conferences lasting several days. No doubt all of them were of deep significance and interest to their special constituencies, but none was more exciting and of broader general interest than the ceremony and related seminars which marked the dedication of Henry E. Ackerson Hall, the new building of the Rutgers Law School in Newark. This event truly glittered with some of the leading legal luminaries of American jurisprudence up to and including the Chief Justice of the United States Supreme Court—Earl Warren.

WHITHER THE SOVIET ECONOMY?

The question of whether the Soviet economy is moving toward capitalism was the subject of one of the earliest of the academic conferences, a discussion of which was held on the New Brunswick campus on April 13. The symposium was held under the sponsorship of the Rutgers Russian Area Committee and the Rutgers Economics Honors Society.

It brought together on the Rutgers campus three men whom Dr. Alexander S. Balinky, professor of economics and chairman of the Russian Area Committee at Rutgers, described as the "most eminent scholars on the Soviet economy and political system in the Western world." They were Abram Bergson, professor of economics at Harvard University; John Hazard, professor of law and government at Columbia University; and Peter Wiles, professor at the London School of Economics. All have written extensively about the Soviet Union and its economy. Dr. Balinky moderated the discussion before a standing-room-only crowd.

The question had been posed by the Soviet economic reforms of the 1960's. Some Western observers had seen in these, wishfully no doubt, indications that the Russians were moving from a planned toward a market economy, or from Communism toward capitalism, "creeping" or otherwise.

What Messrs. Bergson, Hazard, and Wiles had to say on this subject in their Rutgers presentations is published in full in *Planning and the Market in the USSR:* The 1960's by the Rutgers University Press. It begins with a discussion of the subject "Problems and Issues in Soviet Economic Reform," by Dr. Balinky. He opens rather provocatively with the statement that "Western thought has never been entirely free of the theories or myths about the self-destructive propensities of Soviet Society."

The three speakers at the Rutgers meeting were in general agreement that the Soviet economic reforms which some in the West have looked upon as a retreat from Communism are really adjustments providing for more flexibility within a basic Socialist economic ideology, and that the idea of convergence with capitalism is still largely Western wishful thinking.

Answering the main conference question, Peter Wiles gives "a firm but moderate no." Abram Bergson says, "the government is not about to restore capitalism, and Soviet economists have rightly criticized commentators, both in China and the West, who have suggested as much." John Hazard explained the Soviet reforms of the 1960's as consistent with the Soviet principle that "the basic task of the organs of Soviet socialist administration, just as in the case with all other organs of the Soviet State, is the construction of communist society."

THE UNIVERSITY PRESSES MEET AT RUTGERS

From June 12 to June 16 the nation's university presses held their annual convention on the Rutgers campus. The Association of

American University Presses came to New Brunswick partially in honor of the Bicentennial and partially to mark the thirtieth anniversary of the Rutgers University Press.

Some 300 delegates representing 59 academic publishing houses and related institutions gathered in New Brunswick for the five-day meeting. Included in the group were representatives of 54 university presses, as well as the Bolligen Foundation, the Huntington Library of California, the Smithsonian Institution, and the Centro Interamericano de Libros Academicos, a Mexican organization which, as its name implies, distributes academic books throughout Latin America.

The story of the Rutgers University Press was told in some depth and detail in an article which its director, William Sloane, wrote for the July 4, 1966, issue of *Publishers Weekly*.*

Sloane, fifth man to head the Rutgers Press, pointed out that the publishing house had been established by the University's trustees to "assist in the stimulation and publication of faculty and scholarly research in general, and in particular to provide a publishing outlet for the scholarship fostered by the University's Research Council."

He also recalled that the Press began under the direction of the late Earl Reed Silvers, head of the Department of Alumni and Public Relations and an "inspiring teacher with a national background of successful writing and editing." He had on his staff, Sloane noted, the writer Earl Schenck Miers, who was then a recent Rutgers graduate, and Donald F. Cameron, later to become the University librarian, who served as editor. Miers followed Silvers as director of the Press and under his leadership the publishing house undertook to publish a nine-volume set, *The Collected Works of Abraham Lincoln*, which was to bring the Press national and international distinction.

"Even before the publication of this major contribution to the Press and to national scholarship, Earl Miers had found and brought out a group of lively books which found readership outside the normal academic pattern," Sloane wrote. "The most famous, *The Lincoln Reader*, became a Book-of-the-Month Club selection for February, 1946. This volume, the result of the collab-

---

*The complete text of Mr. Sloane's article is found in Appendix F.

oration between Miers as publisher and his historian friend Paul M. Angle as compiler and editor, sold almost half a million copies through the Club and the Press in the first 90 days after publication. Its success marked the emergence of the Rutgers Press from comparative obscurity."

"In those 30 years since 1936," said Sloane, "the Rutgers Press has published some 460 titles. Today the Press is bringing out new books at a rate of 30 or more new titles each year.

"More than half the volumes the Press published are still in print. Many of them have been republished abroad in British editions and foreign language translations and they are to be found in the great libraries of the entire world. Their authors are, more often than not, scholars on other campuses and professional writers. A number are citizens of foreign countries. The publishing scope of the Press today is international and Rutgers books are known and read throughout the world."

Speakers at the A.A.U.P. meeting included Curtis G. Benjamin, chairman of the Board of the McGraw Hill Book Company; Dan Lacy, then managing director of the American Book Publishers Council; John Ciardi, poet, lecturer, teacher, and *Saturday Review* columnist; August Heckscher, head of the 20th Century Fund and special consultant on the arts during the Kennedy administration; Earl Miers, former Rutgers Press director, historian and author; Robert W. Frase, associate managing director of the American Book Publishers Council; Dr. Mary V. Gaver, Rutgers professor of library service and the then president-elect of the American Library Association; and Chester Kerr, president of the Association.

Miers told the gathering of university press representatives that they are "the selected guardians and custodians of what is in the scholar's mind and heart as he struggles to express his aspirations for the future. You represent every shade of regional pressure and prejudices; and collectively, you are a Congress of Culture.

"Unhappily, you have neglected to share this secret with the public . . . why are you, by and large, the country's prize stumble-bums at public relations?"

Miers, continuing, said, "I plead with you to view with dignity and earnest pride what your labors can mean, and must mean, to this troubled land of ours.

"If in years to come we are going to effect a more realistic policy toward China and Africa and our starving sister nations of this hemisphere, the university press books can and must lead the deadened minds of overcommitted professional diplomats into this sunnier intellectual climate.

"If in years to come we are going to achieve the Great Society, then university press books can and must supply the Great Wisdom without which this triumph can never be achieved.

"If in years to come we are going to vitalize that spirit of dissent on which free men thrive—if compassion is not to be a word captured by a political group in a raid on some Texas hamlet called Consensus—the university press books can and must remain the proud spokesmen of our national conscience.

"The fact that you have not always succeeded in putting across this story does not mean you must repeat this deficiency. Perhaps for one looking back over thirty years this is a small message.

"And yet what you continue to do in tapping the intellectual resources in every state of this Union—in what you continue to do to free this nation's intellect from the dominance of political and commercial clichés—is of desperate importance to me, to my children, and to their children.

"Even if this age of higher education must be symbolized by Mark Hopkins sitting on one end of a computer and a student sitting on the other, we want you to continue feeding imaginative information into that gadget."

The *Saturday Review* of June 11, the day before the presses met, had given a most unusual and sympathetic nod to the A.A.U.P.—which in this case was not the American Association of University Professors—to the Rutgers University Press and to Rutgers University.

John K. Hutchens, serving as a self-titled "advance field agent" for the delegates to the annual convention, gave a warm and sensitive "scouting report" on the locale, the host university, and the host university press in New Brunswick.*

---

*Mr. Hutchen's article, "One Thing and Another: Report from Rutgers," which appeared in the June 11, 1966, issue of *Saturday Review* is found in Appendix G.

NORTHEAST BRANCH, AMERICAN SOCIETY OF AGRONOMY

About 150 agronomists took part in the annual meeting of the Northeast Branch of the American Society of Agronomy held on the campus of the Rutgers College of Agriculture and Environmental Science June 19-22. They represented the state universities of the twelve northeastern states, several midwestern institutions, the eastern provinces of Canada, federal and state agencies, and a number of industrial concerns.

The theme of the sessions centered on problems of food supply and of renewable natural resources in the face of an expanding and exploding world population. Dr. Firman E. Bear, emeritus Rutgers professor of soils, and former editor-in-chief of *Soil Science*, presented the keynote address on the topic "Food and Space." Dr. Bear told his audience that the earth has the capacity to meet the food needs of billions more people than now exist.

He said that not only are large acreages of good farming land yet to be brought into production, but that the productivity of much of the land now being farmed could be materially increased by growing better-bred crop plants, by using much larger amounts of fertilizers, and by other means indicated by local conditions.

Dr. Bear saw the development in time of whole new species of crop plants, tailored in accordance with planned specifications and with the help of molecular biology. However, he did warn that there could be less meat for future generations. He pointed out that feeding grain to livestock and then consuming their meat and milk is wasteful in terms of food economy.

On the average, Dr. Bear said, over four-fifths of the energy values of grains are lost by feeding them first to livestock.

He also admitted that any shift toward a vegetarian diet would bring complaints at first, but said that these would gradually die out among succeeding generations that had never known animal-food diets.

However, in Dr. Bear's opinion, there is nothing in sight to indicate that man will not be able to continue producing an abundance of the kinds of foods he is now accustomed to eating, at least until the end of this century.

New Jersey Water Resources Conference

A most practical problem—or more accurately a series of problems—was the subject of the next conference: the New Jersey Water Resources Conference which was held at the University on July 12 and 13, 1966, as a part of the Bicentennial celebration. It was conducted by the University's Water Resources Research Institute, had the endorsement of Rutgers, state, and federal officials, and was supported in part by funds of the Office of Water Resources Research in the U.S. Department of the Interior.

As Brigadier General William Whipple, Jr. (Ret'd.), director of the Institute, has pointed out, the conference was problem oriented. There were 237 persons in attendance and all were selected and invited personally on the basis of their interests and accomplishments in the general field of New Jersey's water problems. Although many specialists and experts attended, they covered various fields.

In General Whipple's words: "This was primarily a conference not of experts, but of policy makers and planners. The conference was aimed primarily to clarify and define the principal water problems of the State and to suggest possible solutions.

"The status of both research and planning were outlined with respect to these goals. From an academic point of view the approach was interdisciplinary, encompassing both the social and the natural sciences. The University benefited by obtaining policy and priority indications for the better orientation of future research efforts; and the action agencies, brought together from various levels of government, were given results of the latest research. To a limited extent this conference also served to polarize and focus public opinion relative to water resource problems and potentialities in New Jersey."

President Gross opened the conference. Federal representatives participating included Dr. Roland R. Renne, Rutgers Class of 1927, director of the Office of Water Resources Research; Dr. A. Heaton Underhill, assistant director, Office of Outdoor Recreation; Brigadier General Harry G. Woodbury, Jr., deputy director for Civil Works, Office of the Chief of Engineers; and Dr. Robert V. Thomann, Federal Water Pollution Control Administration. State government agencies were represented by Commissioner of Con-

servation and Economic Development Robert A. Roe; Commissioner of Health Roscoe P. Kandle; and Secretary of Agriculture
Phillip Alampi, Rutgers Class of 1934.

AMERICAN SOCIETY OF ANIMAL SCIENCE

Late in July some 900 members of the American Society of Animal Science gathered on the Rutgers campus for the annual meeting of that organization. During the four days of their meeting,
which began July 31 and ended August 4, the Society heard a
total of 212 papers presented on such areas of animal science as
nutrition, physiology, genetics and breeding, endocrinology, and
teaching and extension education as related to livestock. The animal scientists and their wives had come to the Rutgers campus
from almost every state in the Union and from a number of foreign countries.

FOURTH INTERNATIONAL BIOMETEOROLOGICAL CONGRESS

Some 35 countries around the world were represented among the
325 scientists who attended the Fourth International Biometeorological Congress which was held at Rutgers August 26 through
September 2. Physiologists, dermatologists, zoologists, patholo-
gists, allergists, and civil engineers—all interested in the effect of
climate and weather on man, animals, and plants—as well as
meteorologists—attended this session, the first time the Congress
had been held in the United States.

Meeting concurrently with the Congress were 125 scientists
who attended the National Conference on Agricultural Meteorol-
ogy of the American Meteorological Society. Both meetings were
convened at Rutgers at the invitation of the Department of Mete-
orology of the College of Agriculture and Environmental Science
as a part of the Bicentennial.

Dr. Mark D. Shulman, Rutgers meteorologist, commenting
on the growing interest in his field, pointed out that "The atmosphere is the most important part of our physical environment in
that it surrounds and thus affects almost all living organisms.

Biometeorology considers these relationships and this is the reason why so many different fields are represented at our meetings."

His words were underscored by the variety of subjects taken up by the conferees. One highly specialized group, made up largely of physicians and physiologists, considered the question of how life can be made safe and bearable for the farmers and industrial workers who exploit the agricultural and mineral riches under the world's oceans.

In another session of the Congress, Lieutenant Colonel F. M. G. Holstrom of the School of Aerospace Medicine, Brooks Air Force Base, Texas, described the results of a study of the effects of high altitude on a group of men who had worked at an Air Force laboratory on Mt. Wrangell, Alaska, at an altitude of nearly 14,000 feet. Colonel Holstrom reported that men over 35 years of age suffered less from altitude sickness than men from 20 to 35.

And in another session Dr. J. St. Lawrence, a physician from Manchester, England, reported that people who live in Jamaica, B.W.I., bear the pain of rheumatism better than fellow disease sufferers in the north of England. The warmer climate in Jamaica was cited as the reason. While Dr. St. Lawrence found joint degeneration greater in the Jamaicans, they lost less work and complained less of pain than did arthritis sufferers in England.

There was one report at the International Biometeorological Congress which, if commonplace to the scientists, was certainly a shocker to the layman. This was a statement that certain plants, particularly the pine tree and the pungent sagebrush, pollute the air more than do all of man's fires, factory fumes, and car exhausts.

Fritz W. Went, botanist at the University of Nevada's Desert Research Institute, Reno, made the statement and estimated that these plants and their relatives put out ten times the air pollution of man. He said that they send into the air molecular substances known generally as terpenes and esters. The same sort of chemical reaction goes on with them as with man-made pollutants and the result is summer haze, often called heat haze or blue haze, Dr. Went pointed out. The botanist said that he estimated nature's own smog produces as much as 1,000 million tons of pollutants a year around the world, or roughly ten times more than man's carelessness and inefficient engines produce.

❧

2,000 MATHEMATICIANS + 5 = 200

The largest learned group to help Rutgers celebrate its Bicentennial were the mathematicians of the United States. More than 2,000 members of the nation's leading mathematical associations came to New Brunswick for five days, August 29 through September 2.

They were here to attend the meetings of the American Mathematical Society, the Mathematical Association of America, the Institute of Mathematical Statistics, the Society for Industrial and Applied Mathematics, and two undergraduate mathematical fraternities, Pi Mu Epsilon and Mu Alpha Theta.

Dr. Louis F. McAuley, Rutgers professor of mathematics who was in charge of the conference programing, estimated that 200 discoveries in the various fields of mathematics were announced and explored in papers presented during the meetings. Most of these have since appeared in the many journals devoted to mathematics in this country and abroad.

In addition to the research papers the mathematicians were given the opportunity to listen to and exchange ideas over some thirty exploratory or expository papers and to view a dozen films on mathematics. One of the highlights was the delivery by Professor Eugene P. Wigner of Princeton University of the John Von Neumann Lecture sponsored by the Society for Industrial and Applied Mathematics. Dr. Wigner, a 1963 Nobel Laureate in physics, lectured on "Statistical Theory of Spectra."

While journal papers on advanced mathematical discoveries do not make exciting reading for the layman, two developments at the conference caught widespread press attention. The first of these was the comment by two mathematicians that their Soviet colleagues are leading the world in two important fields, higher arithmetic and automatic control theory. But the two reporting scientists, Drs. W. W. Comfort of the University of Massachusetts and J. R. Isbell of the Case Institute of Technology, also said that Russian mathematics on the whole lags behind that of the rest of the world.

The two American mathematicians based their report on impressions gained at the International Congress of Mathematicians in Moscow, which was held immediately preceding the sessions at Rutgers.

A discussion by a panel of leading mathematicians about the subject of mathematical education—past, present, and future—earned widespread press attention including a report and an editorial in the *New York Times*.

Harry Schwartz, the *Times* knowledgeable reporter in several scientific fields, including mathematics, had this to say about the panel under the heading "Experts Criticize 'New Math' Trend":

New Brunswick, N.J., Aug. 30—If Johnny doesn't like his "new math" course when school opens next month, he may—in some cases—be showing sound instinct rather than obstinate resistance to progress.

This conclusion emerged here today at a symposium on mathematics education at Rutgers University. Leaders in the field criticized what they called excesses that have crept into the last decade's revolution in elementary and high school mathematics instruction.

Speaking before more than 500 mathematicians at a meeting of the Mathematical Association of America, Professor Andrew M. Gleason of Harvard, Professor Edward S. Begle of Stanford, and Dean Albert E. Meder, Jr., of Rutgers criticized such failings as excessive abstraction, unnecessarily involved terminology, and poor preparation of teachers.

The speakers, who are among those chiefly responsible for the present widespread use of the "new math," made plain that they were not repudiating the movement toward change.

They are proud of the progress made in introducing more modern mathematical ideas into precollege courses, and in helping students understand the "why" as well as the "how" of mathematical operations.

More Changes Expected

They feel future changes will and should be in the same direction, though probably at a slower pace than in the last 10 years.

Professor Begle, whose School Mathematics Study Group has prepared the "new math" textbooks used in many schools, criticized a tendency in some quarters to use excessively esoteric ideas and language from graduate mathematics in courses for youngsters.

As an example he cited a textbook that defines a number in terms of "the equivalence class of ordered pairs of the equivalence classes of ordered pairs."

Professor Gleason, one of the nation's outstanding mathematicians, expressed the hope there would be a retreat from abstract formalism toward better intuitive understanding in the teaching of mathematics.

In private conversation afterward, he and others indicated their belief that some poorly trained teachers had tended to stress secondary aspects of the innovations in mathematics education at the expense of the primary goal.

As an example, the Harvard mathematician deplored the practice in some courses of stressing the difference between a number and a numeral.

The distinction between a given concept—the number—and the symbol by which it is represented—the numeral—is sometimes useful. Professor Gleason said, "but it would be a terrible mistake for the teacher to jump down Johnny's throat" for confusing the two.

The *Times* on September 3 editorialized thusly about the new math:

The "New Math" Reconsidered

The gap between advocates and critics of the past decade's revolution in American mathematical education seems to have narrowed considerably. At a Rutgers University symposium this week, several key leaders of that revolution warned against excesses—too much abstraction, needless jargon and the like.

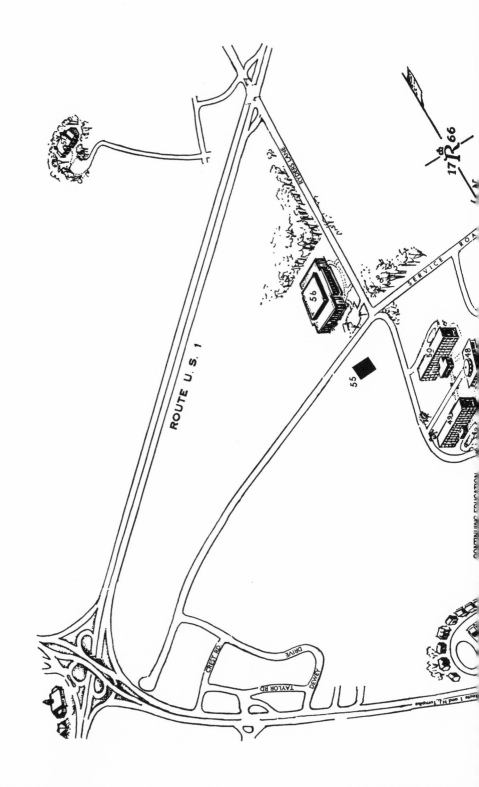

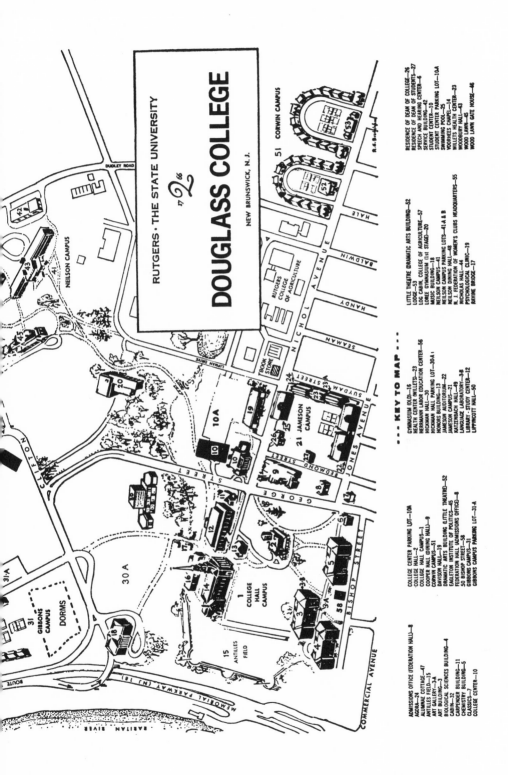

RUTGERS · THE STATE UNIVERSITY

DOUGLASS COLLEGE

NEW BRUNSWICK, N.J.

· · · KEY TO MAP · · ·

ADMISSIONS OFFICE (FEDERATION HALL)—8
AGORA—24
ALUMNAE COTTAGE—47
ANTILLES FIELD—15
ART GALLERY—3-A
ART BUILDING—2
BIOLOGICAL SCIENCES BUILDING—4
CABIN—32
CARPENDER BUILDING—11
CHEMISTRY BUILDING—5
CLASSES—7
COLLEGE CENTER—10

COLLEGE CENTER PARKING LOT—10A
COLLEGE HALL—2
COLLEGE HALL CAMPUS—1
COOPER HALL DINING HALL—9
CORWIN CAMPUS—51
DAVISON HALL—19
DRAMATIC ARTS BUILDING (LITTLE THEATRE)—52
EAGLETON INSTITUTE OF POLITICS—45
FEDERATION HALL (ADMISSIONS OFFICE)—8
50 BISHOP STREET—58
GIBBONS CAMPUS—31
GIBBONS CAMPUS PARKING LOT—31-A

GYMNASIUM (OLD)—16
HEALTH CENTER (WILLETS)—23
HERRMANN LABOR EDUCATION CENTER—56
HICKMAN HALL—30
HICKMAN HALL PARKING LOT—30A-1
MUSIC BUILDING—18
NEILSON CAMPUS—41
HONORS BUILDING—13
JAMESON AUDITORIUM—22
JAMESON CAMPUS—21
KATZENBACH HALL—49
LANGUAGE LABORATORY—38
LIBRARY: STUDY CENTER—12
LIPPINCOTT HALL—50

LITTLE THEATRE DRAMATIC ARTS BUILDING—52
LODGE—53
LOG CABIN: COLLEGE OF AGRICULTURE—57
LOREE GYMNASIUM 11st STAGE)—20
MUSIC BUILDING—18
NEILSON CAMPUS—41
NEILSON CAMPUS PARKING LOTS—41-A & B
NEILSON DINING HALL—48
N. J. FEDERATION OF WOMEN'S CLUBS HEADQUARTERS—55
NICHOLAS HALL—44
PSYCHOLOGICAL CLINIC—19
RAVINE BRIDGE—17

RESIDENCE OF DEAN OF COLLEGE—26
RESIDENCE OF DEAN OF STUDENTS—27
SPEECH AND HEARING CENTER—6
SERVICE BUILDING—42
STUDENT CENTER—10
STUDENT CENTER PARKING LOT—10A
SWIMMING POOL—25
VOORHEES CHAPEL—14
WILLETS HEALTH CENTER—23
WOODBURY HALL—63
WOOD LAWN—45
WOOD LAWN GATE HOUSE—46

By now, the "new mathematics" is no longer so new. Millions of youngsters already have been more or less successfully exposed to the idea of a set, to the commutative and distributive laws of addition and to number systems on bases other than ten. The real question is where American mathematics education goes from here.

The tenor of the remarks at the Rutgers meeting suggested that its participants favor making haste slowly in the years immediately ahead. They are impressed with how much remains to be done before the innovations already made are digested and their potential benefits fully realized.

Such relative conservatism is opposed by radicals among the mathematicians. This group dismisses the changes already made as grossly inadequate, and urges an even more drastic revolution in elementary and high school mathematics in the next few years. The problems exposed by the stormy experience of ten years suggest that the more moderate voices reflect more wisely the lessons that have been learned, some at very high cost.

BICENTENNIAL SYMPOSIUM—INSTITUTE OF MICROBIOLOGY

Three Nobel Prize winners were among the very distinguished scientists who gathered on the campus on September 8 for the three-day Bicentennial Symposium held under the auspices of the Institute of Microbiology. This major scientific meeting of the anniversary year was supported in large measure by the National Science Foundation and was devoted to the subject of "Organizational Biosynthesis." Its proceedings are published in a volume under that title which has been edited by Drs. Henry J. Vogel, J. Oliver Lampen, and Vernon Bryson, organizers of the symposium.

The symposium, which was held at Waksman Hall, named for Nobel Laureate Selman A. Waksman, attracted more than 200 scientists from this country and abroad. They heard some 24 papers on new discoveries in the field of their consideration, which very simply put is the way that plant and animal cells build up key parts of their internal organization from comparatively simple chemicals.

Dr. Fritz Lipmann, Nobel Prize winner of Rockefeller University, opened the meeting with an address on molecular technology. Dr. Feodor Lynen of the Max-Planck-Institut fur Zellchemie in Munich and Dr. Konrad Bloch of Harvard University, Nobel Prize winners in 1964, presided over sessions on the synthesis of membranes and chloroplasts.

Dr. C. A. Thomas of Johns Hopkins University and Dr. S. B. Weiss of the University of Chicago chaired the sessions on organizational nucleic acid synthesis and Dr. Alexander Rich of the Massachusetts Institute of Technology headed up a session on protein synthesis as a heterogeneous process.

Dr. S. S. Cohen of the University of Pennsylvania lectured the first evening of the conference on developments in metabolic integration. This session was conducted by Dr. R. W. Schlesinger of the Rutgers Medical School. Other phenomena of cellular organization were discussed in two sessions headed by Dr. C. B. Anfinsen of the National Institutes of Health and Dr. Noboru Sweoka of Princeton.

Dr. R. B. Roberts of the Carnegie Institution of Washington and Dr. Efraim Racker of Cornell University led the sessions which took up the synthesis of two other fundamental biological particles, ribosomes and mitochondria.

The speaker at the banquet for the participants and guests was Dr. Philip Handler of Duke University, a senior presidential adviser and chairman of the National Science Foundation Board. Dr. Handler discussed "University Scientists and Public Policy."

DEDICATION OF HENRY E. ACKERSON HALL

Thomas J. Hooper, the *Newark Evening News* reporter who covered the dedication on September 10, 1966, of Henry E. Ackerson Hall, the new building of the Rutgers Law School in downtown Newark, wrote that it had brought together "the most distinguished assemblage of notables in the legal profession in the history of New Jersey."

Certainly, no one in the University nor in the legal profession could argue with Mr. Hooper's appraisal of that brilliant lineup of legal talent. In addition to Chief Justice Warren, it included two other justices of the Supreme Court, William J. Brennan and Abe Fortas, Chief Justice Joseph Weintraub of New Jersey, New Jersey's Governor Richard J. Hughes, a former Superior Court judge, a long list of other judges, legal practitioners, and outstanding legal educators including delegates from 37 law schools across the nation who came to pay tribute to Rutgers and its Law School.

The Chief Justice gave the address at the Saturday afternoon dedication, the climax and conclusion of the exercises. Justice Weintraub and Governor Hughes spoke at the luncheon which preceded the ceremony, and Justice Brennan spoke at the dedication banquet on Friday night.

The stage for the dedication had been set on Friday with one of the most stimulating presentations of the Bicentennial. A group of outstanding scholars representing several disciplines as well as the law took part in three seminars which made up a day-long symposium on the subject, "The Projection of an Ideal: The Law School of Tomorrow."

Dr. Robert M. Hutchins, president of the Center for the Study of Democratic Institutions, was the lecturer for the first of the seminars, which dealt with "Law as a Phase of the Humanities and as a Subject of the Behavioral Sciences." Dr. Sidney Hook, professor of philosophy at New York University, and Paul Goodman, author and teacher, were the critics.

For the second seminar, which was titled "Directions for Research, Empirical and Non-Empirical," the lecturer was Harold Lasswell, professor of law at Yale University, and the critics were Mark S. Massel, economist of the Brookings Institution, and Professor James A. Robinson of Ohio State University.

Justice Fortas gave the lecture for the third of the seminars. It took up "The Training of the Practitioner." The critics for this panel were Judge Henry J. Friendly, of the Second Circuit, U.S. Court of Appeals, and Myres S. McDougal, professor of law at Yale University.

Dean C. Willard Heckel presided at the dedication. Governor Hughes presented the handsome new building to the University and Charles H. Brower, chairman of the Rutgers Board of Governors, accepted it on behalf of the University. Professor David

Haber gave an acceptance speech for the faculty and William Greenberg, president of the Student Bar Association, accepted for the student body.

President Gross then conferred the honorary degree of **Doctor of Laws** upon Chief Justice Warren. The citation accompanying the degree read as follows:

> Earl Warren, Chief Justice of the United States—Under your leadership the Constitution of the United States has become a living document that has given legal protection to the most precious values in our democratic society. Your powerful intellect, your committed humanitarian approach to the law, your unfailing energy, have all been devoted to insuring equal justice under law for all men. Your intellectual courage has been an inspiration to men in all walks of life.

In his address the Chief Justice spoke of the tremendous changes in all human society in a relatively short span of years and declared that "the greatest problem of today is that of adapting our democratic institutions to these precedent-shattering changes without disturbing the basic fundamentals of a free society. To a very large extent this adaptation falls upon the legal institutions of our nation, for it is there that the framework of business and society should be equated with the constitutional safeguards of our Government."*

In his introductory remarks the Chief Justice took notice of both the 300th anniversary of the establishment of the City of Newark and the Rutgers Bicentennial, said that it was "icing on the cake to be able to share this happy occasion with my colleague Mr. Justice Brennan," said that the presence of Mr. Justice Fortas added to his pleasure at being at Rutgers and recalled the first intercollegiate football game, drawing from it a legal precept.

Of that contest in November, 1869, he pointed out that "since I am speaking here in the comfortable safety of your presence and not at Princeton, I can take note of the fact that it was Rutgers which prevailed—six goals to four. All of us whose concern is with the law know the importance of rules, for they are

---

*The text of Mr. Justice Warren's address of September 10, 1966, is found in Appendix H.

the very essence of our profession. I should therefore like to add an interesting postscript to my historical commentary. This first intercollegiate football game was played at New Brunswick under Rutgers' rules. Next week a return match was played at Princeton —this time under Princeton's rules—I shall leave it to your surmise who won."

Mr. Justice Warren said in part: "Lawyers must always be among the most influential leaders of opinion in modern society. In this position, it is the responsibility of lawyers to call upon the experiences of the past and to correlate law with history, economics and all of the social sciences available in the solution of human problems. Many law schools are now recognizing this important relationship of law and social science, and the laws enacted by our legislators have drawn heavily on this area. This is reflected in the statutes which regulate labor relations, unemployment compensation acts, and in legislation designed to provide housing for lower income groups.

"The law school of today carries an important responsibility for leadership not only in the training of lawyers, but in the actual development of the operation of our democratic system. This calls for new types of research consisting of programs of critical and analytical examination of the operation and impact of our laws on business and society. The law schools can provide leadership in the development of law itself through unbiased and objective examination of our legal system with long-range planning and perspectives. It is the environment of the law school that extensive factual inquiry can be conducted and where the troublesome areas of the law can be analyzed."

THE UNIVERSITY AND THE WELFARE OF MAN

For the most part the academic meetings and conferences of learned and professional groups during the Bicentennial were held for and by specialists—experts or authorities in relatively narrow fields of academic or professional interest. Certainly the mathematicians, biometeorologists, animal scientists, agronomists, historians, geologists, Russian area experts, and even the directors of university presses were all specialists talking about their specialties.

There was one meeting, however, which brought together a group of men eminent in widely different fields who discussed a topic or, more accurately, a series of topics of wide interest to all mankind.

This was the conference held on October 7, 1966, to discuss "The Environment, the University and the Welfare of Man," about as broad a subject as could have been selected for a day's consideration. It was planned, as its title indicated, to look at the question of what is involved in man's preservation of his environment and his hopes of passing it along to his children in at least as healthy a state as it is now.

The seven speakers who took up this basic question treated it as just that and pointed to some of the complex and basic factors which enter into the care and feeding of the environment from evolution, through genetic endowment, the relationship of agriculture and electrical power to the fulfillment of man's needs, through discussions of aesthetic values and their economic validity, all the way to the argument that many universities need organizational overhaul if they are to be adequate in the role modern society is asking them to play.

The seven speakers of October 7 were brilliant, informed, and broad-gauged in their approaches to their assigned topics. The result was, for the generalist, some of the most interesting discussion of the Bicentennial Year. The cast for this presentation included Wheeler McMillen, former editor of the *Farm Journal* and one of the most knowledgeable men in the country on agricultural problems and prospects; René Dubos, microbiologist of Rockefeller University, one of the nation's outstanding biologists and a former graduate student of Dr. Selman A. Waksman, Rutgers Nobel Laureate in medicine; Paolo Soleri, brilliant and outspoken architect from Scottsdale, Arizona; Colin S. Pittendrigh, noted biologist and dean of the Graduate School of Princeton University; Aubrey J. Wagner, chairman of the Board of Directors of the Tennessee Valley Authority; Michael T. Romano, professor of operative dentistry and coordinator of medical center television at the University of Kentucky; and Dr. Mason W. Gross, the president of the University but who, in this instance, presumably was speaking as a philosopher, a scholar, and a lover of beauty.

Dr. Billy Ray Wilson, chairman of the Bureau of Environmental Science in the College of Agriculture and Environmental Sciences, conceived and arranged the conference and served as its moderator or master of ceremonies.

Mr. McMillen, discussing the important question of whether the environment can provide man with enough food or, more precisely, enough arable land to raise the food he needs, pointed out that "throughout history the rulers of nations, the so-called statesmen, have been strangely blind to the fact that agriculture, everywhere and at all times, is of first importance and in all national considerations should ever have first priority."

He also pointed out that American agriculture had benefited from a recognition of its importance and declared that "the most constructive development in all human history has been the creation by American farmers of a pattern for the conquest of hunger."

He agreed that American agricultural competence cannot be exported readily to hungry nations, but he did state that "what can be exported is the pattern by which our highly productive farming techniques have been developed. Given a reasonable expanse of arable land, the nation that will study its soils scientifically, apply modern genetic knowledge toward developing indigenous or adapted crops and livestock, seriously pursue intelligent experimentation, educate its young farmers, teach them the dignity of agriculture, and leave its people enough freedom and incentive, can within limits begin to feed itself. Then and probably only then can it begin to accumulate capital for other purposes."

Mr. McMillen also said:

"Somehow the race between people and hunger must be won by the people themselves. Application of the American farmer's pattern for plenty would now appear to be one of the most promising means. Restraint of births and changes in outdated customs will assist. More equitable distribution of landownership, and greater incentives for farmers, would help. Perhaps scientists will evolve new solutions not yet imagined. Present predictions say that by A.D. 2000, only a third of a century hence, the face of the earth could be crowded by twice as many people as now. If the demographers prophesied accurately, hunger will increase rather than diminish unless wise and heroic efforts rapidly expand the food supplies."

Commenting on the present-day problems of the cities, Mr. McMillen pointed out that large numbers of people no longer want to live in them as they are now constituted, and he questioned the idea that it is necessary for the city to continue to develop in an ancient mold that was formed because of far different military, transportation, economic, and cultural forces than exist today.

Studies suggest, Mr. McMillen said, "that increasing numbers of Americans do not feel that the big cities are attractive places to live in. They see that the overgrown metropolis can seldom manage the traffic over its streets, control its crime, or eliminate air pollution. It falls short in educating its children, provides intolerable housing for its poor, and rarely can govern itself with honesty and efficiency."

He admitted, however, that the fact that "megalopolis is irrational does not mean that it will cease to exist, nor that it will not continue to grow." This is likely to remove more good and productive land from cultivation and Mr. McMillen suggested as an alternative the building of "new cities, new places in which to live and work, in locations not likely to be of much use for agricultural purposes. Such areas exist—the Pine Barrens of New Jersey, the less rugged portions of mountain ranges, large parts of the southeastern coastal plain, are examples. Their counterparts can be found in many other parts of the nation. Most of them could be made highly acceptable places in which to live."

While the speaker conceded that more and more farmland will be taken out of production, he did not foresee any drastic increases in the prices of farm products at an "early date." He reasons that technological advances, development of new synthetics, and the return of reserves of cultivable land to farming would enable the nation to maintain adequate supplies of needed food stuffs.

Because of his reference to the Rutgers Tricentennial in 2066, Mr. McMillen's concluding remarks are included here in full:

Now, let me conclude these somewhat scattered remarks with a plea—a plea to the student who on the occasion of the Rutgers Tricentennial in 2066, or perhaps even as soon as the 1900's give way to the 2000's—to the student who then on some remote, air-conditioned shelf may encounter the records of this conference.

What sort of student he will be I have no idea; maybe an exchange student from some other planet. First, let him have his laugh. Then let him realize that we have spoken today as well as we know how. To all of us the future is somewhat dim; and our lamps of experience cannot penetrate far.

Had we been ready to respond to an invitation such as this in the college's centennial year of 1866, or even more recently at the birth of the twentieth century, I doubt whether any of us on today's program would have predicted that by 1966 Americans would own horseless vehicles enough to transport the entire population at one time; or that flying machines would cross the nation and the oceans in mere hours, or that sounds and pictures would be transmitted instantly into nearly every home without wires; and even be bouncing from man-made satellites; or that men would circle the earth in outer space in less than two hours; or that the incredible force of nuclear energy would be responding to man's will; or that anti-biotics would be relieving man's ills and extending life; or that things called computers would be doing what they do; or that our country's history would be bloodied by wars fought over-seas.

Had we then been content to predict in general terms that human nature would not change noticeably; that man's curiosity about his environment would grow more intense; that progress in various forms would continue; and that each succeeding generation would manage in some fashion to face up to most of its problems and would postpone others, we could have been on safe ground.

For the student in the year 2000 or 2066 I extend the hope that he will not be troubled about finding enough to eat; that he will not mind too seriously elbowing his way through the crowds of people; that there will remain to him some green land; and that still his will be the priceless American privilege of individual liberty—the right to make a reasonably large percentage of his own choices.

Mr. Aubrey Wagner's topic was "Electric Power for Tomorrow" and he developed the theme that such power frees man from drudgery and gives him the chance for greater individual development.

He said that "electric power combines in one modern, scientific tool man's achievements through the ages in his efforts to free himself from physical toil. Over the centuries he adapted the primitive wheel, the lever, and the wedge to more and more of his labor needs. He used them in many combinations. He expanded their usefulness by applying the power of rivers and their waterfalls to grind corn, lift hammers, and make iron. He captured, in some lands, the power of the winds. He perceived the power of steam and again put it to work performing tasks all the others could not do.

"But in electricity man has found a substitute for muscle power and horsepower which transcends, almost beyond imagination, these past accomplishments. The power of the river is made to extend far beyond the banks of the stream. The power of steam is given greater precision, greater mobility, far greater application. Immense strength can be focused on the small tasks of the household or the titanic problems of weight and speed and heat and cold in great industries.

"Electricity is significant in the context of your Bicentennial conference theme in this way: more than any other present-day energy source, it is the key for unlocking the shackles of drudgery which hold the mind and the will in rigid molds of fatigue and despair. It is thus a means of releasing the forces of the human personality which lead to personal fulfillment, happier people, and a better society."

And in his conclusion, Mr. Wagner added:

"We could expand these thoughts indefinitely to demonstrate that electricity is vital, that it is irreplaceable, and that its promise for the future seems endless. But added examples would only further underscore an already apparent truth: usefully applied, this energy form opens new horizons to the mind and the spirit of man—horizons otherwise totally indiscernible. In freeing him of oppressive labor, it allows the time and opportunity for fullest development of his best inherent qualities. And in multiplying a millionfold the capacity of his memory and the speed of its application, it extends to limitless boundaries the reach of his mind and its ability to serve his most noble purposes."

Dr. Soleri's theme was the physical, aesthetic, and emotional environment of man.

He explained that man must use his technical knowledge to improve his world. He emphasized that, although science can solve many of the problems that man faces, fate and love (the environment of the deeper emotions) also affect his life.

Dr. Soleri urged a fusion between what he calls "environmental" and "synthetic" knowledge. The first deals with facts and the rational and the latter deals with emotion and the creative arts.

He suggested that new buildings should reflect joy and spontaneity as well as technological knowledge. However, he reflected, today's homes are rigid, cities are haphazardly structured, and the result is chaos.

Presenting his personal ideas of what an ideal city might be like, Dr. Soleri outlined the features of one-structure cities which he said retain the advantages of both urban and country life.

"The advantages of both are retained and the disadvantages minimized," he pointed out. "The urban advantages of abundance of facilities, cultural wealth, direct contact are included as are advantages of direct or quick communion with nature, the open spaces, the clean air, the isolation. The time-energy waste of commuting, chaos, and squalor are reduced to a residual."

Dr. Soleri illustrated his talk with slides of preferred construction and presented plans for his one-building city, the "megastructure." Before he began his visual presentation, he declared that "A heartless and pauper environment does nothing more than reflect and denounce the harshness and the indigent condition of our minds and souls. To change all this will require greater things than wealth and determination. It will require a definite moving away from materialism, determinism, and arrogance. It will require a truly reverent attitude toward the sacramentality of all things."

Dr. Dubos began with two propositions: that man—biologically and mentally—has not changed significantly since paleolithic times, but civilizations have changed, are constantly changing, and are creating entirely different ways of life.

Man, he said, is still depending upon the same needs and the same biological mechanisms that characterized the paleolithic hunter or the neolithic farmer. If you argue, Dr. Dubos said, that man is living under far different conditions than he did hundreds or thousands of years ago, you must also understand that "in reality, nothing is changing, because wherever man goes he carries with him, or constructs around him, the kind of physiological environment which is that which became essential to him one hundred thousand years ago.

"To summarize a very large problem, I think we can say without any question that the genetic endowment of Homo sapiens has changed only in minor detail since the Stone Age; and in my opinion there is no change whatever that we can significantly, usefully, or safely modify in the foreseeable future.

"This genetic stability is not only a problem of intellectual curiosity for biologists. In my opinion this genetic stability determines the physiological limits beyond which human life cannot be safely altered by social or technological innovations. So that, in final analysis, the frontiers of technology are far less significant in the life of man than are man's own frontiers, which are determined by the genetic constitution he acquired during his evolutionary past."

Dr. Dubos continued by noting that one of the factors which conditions man's response to his environment is the "genetic uniqueness of each human being."

"Anyone who knows anything of biology will know that each human being—except for identical twins and even there the reservations are large and I shall not discuss them—has a unique genetic endowment that never happened before and that statistically will never happen again.

"Each one of us is a unique event in the history of life."

The conditions under which people live, Dr. Dubos asserted, not only affect their immediate well-being "but also affect what you will become tomorrow—and much more importantly, determine what your children and grandchildren will become."

He quoted from Winston Churchill's defense of the reconstruction of the House of Commons exactly as it was before the war to bring out the extraordinary sentence which ended Sir Winston's presentation: "We shape our buildings, and then they shape us."

Dr. Dubos continued:

"I think the concept of the design of our cities, the designs of our homes, the kind of environment in which we live, is important not only for our comfort for today but is extremely relevant to the distant future, and is, I believe, one of the most important aspects of social planning."

And he went on:

"The evidence is clear that man in the past, or today, uses only a very, very small percentage of his potentiality. All our knowledge about modern genetics shows that at any given time only five percent perhaps of the genes are in an active state, the other parts are repressed, not expressed.

"So, we can feel confident that there is an immense range of potentiality that man has not yet exploited. And this, I believe, should be of large importance in our designing of the environment around us. All experience shows, the varied experience of life, that those components of the genetic endowment that become expressed are those which in some way are stimulated by environmental factors.

"It is well known that if we narrow down—if we run too uniform in our environment—we will limit enormously the range of expression about innate potentialities. From that point of view, I think it is certain that the greatest crime of our cities is perhaps not their ugliness, because one reacts to ugliness, against ugliness; it is not their lack of sanitary conditions, because one protects against them; it's their deadly uniformity—the fact that there are so few stimuli to reach the young growing organism and cause him to respond and thereby express what potentiality he has to himself.

"So, in a peculiar sort of way I do believe that when we come to really formulate an organic, biological structure for environmental development we will have to organize that diversity that is the essential part of true functionalism. I believe we will have to be willing to sacrifice efficiency for the sake of diversity."

Dr. Dubos differed with Mr. McMillen in his attitude toward the city. He argued that "man has always wanted to live in a crowded environment," but admitted that the degree of crowding man will tolerate or possibly enjoy may be a highly variable factor.

The Rockefeller University scientist and thinker summarized his talk in his concluding paragraphs, saying:

"Let me say that a scientific philosophy of mankind can be realized only from the knowledge that man's nature is made up of two statements that are radically different, yet complementary. On the one hand, Homo sapiens has existed as a species with a well-defined genetic endowment for at least fifty thousand years.

"On the other hand, man has continued to unfold his little potentialities ever since that time. This ancient language accounts for the biological limitations of mankind, and also for its immense diversity. The biological limitations inherent in the human species create a collective responsibility for making technological development compatible with the essential needs and wants of man. The wide range of potentialities gives to each of us the chance to select or create his surroundings and ways of life, and thus to develop along the lines he chooses.

"The existentialist faith that man makes himself implies of course the willingness to decide, and the courage to be, but it also demands that action be guided by scientific knowledge of man's nature. For this reason we must create a new science of environmental biology that will help in predicting, and hopefully in controlling, man's responses to the environmental conditions prevailing in the modern world. Entirely new kinds of scientific institutions must be developed to study the effects exerted by the surroundings and the ways of life on physical and mental development, especially during the formative years of life.

"The characteristics of individual persons and of societies are largely determined by feedback reactions between man's nature and environmental forces. Since man has much freedom in selecting and creating his environment, as well as his way of life, he does determine by such decision what he and his descendants will become. In this light man can truly make himself consciously and willfully. He has the privilege of responsible choice of his destiny;

and this probably is the noblest and most unique attribute of the human condition."

Dean Pittendrigh in his opening remarks stated that his purpose was to question "whether or not the universities, with the functions they have to fulfill in the social organism, are really adequately structured to face the challenge of the pace of social evolution." He also made clear that he would not have thought of posing the question unless he had decided that the answer must be a negative one.

Pointing out that biological evolution is inescapable and that "all organisms, or species, by virtue of living must evolve," Dean Pittendrigh declared that, while the process of biological evolution is slow, social evolution, brought on by the mechanism of language, is going on at a fantastic pace.

"The subject of the evolution of language is something that you can say a great deal about, for the standard reason that we know nothing about it. But nevertheless its function is clear in early man. And here is an interesting point: language evolved as a device to transfer information from individual to individual, and immediately became an entirely new mechanism of heredity. As far as the biologist is concerned, this is the significance of the emergence of language in the early evolution of man."

The speaker went on to say that language is the mechanism of social evolution and it is this evolution which will determine the future of man.

"The rate of cultural evolution is going so much faster than the life span of the individual that we are confronted with intellectual obsolescence in the lifetime of an individual," Dean Pittendrigh declared. "And the rate of individual obsolescence itself is increasing at such a pace that it is frightening, to be trite about it. In fact it increases the university administrator's problem acutely in a sense that it makes the amount of dead wood on the faculty greater every year . . ."

Dean Pittendrigh now turned to the problem of the relation of the universities to the social revolution. He gave as a basic premise the assertion that "in a sense the universities are the mainsprings of the new knowledge on which the social evolution depends, and the source of whatever new knowledge, the control or management of social evolution, if it is indeed to be managed—must come from.

"My proposition is, then, or relates to three items of concern: the speed or pace of cultural and social evolution, the role of the universities in that evolution, and my skepticism that the universities themselves as organisms in a way are not organized adequately to respond fast enough to the challenges that social evolution in its great pace presents."

And then, after discussing how university organizations have evolved, the speaker continued:

"I am suggesting that the organizational structure of the university is not something to be taken lightly, and it is not something that relates only to the administrative convenience of deans, and to financial vice-presidents, but rather the organizational structure of the university will dictate the pace at which the university as an institution and an organization can cope with the pace at which new problems and problem areas are defined."

Dean Pittendrigh pointed to the problem of the city as one needing an "interdisciplinary" approach by the universities, but he questioned their ability actually to tackle such problems with the "vigor that they should be attacked, if the university is to discharge its function in contributing to the regulation of social evolution.

"Let me say, then, that I regard this as a very urgent and serious problem. I am not suggesting that there is just something slightly wrong with the universities, or that they irritate us sometime. I am venturing the proposition that we in deep trouble unless the university community as a whole is capable of scrutinizing the way in which it responds to challenges, unless we do something about it. I believe, for instance, that one of the most obvious and serious problems we are facing is that as knowledge explodes—to borrow another cliché—or as the problems become manifestly more diverse, every institution is trying to cope with all of them, and no institution is moving with any of them really adequately. The time has come when universities are going to have to decide what areas they want to tackle, and what areas they do not. No university can cover the whole ground and cover it adequately. And yet, with very few minor exceptions, there is no significant trend in the university world to face up to this. Every one of us has a linguistics department, which is inadequate. Every one of us is seeking a Near Eastern department which is inadequate, etc."

The speaker also advocated that universities plan administrative structures with built-in short life to protect themselves from self-perpetuating departmental or other academic units which have actually outlived their original, and perhaps experimental, purpose.

Dr. Pittendrigh concluded by referring to his original analogy between biological and social organisms and declared that "organisms can live too long for the health of the population of which they are a part."

Dr. Romano discussed the ways in which new advances in communication techniques will aid the academic process. He predicted that many new devices such as picture telephones, picture "guns," and video tape recorders for individual use will be among the communication tools soon available to educators. He predicted varying sizes of viewing equipment, personal viewers for self-study, electronic printers, and devices that will convert the spoken word into printed pages of material. He also forecast that the student of the future will be aided by nationwide information storage and retrieval systems and centralized reservoirs of knowledge, readily available to anyone via television.

"In the next quarter of a century there will evolve a new, more efficient basic communication medium in education," Dr. Romano declared. "We will see the primacy of the word challenged by illustration, graphics, and electronic imagery. It is becoming increasingly clear that we are well into the age of vision. Further, we can predict that men of the future will be forced to develop what can be described as 'visual literacy,' or, the ability to communicate with pictures. Whereas literature, as we now know it, consists primarily of words, reinforced to varying degrees by still pictures, the new, more efficient 'visualature,' as it has been called, will be primarily pictures (still and motion) supported by words."

Automated examinations will allow the student to proceed at

his own rate. He will be able to participate in laboratory experiences and other prescribed activities after he has mastered all the subject matter involved.

University lectures, noted Dr. Romano, now require that all students be on a similar level of development. The new techniques using electronic and other newly developed techniques will make it possible to tailor instruction for individual levels.

Optimum communication, Dr. Romano said, would mean that experts could serve on several college faculties because they could operate from remote locations through "live" television contact. Television, the speaker asserted, could become a "university without walls" and make a "lifetime of learning" more real than it has ever been before.

Dr. Romano declared that instant information, available to anyone, anytime, anywhere, is the key to closing the gap between the demand for and the availability of knowledge. He urged the universities to accept the challenge posed for them by the newest technological advances.

President Gross spoke on "The University and the Welfare of Man," and began his remarks by agreeing with Dr. Pittendrigh that universities have changed very little over the years and "have hardly adapted themselves to the tasks which are currently before them."

"This is nowhere truer than in the general approach to undergraduate education," Dr. Gross added, "and I am going to make the flat statement that I think our concept of how we should conduct the business of educating undergraduates really is still under the domination of two people who died some twenty-four hundred years ago, namely, Plato and Aristotle. Now I don't mean that it goes directly back to Plato and Aristotle, although I think it can be demonstrated quite easily that these are the prevailing concepts."

In pointing out the failings of the universities Dr. Gross criticized the unwillingness of most of the academic world to find out what is really going on in society.

"When we teach sociology courses or economics courses, or courses about the present health of our urban society, we do it from a classroom," Dr. Gross said. "We don't go down into the society if we can help it. We do it from here with the general notion that if we can only work out a better scheme of things, wouldn't that be nice for all the other people. Somehow or other we are out of this thing, we are removed from it. We are not going to get dirtied by it, or anything else. We'll think about it. That's the very important thing that we will do, and perhaps one of these days, things will get a little bit better.

"Well, I suggest to you that this concept of the relationship of man to his environment is radically at odds with our vaguely conceived, vaguely admitted traditional educational objectives."

Dr. Gross continued:

"One thing that we know now is that we are radically interconnected with all the rest of the people in our society. We are beginning to realize, for example, that if we have poverty on our doorstep, if we have misery, it isn't merely bad for those people, it's bad for us too."

He said that people who refuse to see the ugly and the hideous in their environment are cutting down their own capabilities and delaying and impeding necessary reform. He also said that efforts to beautify will not be effective if they "move in from the top," but can succeed only if the effort is directed by someone who understands the interconnections of the hideous and ugly in the environment with his own being.

Dr. Gross said that he expects the undergraduates to catch on to this point of view more quickly than the college faculties, and he cited a number of instances at Rutgers where the students had led the way in the introduction of new courses fitted to the changing needs of their society.

He spoke very movingly about the present-day undergraduate and this young person's concern for all that is wrong in the world from the civil rights issue in this country to the war in Vietnam. He called "insulting" those who would dismiss youthful disgust with the war in Asia as some kind of cowardice.

"What we have to do," Dr. Gross went on, "is to start conceiving of what our educational pattern would be like if we thought of it in terms not of an individual voluntarily entering a new relationship but of individuals already being shaped and formed by all their interrelationships, and then try to make something constructive and creative out of it.

"This need not change too much. But it will not be a matter of acquiring information, whether by the lecture method or by television. It will be by somehow entering into relationships with people, and recognizing those as the relationships which are constructive of our personality at any given moment; and then trying to make something constructive and good out of those, not merely in terms of knowledge but much more in terms of value."

CONFERENCE ON EARLY AMERICAN HISTORY

On the same day that the conference on "The Environment, the University, and the Welfare of Man" opened in Records Hall, some 300 historians from colleges and universities throughout the Northeast were gathering in Kirkpatrick Chapel for the Twentieth Conference on Early American History. This was a special event of the Bicentennial Year.

The principal address of the conference was given on the opening days of the two-day meeting. It was a talk by Professor J. H. Plumb of Cambridge University, who discussed "America's Last King." He referred, of course, to George III, the English monarch who handed down the charter which opened the way for the establishment of Queen's College and thus made inevitable the Rutgers Bicentennial of 1966.

The conference opened on Friday, October 7, with a paper presented by Richard S. Dunn of the University of Pennsylvania. Speakers on Saturday included Stanley Katz of the University of Wisconsin and David Alan Williams of the University of Virginia. Michael G. Kammen of Cornell University spoke at the concluding session on Saturday. Commentators on the papers were Professors Michael G. Hall of the University of Texas, Thomas Barrow of the University of Missouri, and Richard B. Morris of Columbia. Codirectors of the conference were Dr. Richard M. Brown of the Rutgers College of Arts and Sciences and Dr. Alison Olson of Douglass College. Presiding over the several sessions were Drs. Emery S. Battis, Theodore Thayer, and Richard P. McCormick, all members of the Rutgers history faculty.

WHAT'S NEW ON EARTH?

Three days later, October 10-11, the University's geology departments sponsored a conference which drew to the campus some of the world's leading geologists. The topic under discussion was the intriguing question, "What's New on Earth?" which, it seems from the geologist's point of view, is more specifically the question of whether there is "evidence for or against existence, possible causes and mechanics of fracturing, drifting and rotating of continents and ocean basins."

The list of speakers made up an impressive panel of geological experts. It included Dr. William T. Pecora, director of the U.S. Geological Survey, who served as chairman for the opening session on continental geology; Dr. James Afflect, of the Gulf Research and Development Company, chairman of the session on geophysical considerations; Dr. Harry Hess, Princeton University geologist and one of the leaders in the now-abandoned Mohole earth-core drilling project; Dr. H. W. Menard, member of the President's Science Advisory Council and director of the Scripps Institute of Oceanography; Dr. D. W. Collinson, University, Newcastle upon Tyne, England, authority on climate records over the past several thousand years; Robert S. Dietz of the Geological Survey; Charles Drake of the Lamont Geological Observatory, who served as chairman of the session on ocean basins; Bruce Heezen, also of the Lamont Observatory; James Gilluly and Philip King of the USGS; Leon Knopoff of the University of California; Paul Lyons of the Sinclair Oil and Gas Company; John C. Maxwell of Princeton; A. E. Scheidegger of the University of Illinois; and J. Tuzo Wilson of the University of Toronto.

The cochairmen and organizers of the conference were Dr. Helgi Johnson, professor of geology at Rutgers College; and Dr. William N. Gilliland, dean of the College of Arts and Sciences at Newark and professor of geology.

CHANGING PATTERNS IN HEALTH AND PROFESSIONAL EDUCATION

Some 300 persons attended the one-day symposium on "Changing Patterns in Health and Professional Education," held in Newark on October 29, 1966, under the sponsorship of the College of Nursing. Following opening remarks by Malcolm M. Talbott, vice-president in Newark, Dr. Robert M. Farrier, associate director of the Clinical Center of the National Institutes of Health, discussed the constant advances in medical science and their effects on the nursing profession. Dr. Farrier said that a baccalaureate education is a necessary base for professional nurses if they are to be able to work effectively with physicians and modern therapeutic equipment. He was followed by Mrs. Geraldine Ellis, assistant chief of the Nursing Department, Clinical Center of the NIH, who declared that the student nurse should be imbued with "an intellectual curiosity that will last through future advances in knowledge and technology."

Rutgers Provost, Dr. Richard Schlatter, opened the afternoon session speaking about "Rutgers' Role in the Expansion of Professional Education." He said that a university not only has a responsibility to increase the supply of trained professional people but must "set a model of professional education at its best."

Dr. DeWitt Stetten, Jr., Dean of the Rutgers Medical School, spoke about the current trend toward developing relationships between the medical school and the community it serves and cited federal programs such as Medicare and regional centers for heart disease, cancer, and stroke as evidence of this development.

The final speaker of the session, Dr. Rozella M. Schlotfeldt, Dean of the Frances M. Payne Bolton School of Nursing at Western Reserve University, said that the benefits of educating nurses at the college level lies "in the expectation that its practitioners should have a broad view of the behavior of man—his actions, reactions, and transactions under myriad circumstances."

The discussions were followed by a reception at which the Dean of the College of Nursing, L. Bernice Chapman, served as hostess to the speakers, university faculty, and invited guests from the nursing and allied professions.

THE UNIVERSITY AND THE CHALLENGES OF URBAN SOCIETY

No discussions of the Bicentennial Year had more relevancy to actual and pressing problems of society than the three conferences on "The University and the Challenges of Urban Society" which were held in Newark as part of the 200th anniversary celebration. The third and last of these meetings, April 20, 1967, was held only a few short weeks before the tragic "challenges" in Newark during the hot days of July.

The conferences held on December 1, March 29, and April 20 covered a wide range of topics in an effort to define the University's role in the city and indicate the directions it should take.

Vice-President Talbott keynoted the opening session by outlining a dramatic proposal that urban universities such as Rutgers in Newark be given federal support similar to that extended to the land-grant colleges.

Talbott noted that there already are colleges and universities given special support to encourage the development of expertise in agriculture, the mechanical arts, and oceanography.

"Should not present colleges and universities be designated 'urban challenge colleges'?" Talbott asked. "The problems of education in the future are inextricably bound to an urbanized society. Should we not anticipate these problems and build a great network of such urban colleges and universities to share in the solution of such problems?

"The urban challenge university must remove itself from its campus, from its downtown buildings, from its isolation, and must go to the ghettoes or problem housing, problem education, problem employment, problem-ridden government, and pool solutions to vexing problems. In short, the university must sail into *terra incognita*, explore it and develop it for the century ahead."

At the final conference Dr. Schlatter also presented a definition of the university's role in the attack on urban problems. He listed what he termed the three basic functions of the university:

"The first function is education, the training of the young and the preservation of our heritage of knowledge by handing it on to the next generation. The second responsibility of the university is research and scholarship. From one point of view we know so very little. But the recognition of our own ignorance is the beginning of knowledge and we must go on to the discovery of new knowledge and we must do it quickly. The third function of the university is summarized as extension. By extension here I mean service to the community and a concern with the affairs of the community. And extension is always a two-way system. The university must learn from the community, it must find out what problems in the community need to be solved, and then must try to take back to the community some of the knowledge needed to solve those problems."

Dr. Schlatter also called for a balance between the role of the university as a place for contemplation and research and scholarship and as an active force in the community. He stressed the point that "one of the functions of the university is to provide the perspective, the historical perspective which people who are involved in the field so often lack."

Dr. Elmer C. Easton, dean of the Rutgers College of Engineering, speaking at the opening session, discussed the challenges of physical planning in an urban society of the future which might have to house a world population of 100 billion people. Dean Easton made this point to emphasize the need for long-range planning.

Paul N. Ylvisaker, State commissioner of community affairs, returned to a consideration of the role of the university in the second conference.

"Essentially," Commissioner Ylvisaker said, "the university must be a communication and nerve center of society. It must have a highly complex nervous system with thousands of nerve endings extending beyond the ivy walls to pick up and evaluate information.

"I do not feel that the university is necessarily the place where teaching and learning are best carried out. The kids today, for example, go where the action is and that action tends to be away from the classroom.

"I feel that all people have something to teach and that consequently there is a great need to get teachers from outside the academic world. The university must identify these teachers outside of itself and mobilize their talents to best serve the community."

In the same session C. Malcolm Davis, president of Fidelity Union Trust Company, said that in meeting the challenges of urban society no one group can accomplish it alone.

"It takes the cooperation of government, the university, and the business community and that means each of us individually although we operate under different banners. Without the participation of all of us, we will fail because it is truly a Herculean task," he said.

The view that the university must be "smack dab in the middle" of city problems was expressed at the third session by Cyril Tyson of the New York City Human Resources Administration and former director of the United Community Corporation, Newark's antipoverty agency. He said colleges cannot afford the luxury of "research that is just going to rest on the shelf."

Dr. Mario Fantini, program officer of the Ford Foundation, said universities must be overhauled instead of simply adding on programs as federal funds become available. Too many schools try to change what he termed the "casualties" of the system without changing the system itself.

JAPAN-RUTGERS CONFERENCE

Most persons reasonably well acquainted with Rutgers history know that one of its alumni, William Elliot Griffis of the Class of 1869, played an important role in the introduction of Japan to Western culture, and that, as a result, the first Japanese to come to America for education at roughly the college level came to New Brunswick and Rutgers—enrolling at either the Grammar School or the College.

Unfortunately, a number of these young men, who in some instances used assumed names because of their country's opposition to what they were doing, succumbed in New Brunswick and are buried in the cemetery off Morris Street, but several others returned to Japan and eventually assumed positions of leadership there in government, in the military, and in education. In any case, it is important to note here that Rutgers and Japan had an early and unusual relationship. Griffis was the best known of the Rutgers alumni who served in bringing Western ideas and culture to Japan, but there were others who played lesser but important roles in this relationship.

The Rutgers-Japan relationship has barely smoldered at times during the past hundred years since it began but it nevertheless has been kept alive and in recent years has been fanned into greater heat by interest at both Rutgers and in Japan on behalf of establishing a formal program of exchange scholarship.

This interest led to the organization of one of the last of the conferences held at Rutgers in conjunction with its Bicentennial celebration. This was the Japan-Rutgers University Conference which had its basic purpose in furthering knowledge of Japan, but had as its occasion the celebration of both the Rutgers birthday and the centennial of the beginning of the cultural exchange which started when those first Japanese students, Ise and Numagawa—they assumed those names for the reasons already stated—arrived at Rutgers in the fall of 1866.

The Japan Conference was actually held after the Bicentennial Year had ended, on April 26, 27, and 28, 1967, but it had been in planning for several years as an important part of the birthday celebration. Some fifty scholars from Asian centers in this country and in Japan attended the three-day program and heard a dozen major papers dealing mostly with the beginnings and development of the cultural exchange.

Dr. Ardath W. Burks, director of international programs at Rutgers and organizer of the conference, said in summarizing its discussions that cultural exchange between the United States and Japan actually began when Americans went to Japan as employees of the Japanese government as that nation sought to acquaint itself with Western developments, particularly in science and technology. In turn, he noted, Japanese students began in the middle and late 1860's to attend American universities, and Rutgers in particular.

"This first flow of cultural exchange marked a growing to maturity of the American people," Dr. Burks said, "in turning away from the frontier of the United States to the frontier of the world. Americans have always had a strong sense of mission and we went out there to help."

Dr. Burks also pointed out that William Griffis not only was one of the first American educators to teach in Japan but he also brought back to the American people their first picture of an advanced Pacific culture. Several of the conferees referred to Griffis' contributions to the study of Japanese history.

Several of the papers given at the Rutgers conference discussed Griffis' role in the United States-Japan cultural exchange. Professor Yukihiko Motoyama of Kyoto and Harvard Universities said that it was difficult to determine the direct influence of this Rutgers alumnus on secondary education in the Fukui Domain where Griffis taught for a time in 1871. He said, however, that no one could deny that Griffis' influence took many different forms and that there was a definite spiritual communication between the foreign instructor and the people of the feudal domain in which he taught.

Professor Motoyama gave a very vivid account of Griffis' welcome to Fukui as a young man of twenty-eight and of the interpreter, secretaries, personal guard, gatekeepers, and servants who were put at his disposal, and how in turn Griffis demonstrated his determination to repay for these kindnesses by sincerity and effort on behalf of his Japanese students.

Professor Noboru Umetani of Osaka University presented a paper on "William Elliot Griffis' Studies in Japanese History and Their Significance." In it he noted that Griffis throughout his historical works emphasized the role of the Japanese people in history. He also deplored the neglect by Japanese scholars of the historical role of the foreigners who were employed by the Meiji government.

Professor Umetani said that these were two of the important contributions Griffis made to Japanese history. The others were his study of Japanese mythology, which he viewed with skepticism but understanding appreciation of its historical value, and his objective view of "Mikadoism." Griffis was the first, he said, to give this latter subject true historical study.

Robert G. Flershem, a United States Information Agency officer, described in some detail the evolution of the domain of Kanazawa on the coast of the Japan Sea near where Griffis first taught. He said that the developments aimed at modernization and Westernization rested on a solid base of national or domestic interests.

Professor Hazel J. Jones of the University of Michigan, in a very comprehensive paper, discussed the Griffis thesis on the role that foreign advisers played in Japanese history. Griffis, she noted, had written that these foreign employees were "helpers and servants." Other contemporary students of the period, including the

Englishman Basil Hall Chamberlain, had widely different view of the foreigners' position and role. Chamberlain was among those who took the stand that the foreign employees performed a creative role in the remaking of Japan.

In her conclusion Professor Jones said: "In viewing the entire range of foreign employee services and the full implications of the Griffis thesis, the most that can be adduced is that the better foreign employees were cooperators with the Japanese in the relaying of the foundations of Japan."

Another paper related the important contributions of a former Rutgers professor, David Murray, in the Meiji period. This paper, "Contributions of David Murray to Modernization of School Administration in Japan," was presented by Tadashi Kaneko of the National Education Research Institute. It related how Murray, who was then professor of mathematics and astronomy at Rutgers, was called to Japan in the spring of 1873. Murray, who had established a reputation as a successful organizer and administrator, was asked to help modernize its educational system and, as Kaneko says in his opening remarks, "Among scores of Rutgers men who worked for and contributed to the Japanese Westernization policies, Murray was most noteworthy because he occupied the highest position as Superintendent of the Ministry of Education and exercised great influence on the school policies of those days."

Professor Yoshio Sakata of the Institute of Humanistic Studies, Kyoto University, presenting the first paper of the conference on "The Beginning of Modernization in Japan," raised the question of why it was that Japan was alone among the Asian nations in the 1870's in setting out to modernize itself.

He presented the viewpoint that the fundamental factor in this movement was the existence of the samurai, warrior-administrators, as an intellectual as well as a ruling class. He said that the move toward modernization began when the samurai began to fear that if the chaotic state of affairs in Japanese society continued the nation might be ruined by foreign invasion.

The overseas study by Japanese students in Europe and the United States during the early Meiji period was examined by Professor Minoru Ishizuki of Kobe Yamate Women's Junior College. In his paper Professor Ishizuki recalls Taro Kusakabe of Echizen, the first Japanese student to enter Rutgers College. Kusakabe, who came to the United States in 1867, made the following resolution when about to leave his homeland:

"The stagnation of our country is not a recent matter. . . . Under pressure from the Western Powers, the opening or closing of Japan became a heated issue, and the country has become agitated and confused. Our country is surrounded on all sides by the sea. And the Western ships are a hundred times more advantageous than pack horses, and there is no reason to make disputes about policy for the defense of our island. What the Western nations call their enlightenment is simply a technique. If we now exert ourselves and master their knowledge, we have nothing to fear. . . . When at some later date I have completed my studies, I will be truly happy if I can fulfill my duty to the Imperial realm by clarifying the defects in the relations between us Japanese and the foreigners in the light of the international law of all nations and universal principles."

Other papers presented at the Japan-Rutgers University Conference were a discussion of the history of the Fukui Domain, where Griffis started his teaching, by Professor Madoka Kanai of the Institute of Historiographic Research, Tokyo University; "Nakajima Shoen, Leading Women of Meiji Japan," by Hisako Tanaka; and a discussion of the current efforts of the Japanese to establish a set of educational objectives by Dr. Shiro Amioka of the University of Hawaii.

From water resources through the realms of complex mathematical concepts and the broad and difficult questions of whether there will be too many people on this earth or whether there will be a suitable environment for them, the intellectual discussions at Rutgers during the Bicentennial Year covered a great deal of ground. It would be difficult to claim that there was anything earth-shaking in the intellectual pronouncements made at the Bicentennial conferences but, after all, that kind of discovery, intellectual or scientific, comes only rarely in the history of man and is based on a lot of tiny intellectual nuggets laboriously and slowly panned out over the years. A great deal of this slow but inexorable process in man's enlightenment took place in New Brunswick in 1966.

Godspeed in the Centuries to Come

SIR George Pickering, Regius professor of medicine at Oxford University, served as the spokesman of all the 664 delegates of colleges and universities and learned societies from throughout the world who attended the Bicentennial Convocation of September 22, 1966.

He was accorded this privilege as the delegate of the oldest institution—Oxford was founded in 1214—to send a representative to the climactic ceremony of the Rutgers anniversary celebration.

Sir George Pickering

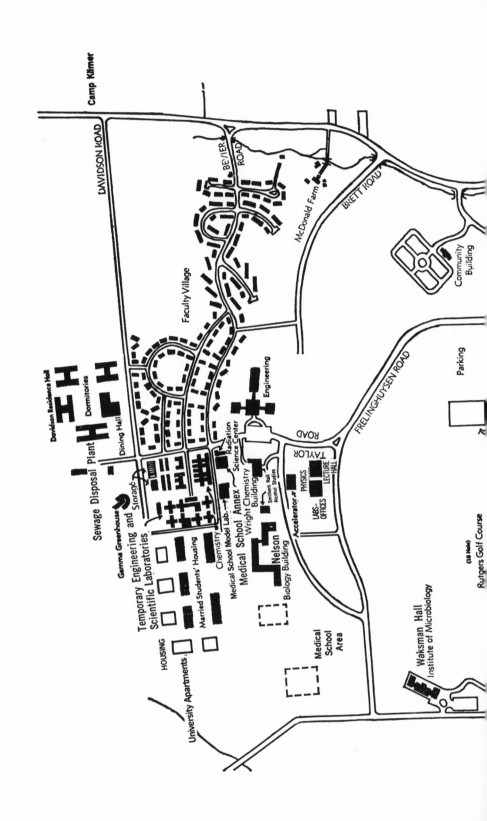

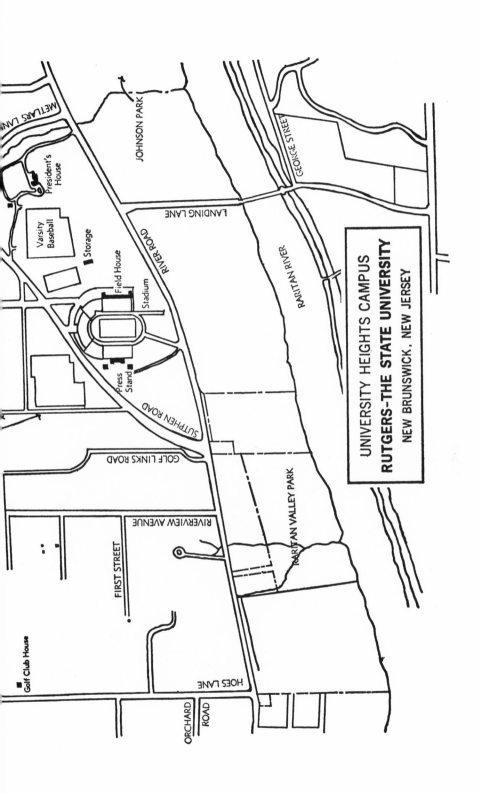

UNIVERSITY HEIGHTS CAMPUS
RUTGERS-THE STATE UNIVERSITY
NEW BRUNSWICK, NEW JERSEY

Sir George, a dapper and courtly gentleman, wore as the crowning touch of his very regal academic costume a large round velvet cap which he frequently doffed in the direction of President Gross. He used it to punctuate his remarks.

It was a significant gesture because it typified the acclaim which Rutgers received that day. That acclaim came from sister institutions and the leading societies from around the world, from the government of the United States, Queen Juliana of the Netherlands, the University of Utrecht, from the State of New Jersey, and from representatives of the Rutgers family everywhere.

Concluding his remarks, Sir George said "my colleagues from the six hundred institutions of learning have come here today to congratulate you, Mr. President, on what you and your forebears have done in making this a great center of learning.

"We congratulate you and we wish you Godspeed in the centuries to come. Floreat Domus."

President Gross, Vice-President Humphrey and Sir George Pickering

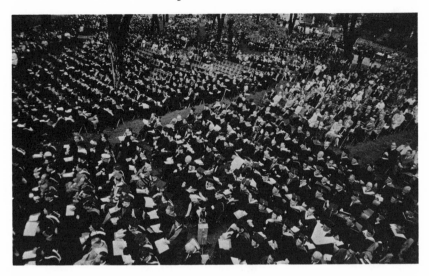

Convocation audience

The speaker's choice of the word "centuries" instead of "years" to come was well noted by those who recalled that his institution could have celebrated its bicentennial some seventy-eight years before Columbus landed on San Salvador.

While Sir George represented the delegates who sat before him in a great display of colorful academic costumes, the other principal bearers of congratulations were the Vice-President of the United States, Hubert H. Humphrey, Governor Richard J. Hughes of New Jersey, the Netherlands Ambassador, Carl W. A. Schurmann, who brought greetings from Queen Juliana, and Dr. A. R. Hulst, Rector Magnificus of the University of Utrecht, the institution which has often been considered Rutgers' academic godfather.

These, with President Gross, the members of the Board of Governors and the Board of Trustees, were the principal dramatis personae of what will be remembered by all those present as one of the most stirring, colorful, and exciting occasions of their lives.

Some 10,000 persons jammed the grassy and shaded Mall between Hamilton Street and Seminary Place to watch the ceremonies which took place on a handsomely decorated platform between Scott and Van Dyck Halls.

Those who arrived early sat through an intermittent and persistent drizzle which was the aftermath of the previous day's downpour. It looked for a time as if the ceremonies might be delayed or possibly moved to the gymnasium which had been made ready for bad weather.

But minutes before the Convocation was to begin the weather broke, the rain stopped, and the sun came through. Truly the "sun of righteousness" of the Rutgers motto shone on her that day.

The members of the Board of Governors and the Board of Trustees, the faculty, alumni, and student representatives, the delegates and distinguished guests had all assembled in their stations by ten o'clock when the Rutgers University Wind Ensemble began playing Beethoven's Military March in D to help set the stage for the ceremony which was about to begin.

A few minutes before 10:30 the bell in Queen's rang out in salute to the Convocation. At 10:30 a sextet of herald trumpeters blew the first notes of Fanfara Canonica especially written for the Convocation by Robert Moevs, Rutgers professor of music, and the academic procession began.

Trumpeters signal beginning of the Bicentennial Convocation.

Academic Procession

With the Provost of the University, Dr. Richard Schlatter, leading, the delegates marched from Queen's down the flagstone walkway through the Class of 1902 Gate across Hamilton Street to their seats on the Mall.

In that gathering of delegates were represented institutions stretching in time from Oxford founded more than seven and a half centuries ago to the Ankara Hacettepe Science Center founded only one year before. In distance they represented colleges and universities in every continent where higher education exists. The 181 societies represented paid tribute to the wide diversity of academic interests in the Rutgers faculty. Truly international in the breadth of their membership and scholarly appeal, they included organizations of scholars and learned men from throughout the world and represented a full spectrum of knowledge. The Royal Society, founded in 1662, was the oldest of the societies there and it sent as its representative Dr. Detlev W. Bronk, former president of Johns Hopkins University and now president of Rockefeller University.

Their costumes were many and varied, from the more austere black gowns of American universities offset only by their colorful hoods to the rich colors and generous braid of European institutions. Academic caps of every size and shape were displayed.

While the delegates proceeded onto the Mall from Queen's, the faculty marched in from stations on Hamilton Street and Seminary Place, each college preceded by its gonfalon.

The Governors and Trustees, the University Senate, the distinguished guests and the guest of honor, Vice-President Humphrey, had assembled in Scott Hall. As the last of the delegates and faculty were seated, this assemblage marched out led by Dean and Vice-Provost Albert E. Meder. As the faculty member with the longest service to the University, he had been elected to carry the University Arms.

Last to be seated on the platform were the Vice-President, President Gross, Governor Hughes, and the chairman of the Board of Governors, Charles H. Brower.

Convocation delegates

Dean Meder carried the
University's coat of arms.

The academic procession approaches the platform.

President Gross, Vice-President
Humphrey and Brower.

President Gross, Vice-President
Humphrey and Governor Hughes

After the playing of the National Anthem, the Rev. Bradford S. Abernethy, University chaplain, gave the invocation:

O Thou to whom men have turned in high moments and low, to beseech, to confess, to deify, to praise, we turn in this high moment to lay before Thee such words as may convey —though never contain—our gratitude for what the years have wrought, and our hopes for Thy continued guidance and favor in the days that are to come.

Kindle, and keep alive in us the memory of those whose desire to see Thee served with the trained mind led to the founding of this college. As for them the search for wisdom began with reverence for the Eternal, so let it be with us, that we, like them, may be discoverers, guardians, and revealers of the truths that make men free.

Bless this University, we beseech Thee, in the years of growth ahead. Let it be ample in service as well as in size. Grant wisdom to those who shall lead it, and vision to those who plan for it. Let no small aims satisfy any who teach or learn here. Because of what is done in this place, and in all institutions here represented, let new hopes for mankind's peace and welfare and brotherhood be born and come to lively fruition.

Establish Thou this work of our hands. Yea, Lord, this work of our hands establish Thou it. Amen.

President Gross welcomed the gathering in a salutation which noted that, while "two hundred years is a good round figure," Jesus College, his own college at Cambridge, could have celebrated its bicentennial in the year in which Geoffrey Chaucer was born.

But age by itself, he said, is nothing. The important thing is still to be motivated at the age of two hundred by the emotions and enthusiasms of youth.

Dr. Gross's Salutation

Mr. Vice-President, Governor Hughes, Mr. Ambassador, Rector Magnificus, Sir George Pickering, distinguished delegates, alumni, and friends:

On behalf of the Board of Governors, the Board of
Trustees, the faculties and the students of Rutgers – The
State University, I extend to you a heartfelt welcome and a
sincere expression of gratitude for the tribute which you are
paying to this University by participating in this Two Hundredth Anniversary Convocation.

It is indeed a joy to see so many delegates from our sister
colleges and universities and from the learned societies. I run
the risk of giving offense by singling out any particular ones

President Gross opens the Convocation.

for special mention, but the date which we are commemorating today reminds us of those struggling colleges which were founded in this country even before the establishment of the Republic. And since New Jersey was the only colony to have two colleges, we greet with special cordiality our ancient neighbor, Princeton University, with the proviso that this cordiality not be extended past 2 P.M. two days hence, at which time the Princetonians will become ravening tigers while we comport ourselves with the mighty valor and chivalric high-mindedness appropriate to scarlet knights.

We salute our sister land-grant colleges, a distinction which we have borne proudly since 1864, and our sister state universities, whose task and responsibilities are so similar to our own. And it is with a feeling of warm friendship that we welcome our sister institutions, public and private, from the various parts of the State of New Jersey. But if I may be forgiven for singling out some of the institutions for special greetings, may I make it clear that we deeply appreciate the presence of all the delegates, from colleges and universities at home and abroad, who share with us the same purpose and the same ideals.

Governor Hughes leads an extremely distinguished group of public officials. May I express to you all our welcome and our gratitude. Rutgers is celebrating its two hundred years today, but we should not forget that it is only ten years since its status as the State University was reaffirmed and clarified, and that many of you here today were of vital assistance in bringing about that change and improvement. We proclaim again our recognition of our obligations as the State University, and we pledge again our resolve to fulfill them.

I am particularly happy to see so many of our alumni present, some of whom I know have traveled very considerable distances to be with us. And I must mention that group of people whose formal connection with this University began when they honored us by accepting an honorary degree. Their presence constitutes a splendid tribute.

Two hundred is a good round figure. That an institution can survive and indeed continue to grow over a period of two hundred years surely marks it as a very important factor in our society, contributing stability in a world which is chiefly characterized now by rapid and pervasive change.

One's feelings of self-congratulations, however, particularly when they are buoyed up by such a distinguished gathering as this is, must be tempered by contrasting humility. A few weeks ago, while we were in frantic preparation for this occasion, I stole time to read *Yankee from Olympus*, Mrs. Bowen's life of Mr. Justice Holmes. In it she records the day when Dr. Holmes, the Justice's father, received his M.D. degree at Harvard. It was a day of special ceremonies, she notes, because Harvard was celebrating its bicentennial. The year was 1836, Andrew Jackson was in the White House, and Martin Van Buren was Vice-President.

Later I was happy to see that there would be a representative here from my own university, Cambridge, whose origins go back to the thirteenth century. I was even more delighted to see that there would be a representative from my own college at Cambridge, Jesus College, which, like my other university connection in the British Isles, the University of Aberdeen, was founded in the decade when people were beginning to hear something about a fellow named Columbus. However, Jesus College upon its founding took up residence in buildings which had been occupied by an earlier institution and had probably been built around the year 1140. Had the inhabitants of those buildings elected to celebrate their bicentennial, it would have taken place in the year in which Geoffrey Chaucer was born.

Still, two hundred years is a long time, and much depends on how that time is spent. We all remember the lesson which Lemuel Gulliver learned about the folly of not welcoming a timely death. His encounter with the Struldbrugs during his travels was almost his greatest shock. These unfortunates were doomed from birth to physical immortality, but they were not immune to the weaknesses and decay incident upon extreme old age. By the time they were two hundred, he records, they had degenerated to the point where no rational communication with their fellow creatures was possible. The only way in which one could determine exactly how old they were was to ask them what kings they could recall by name, just as we recall George III.

It is obvious from this that old age by itself guarantees nothing. Sydney Smith took pains, following Bentham, to expose the fallacy about the sacrosanct wisdom of our forefathers by pointing out that we were in sorry shape if we didn't know more than they did. The secret is to grow old without becoming senile or suffering from some form of hardening of the arteries. Perhaps this is the unconfessed reason why we at two hundred have at last founded a medical school.

The trick is, at two hundred, still to be motivated by the emotions that characterize youth. In the seventeenth century these were listed as wonder, joy, and love of one's fellow man. I would like to believe that Theodorus Frelinghuysen, Jacob Rutsen Hardenbergh and John Livingston, among many others, were excited by these emotions, and that our truest inheritance from them is a capacity still to experience, in all our manifold activities, wonder, joy, and love. If so, then we can face our 201st year with equanimity and confidence, and without the awful dread of the Struldbrugs.

I believe that we can.

Dr. Gross's welcome was followed by the greetings from the delegates, the official greetings from the Netherlands presented by the Netherlands Ambassador, and the greetings from the University of Utrecht given by the Rector Magnificus of that institution.

The greetings from the Netherlands were concluded with a special message from Her Majesty Queen Juliana, who wrote:

"To the chairman of the Board of Governors of Rutgers State University, New Brunswick: Best wishes for your University on the occasion of its Bicentennial celebration. May its Dutch heritage continue to serve as inspiration for mutual respect and understanding between our two countries."

The Rector Magnificus, Dr. A. R. Hulst, on the conclusion of his remarks, presented President Gross with a "congratulation gift," a copy of a rare book on Dutch history in the seventeenth century.

Rector Magnificus Hulst of the University of Utrecht presents rare book to President Gross.

Doctor Hulst said:

Dr. Gross, president of this University, excellencies, ladies, and gentlemen:

I am extremely thankful for the opportunity given to me to present on this festival day to Rutgers University the warm greetings of the University of Utrecht and of nine other universities and colleges of a different kind in the Netherlands and to congratulate you all on the fact that two centuries ago your University was founded.

We understand your gladness and participate in it, the more so as we know that many people whose ancestors came from the Netherlands have contributed to the foundation and development of this famous university. I mention in particular Johannes Henricus Livingston, whose memory certainly is still living here, took the degree of Doctor Theologia at Utrecht University on May 16 of the year 1770 on a thesis, De foederis sinaitici natura, ex ejus fine demonstrata.

The sol iustitiae is found in the seal of this University as well as in mine, and so we may say that this University from the very beginning is allied with the Utrecht University in the Netherlands. It is, Mr. President, our dearest wish that this sol iustitiae, which has been shining upon you and us for so many years, also will radiate now and in years to come on all who are connected with your University—trustees and teachers and students as well—in order that at this University scientific research will go on successfully for the benefit of mankind. God bless you all.

I have now the pleasure to give you, dear Dr. Gross, as a small congratulation gift of the University of Utrecht, a fine copy of an important and rare book about three hundred years old on a subject of Dutch history in the seventeenth century. I hope you will be so kind as to accept this present out of my hands now.

The Governor of New Jersey, the Honorable Richard J. Hughes, who won his law degree at what was later to become the Rutgers Law School, brought greetings from the State and noted that the celebration was a "wonderful day for New Jersey."

Governor Hughes's greetings follow:

President Gross and reverend clergy, Mr. Vice-President, your excellencies, and all of our very distinguished guests from all over the world, Board of Governors, trustees, faculty members and students, ladies and gentlemen:

What a wonderful, happy time it is when one celebrates a two hundredth birthday. So this is a wonderful day for New Jersey and for Rutgers, and we're glad to have our friends with us to share in this special kinship that arises from such a celebration.

As has been said, it's been two hundred years since the Dutch Reformed Church obtained a royal charter from King George III bringing into existence Old Queen's College, now our State University. And that was only ten years, as Dr. Gross says, before the Revolution that was to create the American nation itself. It's fitting, indeed, your excellencies, that representatives of Great Britain and the Netherlands should be present at this Convocation, for they in their way were the parents who oversaw the birth of what is today a great public university of world renown.

Today we in New Jersey and in America are still engaged in another phase of the ongoing American revolution, but not against a mother country. Today our revolution is against the forces of darkness and oppression and against ignorance and hunger and disease and discrimination. In that phase of the American revolution, Rutgers has stood, Mr. Vice-President, for two hundred years now like a beacon of probing intelligence amidst passionate cries for conformity of opinion. Her sons have fought for this nation's freedom in many wars, just as they did when scholars, students, and founders left her halls to fight in the first American Revolution.

And Rutgers has grown with its time, extending itself fully into the community, making great discoveries for medicine and agriculture and science, until today it stands as the keystone of New Jersey's system of higher public education.

Governor Hughes brings greetings from the State of New Jersey.

On its 150th anniversary Rutgers, then a high-level private college, taught about five hundred students, and today, as a state university, ever-increasing thousands receive educational opportunity through her portals. This generation of citizens and public servants has pledged to the next generation that education, indeed, will be the first order of public business. We in New Jersey have already begun to honor this pledge, and Rutgers will play a large part in redeeming it.

So I hope that this 200th anniversary will be the signal for the coming together not only of the friends of Rutgers but of the friends of education and progress throughout New Jersey and the nation. And one of those great friends, the Vice-President of the United States, I particularly welcome here again to New Jersey, where he is not a rare visitor. We're just delighted to have him. He pays us a great honor to come here with us, as indeed do all of our other distinguished guests, including everyone in this beautiful vista which I see before me now. Thank you very much.

President Gross conferred the honorary degree of Doctor of Laws upon the honored guest, Vice-President Humphrey, reading a citation which noted that the recipient did indeed fulfill the requirements of the earliest tutors of Queen's College, the literal ancestor of Rutgers University, that its graduates be "a pleasure to their friends and an ornament to their species."

The text of the citation follows:

Hubert H. Humphrey—Born in the heartland of America, you have inherited the conscience and spirit of your political forebears, the Populists, and, like them, you have never been content with old answers to new problems or easy answers to vexing ones. Throughout your distinguished career, and especially now as our Vice-President, you have faced the problems which bewilder and disturb the nation with brilliance, imagination, and above all, a profound love for your fellow man—whatever his country, his race, or his situation.

For two hundred years this University has striven to send forth graduates, who, in the words of its earliest tutors, were

"a pleasure to their friends and an ornament to their species."
The tutors would be as proud and honored as are we in saluting you as an honorary graduate who has fulfilled that require-
ment for a degree with distinction.

I am pleased, at the direction of the Board of Governors
of the University, to confer upon you, *honoris causa*, the
degree of Doctor of Laws.

In his acceptance speech, the principal address of the Convocation, the Vice-President spoke against the backdrop of a violent
and heated political controversy which had dragged the University into the gubernatorial campaign of 1965 and had pushed it
into national prominence on the matter at issue—academic freedom.

A Rutgers history professor—his name was Eugene D.
Genovese—in the spring of 1965 had said at a teach-in on the war
in Vietnam that he would "welcome" a victory by the Vietcong.

Professor Genovese later explained that what he actually
meant was a political rather than a military victory for the Vietcong, but this very important distinction made little difference to
those politicians and others who clamored for his head.

The Rutgers Board of Governors, under pressure from many
quarters to fire Professor Genovese, took the Voltairian position
that, while they disagreed with what he had said, he had done
nothing "that would constitute grounds for preferring charges
against him."*

Governor Hughes, campaigning for re-election, stood
staunchly by the University's right to handle the situation as it
saw fit and was re-elected by a handsome majority.

In his address the Vice-President took notice of the Genovese
controversy and of Rutgers' defense of the right of dissent and
then went on to his own defense of the "right to challenge established orthodoxies." And as he started to speak, he too was subject
to dissent as a handful of youthful demonstrators against the war
in Vietnam walked out of the audience.

---

*A Report on the Genovese Case—Prepared for presentation to Governor Richard
J. Hughes by the Board of Governors of Rutgers–The State University, August
6, 1965 (Appendix N).

Vice-President Humphrey gives
the principal address of the
Bicentennial Convocation.

The Vice-President surveys the
Convocation crowd.

War protesters

Address of Vice-President Hubert H. Humphrey

Dr. Gross, Governor Hughes, Mr. Brower, Ambassador Schurmann, Dr. Hulst, and the many distinguished delegates from colleges and universities throughout the world, members of the faculty of Rutgers, fellow students, and friends and neighbors:

I am sure you must know what emotions are mine at this moment—the sense of exhilaration and of joy that I now experience at being here with you on this particular important occasion and to be so honored by this honorary degree.

I wish to say to my fellow students that it's a lot easier to get a degree this way. I'm also somewhat in a quandary as to the location of this gathering and this address, because I note to my left and your right there's William the Silent, and that has no relationship to me in any way. But I've been informed by the distinguished Ambassador that William the Silent was only silent when an ambassador of another nation was trying to pry a secret from him. That he, indeed, was a great orator and that his countrymen in the years of the noble history of the Netherlands look upon him as a vocal, vociferous and active leader so, at least possibly, the speaker of the day is not out of step with William the Silent.

Now as many of you know, I am a refugee from the classroom, and every chance I have to return to a great university—not to mention the chance to get an honorary degree—helps me to keep my credentials in order as a political science professor. In fact, my first experience as a vice-president was as vice-president of the American Political Science Association.

I mention all of this because the business of politics is not the most secure in the world and it doesn't hurt to have a little insurance and to update your credentials. And, Dr. Gross, I'm not applying but I'm just indicating, in case. I've always thought well of this University.

Rutgers University is today celebrating a great birthday, its bicentennial as a strong and free institution of learning only a very short time after the strength and freedom of this great academic institution was directly threatened. In fact,

The Vice-President checks his speech.

a year ago in the heat of political controversy, and under the threat of dire retribution, your distinguished, courageous president, faculty, and Board of Governors—supported by an alert and dedicated student body and a courageous governor of this State—were adamant in protecting academic freedom, the right of dissent. You were adamant, I might add, even though many of you—possibly most of you—as I did, disagreed with the dissenter.

But you and your governor were vindicated by the people at the polls. The people of New Jersey thought well of you. And I have been informed today by an associate of this University that the Ninth Alexander Meiklejohn Award in recognition of conspicuous service to the cause of academic freedom was given by the American Association of University Professors this year to President Mason Gross and the Rutgers Board of Governors. I can think of no institution nor of any university president more fully deserving of this high honor.

You gave concrete meaning to the spirit of the Bill of Rights and you gave active defense to the eloquent proposition of Henry Thoreau. You remember his words:

"If a man does not keep pace with his companions, perhaps it's because he hears a different drummer. Let him step to the music which he hears, however measured or far away." That is freedom beautifully expressed in prose and poetry.

And I should like on this occasion to say a word or two about the place of dissent and of academic freedom and academic responsibility in a democratic society. First of all, academic freedom is not just an academic matter. Nor is it just a matter to be the special prerogative of teachers and professors and trustees and university presidents. Academic freedom is both the symptom and the cause of other freedoms we enjoy. As John Milton and John Stuart Mill understood in past centuries, the right of free inquiry and of responsible dissent is society's self-correcting mechanism. In a more modern idiom it is our self-regulating system of "feedback."

There is no party, no Chief Executive, no Cabinet, no legislature in this or any other country wise enough to govern without the constant exposure to informed criticism. If responsible political leaders do not always follow the advice of dissenters, may I assure you it is not because such advice is ignored or summarily dismissed. Rather it is because in submitting the advice to the test of the perceivable consequence, it may not at a given moment seem to make sense.

I know from rather long experience in your nation's capital that very few responsible academic proposals are actually lost. Some are diffused; most are modified by the dialectic of academic as well as political discourse. But as Lord Keynes once pointed out, in terms of fundamental origins, public policy is largely the product of some "academic scribbler," and there are many of them here today.

Now, it seems to me that academic freedom permits universities at their best to perform three cardinal services for government and for society as a whole. First, it enables our great universities to challenge established orthodoxies. Second, it enables them to fashion the laws of nature, including the laws of human nature. And, third, it enables them to promulgate options. Now, let me say a word about each of these.

An example, I think, is appropriate at this moment. Twenty years ago President Truman signed the Employment Act of 1946. That act, as you remember, established the Council of Economic Advisers and set up the Joint Economic Committee of the Congress. And it mandated the President to submit to the Congress each year an Economic Report which would describe the economic state of the Union and would recommend policies aimed at promoting maximum production, employment, and purchasing power.

Now, the background of this Act and the policy recommendations which emerged from the Council since its passage are rooted largely in academic challenge to economic orthodoxy. For generations classical economics had rested on the assumptions that market mechanisms were automatic and immutable and that government interference in the operations of the market should be limited essentially to credit adjustments by the Federal Reserve and to cutting public expenditures in times of depression.

I need not trace for this audience the intellectual and policy battles of the past generation associated with the so-called Keynesian revolution. I can only say that this battle—begun by academic scribblers—has produced a revolution in economic thought and public policy and has immeasurably benefited our country. It is called the new economics for a progressive nation.

Now, if universities break ancient molds, as they have, they also create new truths. The investments in university research by your federal government are substantial, in fact huge. The research of the National Science Foundation, National Institutes of Health, Department of Defense, Office of Education, Atomic Energy Commission, NASA, and other federal agencies is testament to the key role that new knowledge plays in human progress—both technical and social. And I am convinced that much of the recent progress of this nation—economically, scientifically, and technologically—is due to the vast investments in university research by both public and private agencies.

A few years ago when Nikita Khrushchev visited the United States he was astounded by our agricultural productivity. American agriculture is in large part a success story because, for generations, federal and state governments have supported our land-grant colleges and their agricultural experiment stations and county extension services. Our agricultural scientists discovered new truths. They did away with old orthodoxies. They have uncovered laws of nature which have unlocked the secrets of plant and animal productivity, and today American agriculture stands as the wonder of the world.

As chairman of a newly created National Marine Sciences Council I have great hope that we may develop our marine resources just as we have developed our agricultural resources. There is, as you may know, pending in Congress right now legislation to create sea-grant colleges to develop and to bring new knowledge to America and to the whole world for the exploration of that four-fifths of the earth's surface known as the seas.

And there is no question of the roles that our universities have played, and are playing, in developing new materials, processes, and management techniques in our vast federal space and atomic energy programs. An age of exploration unprecedented is now with us, and we are the new explorers and adventurers.

I predict a revolution of educational theory and practice in the next two decades that will revolutionize teaching techniques and much of educational habit as a result of public and private investments in such fields as motivation and learning.

Social psychology, modern genetics, and the new exciting subfield of zoology known as ethology are making astounding breakthroughs which cannot help but affect the future policy of this land and the fate of the human race. And President Johnson's unprecedented support of education at all levels attests to this government's belief that truth, truth perseveringly sought after, will make us free, and it also attests to our belief that both the quantity and the quality of education must be increased and improved if the frontiers of human knowledge are to be extended.

But for the responsible policy maker in government, perhaps the university's most immediate contribution is not the challenging of ancient orthodoxies, or even the discovery of new truths, but the creative construction of policy options for this land of ours. More and more our government turns to the learned professions and to the universities for guidance in forming new programs, domestic and international.

A half-century ago, the University of Wisconsin, under the leadership of John R. Commons, was the policy center of America in such fields as social insurance and welfare economics. Virtually everything that has happened since in the field of humane public policy is the legislative derivative of that pioneering work.

And you recall it was President Franklin Roosevelt who gave currency to the term "brain-truster" or "brain trust." His major advisers in developing the experimental policies of the New Deal were university professors. And since that time professors have become more popular, in fact much more acceptable, and professors have steadily increased their influence in both public policies and private life.

By the way, there are no fewer than seven ex-professors in the President's Cabinet of twelve, and the term "in-and-outer" has become almost as well known as "brain truster." Today Washington is brimming with visiting advisers, witnesses, consultants, and technical experts from our universities in every field of human knowledge. Washington National Airport will at any point of time during the day include in transit a whole faculty which—if kept together—would create one of the world's most distinguished institutions of higher education. And, by the way, considering the long delays in flight take-offs, we might be able to organize a seminar or two.

Now, these professors are valuable to Washington precisely because they are unfettered and because they have the opportunity to see beyond the immediate urgencies and rigidities of ongoing operations. And for the same reason they are increasingly being put to work by progressive private corporations, financial institutions, labor unions seeking the objective, unbiased view in their decision-making process. If these professors were controlled and cowed, they would be valueless. They can produce policy options precisely because they are once removed from the inertias and the compulsions of operating assignments.

President Gross welcomes the Vice-President and Governor Hughes.

And here let me become specific and immediate. In the past months and years no problem has burdened the minds of your national political leaders more than the painful conflict in Southeast Asia. Men of good will both in Washington and in the academic life have differed strongly in diagnosis, prognosis, and therapy. It would be tragic if any authoritarian government were to mistake our discourse and dissent for weakness, for our diversity is the basis for our unity. As John Kennedy once said, our national goal is to make this world safe for diversity. And our intellectual pluralism is the friend rather than the enemy of responsible political decision-making.

Our goals in Southeast Asia and elsewhere are clear: They are to help the nations of that part of the world maintain their independence and to help them build strong and progressive societies. But our means toward these goals are both flexible and pragmatic, obviously open to discussion and disagreement. Military force, at this juncture, is necessary. It is necessary not because it is alone adequate, but because it establishes minimal conditions for undertaking long-range political, economic, diplomatic, and social accommodations which are the only ultimate guarantors of long-range stability and independence in that part of the world.

It is in these complex areas of long-range accommodation that your government needs all the help that it can possibly get from the thinkers, from the academic community. We need the help of universities in breaking orthodoxies in our own thinking—yes, to challenge us to disagree, to put us through the refiners' fire of competition of ideas. But we also need scholars to tell us about the orthodoxies, stresses, strains, and motivations of Asian powers with which we are presently at odds. Above all, we need the help of our universities in thinking through viable, practical, pragmatic options aimed at securing our long-range goals in Asia. We need the continuity of this dialogue between government and free men; we need to talk to each other, we need to seek truth and not merely win points in debate.

I have said many times, since my recent missions to Asia

and the Pacific, that one of the highest priorities in our country should be the expansion, both in quantity and in quality, of our programs of study concerning the Pacific and Asian areas. For, no matter how much we would deny it, the great majority of us are comparatively ignorant when it comes to any part of the world but Europe and North America.

Our universities, and our secondary schools as well, must expand their programs of Asian and Pacific studies, just as you are doing here at Rutgers. They must, in fact, expand their programs of study concerning all of the unfamiliar, overlooked parts of the world. There is always the possibility that in these unfamiliar places—unseen and misunderstood—can grow a larger conflict which might threaten the general peace. In the nuclear age we can no longer afford the luxury of international ignorance or blind spots of understanding. Nor can we, as a world power, afford a half-world knowledge, which is just about where we are in our current international education.

Now, let me say then two things in conclusion. First, the need for the university concern and help is just as urgent in meeting our problems at home as it is in meeting those in the world, because ultimately foreign policy is but the extension of national policy and the conduct of our foreign policy will be no better than the moral fiber of our domestic policy.

Rutgers is in the middle of one of the greatest urban agglomerations in the world. Your Urban Center and your Eagleton Institute are already nationally recognized for their concern with the politics and the administration of state and local jurisdictions. But my guess is that Rutgers would be the first to admit that it has only scratched the surface of its responsibility to the surrounding communities.

Transportation, air and water pollution, slums, poverty, ill-health, racial discrimination, inadequate schools, and truncated opportunity, unfulfilled lives—these social cancers of our nation cannot be wished away or just washed away. They're here, they have to be worked away, thought out, and solutions must be found. The total resources of our universities will have to be mobilized against our urban problems if old orthodoxies are to be broken, new truths to be found, and new policy options to be developed. Just as isolation in the world is something our nation cannot afford, so isolation in the community is something that our universities cannot afford. There are far too few universities today in America which have committed themselves to meeting the problems of their communities.

Most of our universities are aware of the availability of federal funds for studies and activities in urban environment, and a few have made use of these funds. But more of our own universities should be committing their own resources to the problem of urban and metropolitan life. More of our universities should be putting to work some of the lessons learned in space-age technology and management, the lessons of interdisciplinary cooperation, the application of the systems approach to a problem in meeting the more earthly challenge of urban life. Oh, if our universities would become as interested in putting a man on his feet on this earth as we are in putting a man on the moon in this decade, how fortunate it would be! And I might add that a nation that is capable and willing to invest billions of dollars of its resources in that great scientific exploration of a man on the moon in this decade ought not to hesitate to make whatever investments are necessary to help God's children right here where we live on this earth.

Now, some of you may regard me as being a bit too much of an applied scientist and not enough of a theoretician, but I am going to be quite frank with you. I have never believed that knowledge should be the special prerogative of anyone and remain hidden in books or in the minds of the few. I believe that knowledge is here to be put to work and it should be used, used and reused for the benefit of the many and not for the pleasure of the elite.

Earlier this week I spoke at the centennial celebration of Howard University. I offered a few suggestions. Among them I said that I believe universities, working with business and labor, should seek immediately new ways to train unskilled and hard core unemployed workers. What are you going to do, my fellow Americans, with the twenty-seven percent of the Negro teen-agers that are unemployed, that remain unemployed this year despite the fact that we were able to find 1,250,000 new jobs for needy teen-agers?

What are we going to do about the fact that with 3,000,000 more adult workers being employed in two years the rate of Negro unemployment goes up? It does us no good to cry about it. We must put our minds to it and our national policies directed toward it.

I believe that universities should send both faculty members and students into our urban ghettos to help overcome generations there of educational and cultural deprivation. Where, I ask you, could you find a better place for "laboratory" work? On the job, on the scene of the battle.

I believe that universities should take far more seriously their responsibilities to the quality of teaching and research at our small colleges and schools who are without adequate resources.

I believe, in short, that our universities should see as their responsibility the problems of twentieth-century urban society, see these problems which crowd in many cases right up to the edge of their well-tended campuses. I believe the universities can profit from being active participants in the community.

They ought to be where the action is and not serene retreats for constant meditation and reflection without the roar and the din of battle that goes on in everyday life. The combination of theory and reality is an appropriate formula for education in the second half of the twentieth century.

There is no question that academic freedom and academic responsibility are joined together. You showed that academic responsibility a year ago, as I said, when you stood firm when there were those who threatened the right of dissent.

But there are other kinds of academic responsibility.

One of those I have alluded to: the responsibility of the academic world not to draw apart from the real world. Join it, be a part of it, get into the line of battle.

There is above all the responsibility of those in academic life to base their pronouncements upon fearless and objective examination, because you occupy a role of leadership and respectability, and as such you are expected to be responsible. Unless recommendations stem from knowledge rather than untutored emotion, unless a sense of concern is matched by the capacity for hard analysis, the academic dispenser of ideas or giver of advice does himself a disservice and dishonors his profession. The world is filled with the noise and clash of opinion. It is woefully shy of dependable knowledge.

In a society which needs and values your independence —your own "league of notions"—the greatest threat to academic freedom would be the failure of those who prize it the most to live up to their own canons of responsibility.

Let me be very clear. I do not believe that our country is passing through a period of academic irresponsibility. Quite the contrary, we're indebted to our great academic thinkers and leaders.

But I do believe that we cannot, in this age both of danger and of promise, demand anything less of ourselves than the most stringent standards. Simply put, excellence; there is no room for mediocrity or subjectivity. The standard must be one of excellence and objectivity.

Now, more than ever, the great challenge and the great work of challenging orthodoxies, discovering new truths, establishing new options is a necessity for human survival and progress. Your government looks to you. The people that make possible this university depend on you.

Therefore, may we approach that work with humility, with self-discipline, and with responsibility. In so doing, Mr. President, we shall make our freedom the more secure, and life, liberty, and the pursuit of happiness shall not only be the hope and promise of America but the living reality of our generation.

The benediction by Chaplain Abernethy and the Recessional concluded the impressive ceremonies on the Mall.

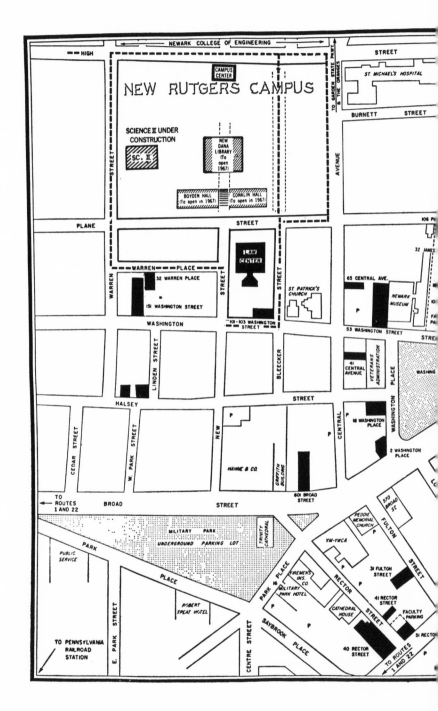

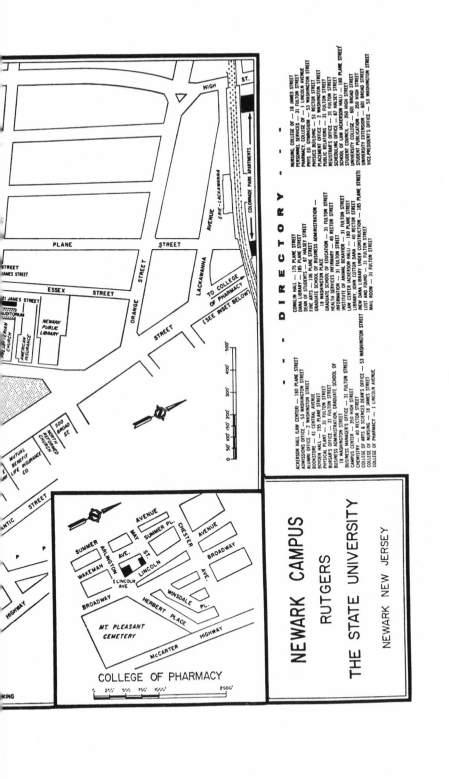

NEWARK CAMPUS
RUTGERS
THE STATE UNIVERSITY
NEWARK NEW JERSEY

COLLEGE OF PHARMACY

- - - D I R E C T O R Y - - -

ACKERSON HALL (LAW CENTER) — 180 PLANE STREET
ADMISSIONS OFFICE — 53 WASHINGTON STREET
ALUMNI OFFICE — 2 WASHINGTON STREET
BOOKSTORE — 41 CENTRAL AVENUE
BOYDEN HALL — 195 PLANE STREET
PHYSICAL PLANT — 31 FULTON STREET
BURSAR'S OFFICE — 31 FULTON STREET
BUSINESS ADMINISTRATION, GRADUATE SCHOOL OF 18 WASHINGTON STREET
BUSINESS MANAGER'S OFFICE — 31 FULTON STREET
CAMPUS CENTER — 350 HIGH STREET
CHEMISTRY — 40 RECTOR STREET
COLLEGE OF ARTS & SCIENCES DEAN'S OFFICE — 53 WASHINGTON STREET
COLLEGE OF NURSING — 18 JAMES STREET
COLLEGE OF PHARMACY — 1 LINCOLN AVENUE

CONKLIN HALL — 175 PLANE STREET
DANA LIBRARY — 185 PLANE STREET
DEAN OF STUDENTS — 87 HALSEY STREET
FINE ARTS — 106 PLANE STREET
GRADUATE SCHOOL OF BUSINESS ADMINISTRATION — 18 WASHINGTON PLACE
GRADUATE SCHOOL OF EDUCATION — 31 FULTON STREET
HEALTH SERVICES INFIRMARY — 40 RECTOR STREET
INFORMATION — 31 FULTON STREET
INSTITUTE OF ANIMAL BEHAVIOR — 31 FULTON STREET
LAW CENTER (ACKERSON HALL) — 180 PLANE STREET
LIBRARY, JOHN COTTON DANA — 40 RECTOR STREET
(NEW DANA LIBRARY UNDER CONSTRUCTION — 185 PLANE STREET)
LOST AND FOUND — 31 FULTON STREET
MAIL ROOM — 31 FULTON STREET

NURSING, COLLEGE OF — 18 JAMES STREET
PERSONNEL SERVICES OF — 31 FULTON STREET
PHARMACY, COLLEGE OF — 1 LINCOLN AVENUE
PHYS. ED. GYMNASIUM — 53 WASHINGTON STREET
PHYSICS BUILDING — 51 RECTOR STREET
PLACEMENT OFFICE — 2 WASHINGTON STREET
PUBLIC RELATIONS — 31 FULTON STREET
REGISTRAR'S OFFICE — 31 FULTON STREET
SCHEDULING OFFICE — 87 HALSEY STREET
SCHOOL OF LAW (ACKERSON HALL) — 180 PLANE STREET
STUDENT COUNCIL — 350 HIGH STREET
UNIVERSITY COLLEGE — 601 BROAD STREET
STUDENT PUBLICATION — 350 HIGH STREET
UNIVERSITY EXTENSION — 601 BROAD STREET
VICE-PRESIDENT'S OFFICE — 53 WASHINGTON STREET

A luncheon in a large tent on the field behind the College Avenue gymnasium concluded the day's events. Participating were most of the distinguished guests, delegates, and representatives of the principal branches of the Rutgers family. President Gross cut a large birthday cake which had been baked and decorated for the occasion by a most considerate and inspired group of young people in the Middlesex County Vocational and Technical High School.

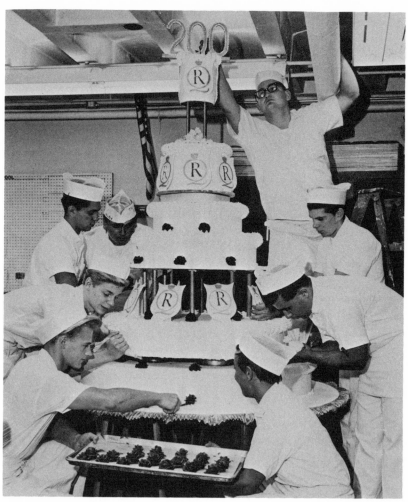

They baked the birthday cake.

"Sincere Esteem and Respect"

IT is a tradition and a pleasant custom in the academic world that important and historic occasions in the life of any college or university are marked by appropriate tributes from fellow institutions. As Rutgers celebrated its 200th anniversary, this happy practice was followed in generous measure and with apparent enthusiasm by institutions in all parts of the United States and around the world.

The tributes that flowed to Rutgers in its Bicentennial Year took on many forms. There were hundreds of institutional greetings from the universities and the learned societies, but homage was also paid to the University in honors conferred upon its President, in special editions of newspapers and magazines, in the attendance of hundreds of delegates at the Bicentennial Convocation on September 22, and in the presentation by the Raritan Valley Chapter of the Society for the Advancement of Management and the New Brunswick-Raritan Valley Chamber of Commerce of a specially designed ceremonial mace which will grace many future Rutgers ceremonies.

In the two hundred years since it had been so modestly started, Rutgers had reached into almost every institution of higher learning on the globe, and in 1966 hundreds of them gave recognition to this fact. Rutgers graduates were teaching in many of them. For many others the results of Rutgers research had been close or complementary to their own. Microbiologists all over the world had learned of the work of Selman Waksman, winner of the Nobel Prize in 1952 for his contributions to the knowledge of antibiotics, agricultural scientists everywhere knew of the soil studies of Jacob Lipman and Firman Bear, and so it went through a wide and impressive variety of scientific and scholarly explorations and discoveries. The academic fraternity in every part of the world had an acquaintance with Rutgers and its accomplishments. Now in 1966 they sent their hearty greetings to this institution which had achieved distinction as well as a revered anniversary.

In all more than 250 academic institutions, learned societies, and foundations took notice of the Bicentennial and sent greetings, some of them most elaborately fashioned and others plainer but equally sincere in their wishes for continued scholarly and scientific achievement.

A list of those sending greetings is included in Appendix I, but some of the more unusual and spectacular tributes deserve specific mention here as characteristic of the color, warmth, and sincerity of all of them.

The University of Bologna, founded in 1088 and generally considered to be the oldest of them all, sent greetings in Italian to Rutgers' "Illustrious President":

> On the occasion of the celebration of the 200th anniversary of the founding of the institution, this institution of higher learning in Bologna would very much like to be represented (at the Convocation) but circumstances prevent our participation.
>
> In the name of the Senate and the Academic Corps, the Rector of one of the oldest institutions of higher learning expresses its affection to a younger one—namely, Rutgers University—and congratulates it for its contributions to the sciences and to the major contributions for the benefit of advanced studies in a serene atmosphere of fraternity. This is given at the hand of the Rector, March 8, 1966.

This tribute from a very older brother was signed by the Rector, Professor Felice Battaglia.

All of the other eight colonial colleges—Harvard, Brown, William and Mary, Yale, Dartmouth, Columbia, Princeton, and the University of Pennsylvania—were included among the well-wishers.

The greetings from Yale University, signed by its President, Kingman Brewster, Jr., took appropriate note of the Yale men who had served Rutgers so well in its history and also recited the contributions of a Rutgers man to Yale. Mentioned in this unusual tribute were the Rev. John Henry Livingston, who received his Bachelor of Arts degree from Yale in 1762 and served as President of Queen's College from 1810 to 1825; Abraham Bruyn Hasbrouck, who was graduated from Yale in 1810 and served as President of Rutgers College from 1840 to 1850; the Rev. Jacob Cooper, Yale graduate in 1852, who became one of Rutgers' most outstanding teachers in the years from 1866 to 1904, serving as professor of Greek and also of logic and metaphysics; and Austin Scott, who graduated from Yale in 1869, was Rutgers' professor of history, political economy, and constitutional law from 1883 to 1890, and served as President of the College from 1891 to 1906.

And, the tribute from Yale continued:

"Outstanding among Rutgers men who have served Yale was Albert Stanburrough Cook of the Class of 1872, professor of the English language and literature from 1889 until his retirement in 1921."

Columbia sent "most cordial greetings" signed by its President, Grayson Kirk. Translated from the Latin, Columbia's message said in part:

"We rejoice that through these years of achievement your University has won such praise in its effective promotion of liberal studies. We rejoice that from your noble seat of learning there have gone forth to meet the responsibilities of life so many possessors of talent, trained to spread the uplifting influence of the arts which conduce to the safety and concord of all mankind. For it is precisely from such studies that there has flowered the liberty, alike of thought and of political action, which you and we have long enjoyed together. We would fain have this liberty more and more securely established by that search for truth through which alone human beings can understand the nature of their relation to the entire universe of which they form a part."

One of the most colorful of the salutations came in a specially made wooden slip case. It came from the Polytechnical Institute of Bucharest, Romania. The greetings on parchment were beautifully decorated in colors laid on by hand and were given in Romanian on one side of the sheet and in English on the other.

Another very unusual greeting was sent by Chung Chi College, the Chinese University of Hong Kong. The message was written in the form of a poem which was hand painted in Chinese calligraphy on gold-flecked "firecracker"-red paper. The paper was mounted on a protective cloth backing which was rolled into a scroll and fitted into a special case.

Dr. C. T. Yung, President of the college, in a letter to President Gross reported that he had appointed Professor Noah E. Fehl as the institution's delegate to the Convocation and provided the following as a "rough translation" of the greetings:

> In New Jersey your University was established using the good name of Rutgers.
>
> It has had a long history covering wide fields of learning, with Colleges of Engineering, Commerce, Arts, Science and Agriculture, in a comprehensive search for truth. Its reputation has spread far.
>
> The University was started with a charter from a British King and commemorated the name of a wise man.
>
> Days and months have passed for two centuries. Now this happy anniversary will add to your honor and distinction.
>
> We, though separated far, travel the same road with you in the advancement of learning.
>
> May your daily progress be without limit until you rest in the highest excellence.
>
> We are happy to take part in this ceremonial and submit greetings to express our sincere esteem and respect.

Writing to President Gross after the Convocation, Professor Fehl, who teaches world history at Chung Chi College, explained that brush writing is still cultivated by Chinese educated in science and added that President Yung received his doctorate in botany from the University of Chicago.

The greetings from the University of Mysore, India, were enclosed in a polished bamboo tube. Many of the greetings were sent in paper tubes or cases, many bore large wax seals, and most were specially printed. There were, however, a few hand-written greetings.

Universitas Cantabrigiensis sent its greetings on a sheet of parchment to which was attached a large gold seal. Many of the seals were in themselves notable works of art and in at least one case—the greetings from the University of Utrecht—the elaborate wax seal was protected by a small metal case.

The birthday message from Oxford University—in Latin— had a special kind of dignity. It was printed on a sheet of fine paper to which was attached a heavy cross-grained ribbon in dark blue to which was affixed a large wax seal.

The University of Strathclyde sent a small hand-painted re-production of its coat of arms, and the Slovak Technical University in Bratislava, Czechoslovakia, a very attractive and heavy crystal letterweight along with a message from the Chancellor, Professor Dr. Josef Trokan, expressing his regrets for not being able to "come to New Brunswick (for the Convocation) as the distance is too great and transport expenses are beyond my means."

THE PRESIDENT IS HONORED BY THE SALMAGUNDI CLUB

Rutgers was honored too during the Bicentennial Year as its President received special honors. In March the Salmagundi Club of New York, founded in 1871 as a haven of fellowship for artists, people in creative fields, and patrons of the arts, awarded Dr. Gross its 1966 Citation and Medal in recognition of his efforts to spur a new interest in culture among Rutgers students and the people of New Jersey.

In announcing the club's selection for an award which had previously been presented to Thomas Hart Benton, Huntington Hartford, John Daly, Howard Lindsay, and Russel Crouse, Fredric March and Florence Eldridge, Francis V. Kughler, New York artist and president of the club, noted that "not the least of the great gifts Mason Gross has brought to the presidency of one of the nation's large universities is his deep and abiding love of beauty and the arts.

President Gross receives 1966 Salmagundi Club
medal from Club President
Francis Vandeveer Kughler.

"He has insisted that all of the arts be given an important
place in the educational program of the State University and by so
doing has insured that there will be a steady flow of young people
who have an understanding and appreciation of the arts and their
place in a full life. At the same time, he has repeatedly called New
Jersey's attention to its needs for cultural identification and development."

The medal which Dr. Gross received at the society's award
dinner on March 10 bore the following citation:

"For distinguished accomplishment in the field of education,
for his development of the Fine Arts in the University and his
program of art appreciation."

In responding, President Gross recalled his frequently quoted
and sometimes misquoted "cultural desert" speech of some years
earlier in which he had discussed the parlous health of the arts in

New Jersey. He said that he could no longer make that same speech, that there had been a cultural awakening in New Jersey as demonstrated by a host of developments from the construction of a new State Museum in Trenton to the lively interest being shown throughout the State in ballet, symphony, painting and sculpture, and choral singing.

Cultural interest in New Jersey, he said, was no longer near death, but stirring into new vitality. On the Rutgers campuses, he went on, it is very much alive, and he pointed to a variety of artistic and musical opportunities which are being made available to Rutgers students and, in most instances, to the public as well.

He quoted from Alfred North Whitehead, a selection of whose writings he had edited in collaboration with Professor F. S. C. Northrop of Yale in 1953, on the subject of culture. Whitehead, in his imperishable essay on "The Aims of Education," had said that "culture is activity of thought and receptiveness to beauty and humane feeling."

In a speech which must have reached deep into some cerebral corners in that gathering of artists and art lovers Dr. Gross considered the matter of beauty philosophically and said: "I suggest to you that when we use the word 'beauty' meaningfully, we mean it to be the same sort of thing—a word which indicates something which we value of itself alone, and, as such, never value because of some other qualities which might come in its train.

"We might find a beautiful object to be useful in decoration, but here we are assessing the contribution which one beautiful object would make as a factor in a larger and more beautiful whole. The courtship tactics of a peacock might suggest that the male, at least, considers the beauty of his tail-feathers as primarily utilitarian, but at less tense moments his strut would suggest that he too admires its beauty for itself alone. But if this example, and with it the whole field of cosmetics, suggests that beauty is on occasion useful in producing results beyond itself, that is no bar to our claim that, regardless of this, beauty is always and everywhere self-justifying."

Dr. Gross said that when the word "beautiful" is used it is not trying to measure a particular quality and is not trying "to say something about our own sense of pleasure," but instead is being used to "describe a situation in which we find ourselves, which is characterized by an overwhelming sense of value, a situation which contains many factors all interrelated, some appearing irreducibly objective and factual, and thereby of great importance and meaning for us, with other factors at the same time undeniably subjective, such as the sense of joy and exultation—personal feelings, no doubt, but not exclusive, because we instantly want others to share them with us. But the sure mark of beauty of such a situation is that we require nothing more of it than, hopefully, its continuance. It is wholly self-justifying. It is completely an end in itself, and even if in fact it is only a prelude to something further, we never require that this should be true. The immediate value of the present is all that seems of importance to us. It is a resting place for the soul."

Dr. Gross went on to say that if a civilization became completely absorbed with utility and were to ignore the things of beauty which are their own justification, then that civilization would collapse.

"I personally feel, therefore," he continued, "that it is an important part of the task of the contemporary American college or university to do all it can to encourage the development of the arts both on the campus and in the surrounding society."

He said that wherever possible this should be encouraged by actual studio work and declared that "the vital thing is to awaken the sense of beauty."

"Events of the last quarter century have proven to us all too thoroughly that our civilization is perilously thin. The murder of six million Jews, the slaughter of over a hundred thousand people suspected of Communist sympathies in Indonesia during these past few weeks, the horrible events following upon political overturns all over the world, as well as the frightening events at Watts and elsewhere in our own country, can support no feelings of complacency about the progress we have made since we came down from the trees.

"But we have achieved at least this much that is human and civilized—the sense of beauty and of self-sustaining value. We learned this first as cavemen, and our knowledge has progressed in subtlety and refinement since those early days. In this sense of beauty, and its concomitant sense of goodness, lies our only ultimate hope of victory and meaning. Let us go tell it on the mountain."

Newcomen Society Honors Dr. Gross

On September 29 President Gross was the guest of honor and speaker at a reception and dinner held on the campus by the Newcomen Society in North America in a Bicentennial tribute to the University. The dinner was held in the faculty dining room of the University Commons.

The Newcomen Society has strong Rutgers connections. Dr. Gross is a member of the Society's New Jersey Committee and the organization was founded in 1923 by an 1877 Rutgers graduate, the late Leonor F. Loree. Loree at that time was known as the "dean of American railroad presidents," and as a trustee of Rutgers was a leading voice in the affairs of the institution.

The Society takes its name from Thomas Newcomen, an eighteenth-century English pioneer in the development of the steam engine. The Newcomen Society in North America is affiliated with the original Newcomen Society in England.

In announcing its plans for the Rutgers dinner, the Society noted that the University was the eighth oldest of American colleges and "is also marked by the distinction that alone among the Colonial colleges it has developed into a land-grant college and finally a state university." It also pointed out that now as Rutgers looks back on two hundred years of accomplishment "it is among the giants of American higher education, enrolling more than 25,000 undergraduate and graduate students," and that as it celebrated its 200th anniversary it has pride in its past "but its deepest concern is reserved for the present and, above all, the future."

Dr. Gross suggested that just as the combination of the agricultural research of the land-grant college program and agricultural extension had provided the means of making American agriculture the most productive in the world, an application of this principle of research brought effectively to the point of need could do much to solve the mounting problems of urban life.

He noted that Rutgers was already deeply involved in this effort to develop first a body of knowledge about the cities and then to create an effective means of bringing this knowledge to the people who need it.

Dr. Gross also told his audience of businessmen and industrial leaders that financial aid from private sources can help to keep the universities from too great a dependence on federal support which he indicated might result in programs geared to or guided by the needs or wishes of the federal government rather than to free scholarly or scientific inquiry. He suggested that business can team up with the University, federal and state agencies to support programs of mutual interest and enable the academic institution to maintain its independence. As an example, he pointed to the support the University had received from these several sources in installing the 16-million-electron-volt tandem Van de Graaff accelerator which has done so much to push Rutgers research in physics to new standards of excellence. Without the support of the Bell Telephone Laboratories, he said, the University might have built a 12 million volt accelerator, a fairly common piece of laboratory equipment. With support from Bell, the more intricate, more sophisticated equipment became possible and the Rutgers Physics Department is now the recipient of a "Center of Excellence" grant from the National Science Foundation of nearly $2,700,000 to carry its work in this field to still higher levels.

ॐ

GOLD MEDAL FROM THE HOLLAND SOCIETY

In early November The Holland Society of New York, an organization dedicated to the perpetuation of the memory of the Dutch settlers who participated so vigorously in the founding of that city, paid a singular tribute to the one university in this country which owes its existence and its name to those same hearty settlers. On November 7 the Society presented its Gold Medal to President Gross for distinguished academic leadership.

The Society's interest in Rutgers extends over a long period of years. In 1928 it had presented the University with its most famous statue, the bronze likeness of William the Silent which stands on Queen's Campus and is a familiar landmark to thousands of Rutgers sons.

In accepting the Society's Gold Medal, Dr. Gross reached back into the history of the founding of the colonial colleges including Rutgers to point out that the aims of the men who struggled to bring them into being are not very different from the real goals of today's colleges and universities.

"The freedom of the individual, the freedom of our society, because of the freedom of its members, the freedom from fear which comes about through knowledge, and most of all, the creative freedom of the human spirit. These are the goals to which —once every two hundred years at least—we must rededicate ourselves." (The full text of Dr. Gross's Holland Society address is found in Appendix J.)

By educating the newcomer to society so that he can develop native skills and talents, we give him the opportunity for economic freedom, Dr. Gross said. On another level the educated man makes a contribution to his society which helps others to freedom. Then, he continued, there is the freedom which comes about with the mastery of the secrets of nature.

But, Dr. Gross added, "A more difficult level of freedom is that which we both achieve and contribute to through the gradual understanding of people of other races, religions, and colors than ourselves. If the kind of political slavery which we knew in this country until the close of the Civil War was a hideous phase of history that we had to grow out of, it was, in my opinion, far less hideous than the defenses that are put up nowadays against recognizing the just claims of our fellow human beings. On the Election Eve, 1966, we can only contemplate with horror and shame the political cries that are being used to justify downgrading and maltreating our fellow citizens of this free republic.

"But if the damage to these minorities is great, how much greater is the damage to the spokesmen for the oppressors. They have willfully turned their backs on the power of the intellect and have sold out to those evil, lying, and prejudicial emotions whose domination constitutes human bondage. The shoe is now on the other foot and the oppressors are now, in the fullest sense of the word, the slaves.

"But the final freedom which I would mention is one which a college teacher learns to recognize and to cherish. We all know the student in our classes who is competent and intelligent, but unconcerned. Then the great moment occasionally comes when suddenly the student catches fire and is off on his own in a glow of wild excitement. It makes little or no difference what his subject is—mathematics or literature, physics or the arts. Suddenly his creative energies are summoned into action, and he probably experiences the greatest freedom he can ever know."

These several freedoms, Dr. Gross concluded, are the goals to which colleges and universities must rededicate themselves.

Early in the Bicentennial Year Dr. Gross received in his office a delegation of executives from the New Jersey Bell Telephone Company. It was headed by its president, Robert D. Lilley. They brought a much-appreciated birthday gift: a new oil painting of Queen's which the company had specially commissioned as an artistic salute to the University.

The representation of Queen's campus had been painted by Marvin Friedman of North Brunswick in a bright, contemporary style. The painting included in its composition the historic Queen's building, the front and one side of Geology Hall, and a corner of Winant's Hall. The browns and reds of the buildings are contrasted strongly with the bright blues and greens which Mr. Friedman used in the sky and lawn.

The painting now hangs in the entrance lobby of Old Queen's, but its more important significance is that it was the choice of the company for the cover design of all the 1966 directories printed for the State of New Jersey. More than four million copies of thirty-eight different editions of that book were distributed throughout the State and only an astronomer would dare to calculate the number of times the picture of Old Queen's was viewed by telephone-number-seeking New Jerseyans.

Mr. Friedman's work was also used as the cover design of the February issue of *New Jersey Bell*, the company magazine which told the story of Rutgers and its Bicentennial as its feature article.

In an editor's note which accompanied six pages of narration and photographs, the magazine pointed out:

Friedman's Queen's

"Our company numbers among its employees some 177 Rutgers graduates. Richard Levis, Sales Methods Supervisor, Planning and Promotion, is chairman of the Rutgers Alumni Bicentennial Celebration Committee. Thomas M. Geisler, Assistant Secretary and Assistant Treasurer, is also a member of that committee. Harold G. Lundberg, Sales Staff Supervisor, is a member of the Executive Committee of the Rutgers Alumni Association, which is active in the celebration."

The telephone company's tribute through its directory was unique because it reached into every business establishment and most of the homes in New Jersey, but it was only one of many similar salutes to the 200th anniversary by newspapers, magazines, and radio and television stations.

Newspapers from one end of the State to the other gave wide coverage to the Bicentennial and its principal events, and many newspapers published special sections or editions to note the celebration. Foremost among these was the very extensive special Bicentennial Edition of the New Brunswick *Home News* which on

September 18, 1966, published a 40-page edition. It included articles and pictures on the University's history, present-day progress, and plans for the future. Other notable special editions or sections were published by the Perth Amboy *Evening News*, the Plainfield *Courier-News* and the Newark *Star-Ledger*.

Many others used considerable amounts of copy on the Bicentennial, making liberal use of a large package of articles, pictures, and cartoons which had been prepared by the University's Public Relations Department and distributed to some eighty papers in all parts of the State.

On June 26 the *Sunday Magazine* of the *Newark Evening News* carried five pages of pictures and text on the anniversary by David C. Schreiber, a 1960 graduate of the Newark College of Arts and Sciences, who has reported the principal Rutgers news of recent years.

The list of special publications or articles about the Bicentennial runs to considerable length, but some of the more notable include a special edition of the magazine *Newark Commerce*, an article in the June 11 issue of the *Saturday Review* which tied the Bicentennial in with the opening of the annual meeting of American University Presses on the Rutgers campus, the entire January issue of *Soil Science* magazine devoted to Rutgers, an article in the International New Jersey magazine supplement to the *New York Times*, a special edition of the magazine *New Jersey Business*, a special edition of the magazine *Business Farming*, and a four-page article saluting Rutgers in the October issue of the *Review* of the New Jersey Education Association.

Three New Jersey companies saluted Rutgers with pictures and copy in folders sent out to their customers: New Jersey Bell in February, New Jersey Blue Cross-Blue Shield in May, and the New Jersey Natural Gas Company in July-August.

Even the University's philatelic enthusiasts had a part in helping the University celebrate. The Federated Stamp Clubs of Central New Jersey devoted its October 7-9 convention to a "Salute to Rutgers." The organization serviced, canceled, and mailed a special Bicentennial cachet for the show. This cachet, hopefully treasured now by many stamp collectors, featured on its cover the Bicentennial logotype.

It was early for the Bicentennial Year, but one of the major sections of the New Jersey Pavilion at the New York World's Fair in 1965 saluted the Rutgers birthday. At least two million persons, from every state in the nation and from many foreign countries, visited this exhibit which featured a panel noting that New Jersey was the site of two of the original nine colonial colleges, Princeton and Rutgers.

The theme of the display was a twist on the expected, for in it Rutgers saluted its sister colleges in New Jersey. The official medallions or seals of the 28 four-year colleges in the State were most attractively executed for the display by Charles E. Blackwood, Rutgers director of graphic arts, and his gifted associate, Gus Szasz.

Mr. Szasz was also commissioned by the State of New Jersey to create the six-foot high Great Seal of the State of New Jersey which graced the entrance way to the New Jersey Pavilion.

For Rutgers Day at the Fair, September 18, President Gross was the principal speaker, the Scarlet Rifles and the Queen's Guard, the crack drill teams of the Army and Air Force Reserve Officer Training Corps, respectively, performed, the Douglass Choir sang, there were selections by the Mummers, the drama group from the Newark College of Arts and Sciences, and the Chorale Group of the College of South Jersey, and talks by Dr. Richard P. McCormick, Rutgers University historian, and Earle W. Clifford, Jr., dean of student affairs.

When the Raritan Valley Chapter of the Society for the Advancement of Management and the New Brunswick-Raritan Valley Chamber of Commerce decided early in 1966 that they would honor Rutgers at their annual dinner on November 12, they looked about for an appropriate and unusual gift to mark their esteem for the State University.

The choice finally settled on certainly qualifies in both characteristics. It is a handsome ceremonial mace, especially designed by one of the foremost manufacturers of fine silverware and precious metal awards.

The mace was financed by contributions from the business and industrial leaders of the community, in a very warm and thoughtful gesture to the University.

The Rutgers Mace

The Rutgers mace, which was presented with all due ceremony, is truly a work of art and fine craftsmanship. It was designed by J. Russell Price, director of design for the Gorham Company of Providence, Rhode Island, and was produced by the Gorham silversmithing department.

Measuring nearly fifty inches in length, the mace takes as its motif various symbols associated with Rutgers, its historical foundations and its connections with the State of New Jersey. The crown and cross at the head of the mace was inspired by Queen Charlotte's crown which rests upon a ring of ermine carried out in sterling silver and deep enamel.

The shield on the front of the mace directly beneath the crown is the new heraldic shield of the University. The reverse side carries the Rutgers seal with its Latin legend. Sprays of ivy as symbolic of universities of learning decorate the area between shield and seal.

Beneath the segment bearing the shield and seal there is a band of gold and red enamel which carries the University's motto, "Sol iustitiae et occidentem illustra," and this rests upon a cushion of white oak from the tree which inspired the poem "Trees" by Joyce Kilmer.

The shaft of the mace is made up of four sections, two of richly colored and finely finished oak placed above and beneath a golden shaft decorated with violets, the State flower of New Jersey. The base of the mace repeats the oak leaf and ivy motif in two bands.

The Gorham Company says that this beautiful object is the most impressive thing that it has ever made and there are good reasons to accept this somewhat subjective opinion. In taking on this unusual commission the designers, artists, and craftsmen faced the challenge of meeting the centuries-old standards of British craftsmen who had been creating maces ever since the early ones were used in knightly mayhem. Gorham set out to do the British one better in the mace department. The impressive Rutgers mace, which will be carried at commencements and other major academic ceremonies, demonstrates that they have done so.

There was another touching and thoughtful Bicentennial tribute. On Sunday, April 17, the New Brunswick Theological Seminary, which shared a common parentage with Queen's College and was linked with it for many of its earliest years, and the Reformed Churches of the area re-created a Dutch Reformed Church service of colonial days.

The details of the service, held in Kirkpatrick Chapel, were worked out cooperatively by the Rev. Wallace C. Jamison, president of the Seminary, and the Rev. Bradford S. Abernethy, Rut-

Eighteenth Century Service on April 17, 1966

gers chaplain. The service was authentic to the point of using costumes of the period, the Dutch language for part of the service, and the congregational singing of the Psalms in English, as did the Dutch in 1766.

Representatives of nearby Dutch Reformed churches antedating 1766 took part and four Reformed clergymen conducted the service. Strictly out of character with the reproduction of a church service of 1766 was the provision of closed circuit television to accommodate the overflow crowd attending in nearby Scott Hall.

Rutgers Around the World

IN Nairobi, Kenya, a Rutgers professor of entomology on leave with the East African Agriculture and Forestry Research Organization gave a party for a group of his colleagues; at Ithaca, New York, a group of Cornell University graduate students gathered for an impromptu party; in New York City some 318 persons in formal dress dined by candlelight at the New York Hilton; in Tokyo 37 Japanese and Americans had a party at the Gakushi-Kaikan; and in Milan, Italy, a group of six lively ladies got together to eat banana splits and drink vintage wine.

Nov. 10, 1966—Nairobi, Kenya. Dr. Ordway Starnes entertains friends at Charter Night party.

There were at least 74 of these parties on a single day in mid-November of 1966. There were formal dinner parties, informal get-togethers, luncheons, and just a "toast or two" at some friendly bar. They varied widely in format, in size, in the cuisine and the beverages, and in the geography of the place. But all had one common denominator. They were all a part of "Rutgers Night Around the World," the imaginative and unusual festivities of November 10, 1966, which had been conceived as a demonstration of the worldwide distribution of Rutgers sons and daughters and the solidarity of the alumni family.

Nov. 10, 1966—Cochabamba, Bolivia

Nov. 10, 1966—Belgrade, Yugoslavia

The worldwide "party" certainly achieved these goals for the University. Although the number of celebrants was small in relation to the total alumni body, "Rutgers Night Around the World" has given Rutgers the right to paraphrase the claim of the former British Empire and say that "the sun never sets on some Rutgers alumnus or alumna."

Nov. 10, 1966—Seoul, Korea

The "Rutgers Night Around the World" stretched from the campus on a zigzag trail across the country, through Chicago, down to Phoenix and Tucson, across to Los Angeles, San Diego, and San Francisco, hopped across the near Pacific to Honolulu, then across the far Pacific to Tokyo, on to Seoul, Korea, and Bangkok in the Far East, to Belgrade, Yugoslavia, to Milan, Madrid, to London, and then back to New York.

Actually, this longitudinal lineup is only a partial listing of the sites of the parties on that memorable night in Rutgers history. There were many other gatherings in South America, throughout the United States and closer-by in New Jersey. (A full listing—as far as can be determined—of the "Rutgers Night Around the

Nov. 10, 1966—Honolulu, Hawaii

World Parties" is found in Appendix K. It was prepared by George J. Lukac, editor of the *Rutgers Alumni Monthly*, for original use in that publication. Mr. Lukac has graciously given permission for its use in this volume.)

The "Round the World" parties were as varied as the locations in which they were held. It isn't too surprising that the groups in Boston, New York City, and Bergen-Rockland Counties straddling the New York-New Jersey border, wore formal attire while the Rutgers celebrants in Miami held an outdoor barbecue and in Honolulu the men wore brightly colored floral shirts and the women the long and comfortable muumuus.

The cuisine and the beverages sometimes took on local color. While roast beef and steak were the favorite by all odds, in London the menu featured roast duckling à l'orange, at Penn State it was haddock—that's about as far from haddock habitat as you can get, and in Kingston, Jamaica, barbecued chicken.

When the idea of the "Rutgers Night Around the World" was first proposed, Bicentennial Coordinators Ingham and Durham had suggested that November 10, 1966, should be the night on which wherever two or more Rutgers sons or daughters congregated they would get together to drink a toast to Alma Mater. Reports from those 74 parties and many individual alumni make it clear that this suggestion was heartily endorsed.

The beverage for the toast ranged over the full gamut of liquid potables, including those commonly and some not so commonly used for this purpose. Where geography and availability indicated a break with the usual Scotch, gin, rye or bourbon, Rutgers sons and daughters adopted the Good Neighbor policy and toasted in local favorites. For example, the group in Milan which celebrated with banana splits, apparently in the interest of maintaining an "American" atmosphere, washed that confection down with a good local wine. The reports from Around the World indicate that Rutgers was toasted on November 10, 1966, in a variety of beverages foreign and domestic. The basic raw material of those "toasts" included champagne, tequila, many kinds of wine, the virile beers of Australia, the gentler brews of the Netherlands, and a long list of American brewery products. The stuff of the toasting was as cosmopolitan as the toasters.

The programs were different and varied too. A number of the parties called on Rutgers faculty and staff for the formal part of their programs, but the majority filled out local arrangements with the filmstrip specially prepared on campus for the occasion.

President Gross, Charles H. Brower, member of the Class of 1925 and chairman of the Rutgers Board of Governors, and U.S. Senator Clifford P. Case '25 were the speakers at the largest of the off-campus dinners, a gathering of more than 300 at the New York Hilton. Director of Athletics Albert W. Twitchell '35 spoke at the Chicago meeting. Frederick E. Gruninger '53, assistant to the director of athletics, and Leslie H. Unger '52, director of sports information, spoke at the Boston party.

Nov. 10, 1966—Phoenix, Arizona

Nov. 10, 1966—The Hilton Hotel, New York City

The filmstrip provided to some sixty of the celebrating groups was designed to give the alumni a visual and vocal report on present-day Rutgers and the Bicentennial. In full-color photographs accompanied by a recorded message from President Gross it told of the present size and strengths of the University, some of the highlights of the anniversary celebration, particularly of the Bicentennial Convocation, and of Rutgers' plans and hopes for the future.

Topping off the programs of the Rutgers parties Around the World was a fresh message from President Gross carried by telegram to each of the celebrations. Enthusiastically received everywhere, the telegrams brought "Greetings from the Banks. You are among several thousand loyal sons and daughters of Rutgers assembled this evening in more than seventy places around the world. Best wishes from everyone here on the campus."

Several of the parties included in their programs a showing of the new film *Rutgers—From the Inside*, a full-color documentary motion picture completed during the Bicentennial but not an integral part of the celebration. It was produced by Robert Bell '44, professional film maker, to capture the spirit of Rutgers and perhaps, more importantly, the whole spirit of learning.

Rutgers—From the Inside is a sensitively handled motion picture which is notably free of all the usual and expected clichés and devices of films of this sort. It does very little "selling" in the public relations sense, but does portray the excitement of learning, the thrills of intellectual discovery and artistic creation, the real significance of the student-teacher relationship. If it "promotes" anything, it is the wonderful process of opening up young minds to the power and excitement of intellectual pursuit, the spiritual release which President Gross in his Holland Society speech had described as the "greatest freedom" man can ever know.

While Rutgers alumni were celebrating, literally around the world, the Rutgers family was having a birthday party on campus. Several hundred members of the faculty and staff, including, of course, both alumni and nonalumni, took part in this "family" affair in the University Commons. There they heard President Robert F. Goheen of Princeton University pay generous tribute to a long-time neighbor.

Dr. Goheen's address* that evening was testimony to the fact that, while Rutgers and Princeton are and probably always will be fierce rivals in athletic competition, they share a common heritage and a common purpose and must inevitably come closer in the years ahead to achieve that goal.

In his introductory remarks Dr. Goheen noted that the two institutions have shared in New Jersey's history over the past two centuries and that during those years the "relationships between the two institutions have been close and sometimes curiously inter-mingled."

President Goheen recounted some of the histories and backgrounds of all the colonial colleges and then recalled the early struggles and growth of Rutgers and Princeton, bringing this historical narrative to the point where "we stand today, no longer two provincial colleges, but universities, with national and international responsibilities. . . . I do not hesitate to predict that these two universities will contribute more, and be of greater influence, within the State of New Jersey in the decades ahead than ever in the decades past."

He said that it is the mission of the modern university to teach, to conduct research, and to engage in public service.

"If the imaginative and persevering search for new knowledge, the effective passing on of that already known, and a deliberate application of learning (both new and old) to the public benefit constitute the mark of the powerful university, then clearly Rutgers is powerful. Indeed, those of us who are concerned with such things find it hard to exaggerate the accomplishments of Rutgers and its most recent presidents.

"They are the more remarkable because the great power-house which is current-day Rutgers—with lines that extend near and far, generating, conveying, and putting to use ideas and skills —this great power-system has been brought into being despite very great budgetary limitations and with all too little understanding and encouragement from the people of New Jersey and their representatives."

Dr. Goheen then said that the "long-standing parsimony of

---

*Appendix L—Address by President Robert F. Goheen of Princeton at the New Brunswick Charter Night dinner, November 10, 1966.

the State toward public higher education has been fading—fading quite fast," and went on to predict the adoption of the legislation which has since provided for a reorganization of the structure of public higher education including the establishment of a new State Department of Higher Education.

He said:

"Within the statewide system for public higher education conceived in New Jersey Senate Bill 434 [the reorganization legislation] and under the sort of forward-looking master-plan that we need, much room will be left open for institutional initiative and autonomy. And in any comprehensive system which develops in New Jersey, I am confident that Rutgers will continue to be living witness to the importance and efficacy of these prerogatives of vital educational institutions."

Concluding, Dr. Goheen said: "Rutgers is important, critically important in her own right, and she is important because of the pivotal point she must occupy in any coordinated system of higher education in this State.

"Two hundred years of history declare her mission—past, present, and future."

In a tribute to Dr. Goheen's work on behalf of better public higher education in New Jersey, President Gross presented the guest speaker with the Rutgers Medal, and a citation which reads as follows:

The medal we present you here is of a coinage two hundred years old. Our intention is both general and particular. It is general because of the eloquent words and generous deeds by which you have supported our common faith that public and private higher education are the two sides of a single noble coin. Your strong leadership has been a summons to men of good will to support that truth. It is particular because, while we are celebrating tonight a Rutgers past and future, we are also honoring you as a friend of higher education in the entire State. By this medal you are seized of the company of Rutgers men and women everywhere.

Dr. Goheen was the founder and chairman of the Citizens Committee for Higher Education, a group of the State's leading

Rutgers Medal to Princeton President Goheen.

citizens organized to "arouse the public to the urgent problems of the State's inadequacy in the whole range of higher educational services, and to support measures which will ensure a sound long-term solution."*

While the founders of the little college originally known as Queen's were Dutch colonials, it was, after all, the English who gave it its charter, and it was most appropriate that the other guest speaker at the family Charter Day dinner should be a representative of Great Britain. He was Paul M. G. Wright, director of the British Information Service. Mr. Wright made humorous and affectionate comments about King George III, the English monarch in whose name the charter was handed down by his representative Governor Franklin, just two hundred years before.

---

*From *A Call to Action*, published by the Citizens Committee for Higher Education in New Jersey, 1 Palmer Square, Princeton, 1965, p. 2.

MR. LENKEY'S FILLIP

John Lenkey III is a Rutgers graduate who likes mountain climbing, travels a great deal, and was determined to add an unusual fillip to the Bicentennial celebration. As this is written, Mr. Lenkey is already well on his way to adding that extra something.

The "fillip" which Mr. Lenkey came up with was the proposal that he and some other alumni assistants plant the Rutgers flag on the summits of some of the largest mountain peaks in the world. He announced the plan at the Charter Day dinner in Los Angeles and called on all Rutgers men with a high disregard of life and limb and equally high spirit of adventure to help him in the project.

"By showing our colors proudly to the world," Mr. Lenkey explained, "we Rutgers men will demonstrate our great pride in our University as it starts its third century of service and education."

Mr. Lenkey was inspired in the flag-placing project by the exploits of members of the Rutgers University Soils and Crops Department who had in recent years placed Rutgers flags near both the North and the South Pole. Last August in what will certainly be the northernmost observance of the Rutgers Bicentennial, Dr. John C. F. Tedrow, professor of soils, and Grant F. Walton, instructor, carried the Rutgers flag to Inglefield Land, about 600 miles from the North Pole as they made studies of the soil there for the Arctic Institute of North America and the U.S. Army Materiel Command. Dr. Tedrow had previously placed the Rutgers flag within a few hundred miles of the South Pole—atop Mount Erebus, the only active Antarctic volcano.

With the Rutgers flag already at or near the two poles, Lenkey declared from Los Angeles that he would plant it on the most famous mountain peaks of four continents as well. The targets selected are Mt. Kosciusko, Australia's highest peak; Mt. Fujiyama near Tokyo; Mt. Everest in Nepal; the Matterhorn in Switzerland, and Mt. Whitney in California.

Lenkey quickly followed up his plan with action and by early March of 1967 had "conquered" both Mt. Kosciusko and "Fuji." The Australia peak didn't provide much of a challenge beyond some exercise, but climbing Fuji in midwinter is a different and dangerous undertaking.

In letters to Colonel Vincent Kramer of the Alumni Relations staff, Lenkey told of his Mt. Fujiyama climb with enthusiasm and wit:*

Our expedition to place a Rutgers flag atop Mt. Fuji has proven to be a resounding success and full of honors for Rutgers.

At long last we reached the crest of that great hollow, icy volcano, pulling ourselves hand-over-hand through the top gate and we rested a few minutes. I had been able to snap a few pictures of the climb up to station eight, but it was too dangerous above that. Now we broke out our Rutgers flag and snapped one picture. It was 5:30 P.M. and we were again in sunlight. But the official hoisting was to be postponed for the Rising Sun, of course. . . . The next morning at 7:30 A.M., March 8, 1967, year of Showa 42, the Scarlet flag greeted the rising sun with the American and Nippon flags at 12,535 feet, held squarely on the marker showing the highest point in Japan.

Having successfully climbed Mt. Fujiyama in the depth of winter, Lenkey typically wondered whether his proposed target in Europe, the Matterhorn, was a big-enough challenge. Should he change his goal, he asked, to Mont Blanc, the highest peak in Europe, or to the Zugspitze, "which lies in two countries and we can salute Austria and Germany by standing on one side and then the other."

Lenkey got a surprising answer to this question in late June, but before he reached Europe of the Matterhorn he had had his encounter with the mightiest of all mountains, Everest, and had in a sense achieved his purpose there.

He never seriously considered climbing Everest. He had conferred with Sir Edmund Hillary, the famed New Zealander who led the first expedition to scale that awesome pile of rock and ice,

*Appendix M: John Lenkey III's letter to Colonel Vincent Kramer describing the climbing of Mt. Fujiyama, Japan, to place the Rutgers flag on its summit.

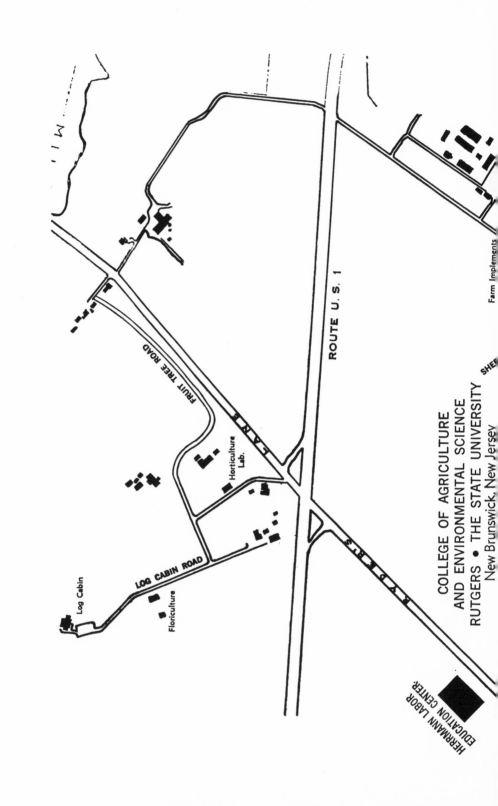

COLLEGE OF AGRICULTURE
AND ENVIRONMENTAL SCIENCE
RUTGERS • THE STATE UNIVERSITY
New Brunswick, New Jersey

HERMANN LABOR
EDUCATION CENTER

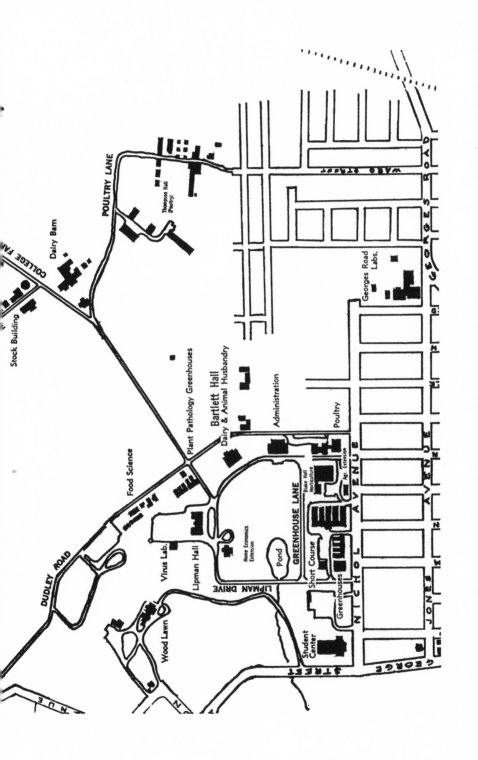

and had, on the basis of Sir Edmund's advice, decided to drop the Rutgers flag from an airplane.

Lenkey himself went to Darjeeling, India, the hill station where the Everest expeditions had started. There he visited with Tenzing Norgay, Hillary's partner on the first successful Everest climb and probably the world's best-known Sherpa. He also met Sherpa Nawang Gombu, the only man ever to stand on the top of Everest twice, and S. K. Sanyal, secretary of the Himalaya Mountaineering Institute. Tenzing and Nawang signed Lenkey's Rutgers flag for luck but they were unable to help him on his avowed project. Lenkey, they said, would have to get a plane from Kathmandu, Nepal. This was his next stop, and there he managed to persuade a 1949 graduate of Utah State, Harry J. McCarty, director of forestry work for the U.S. AID Mission, to plant the Rutgers flag on Mt. Everest.

McCarty and his son, Gary, carried the Rutgers flag to the 18,000-foot elevation and raised it on a 12-foot flagpole. Hopefully, it is flying there now.

Lenkey now moved west through the Middle East and Middle Europe and arrived in Switzerland in June only to find that the

John Lenkey carries Rutgers flag to top of Mt. Fuji.

Spirit of 1766

climb up the Matterhorn was too dangerous because of late snow —Matterhorn climbing for tourists usually begins in July.

One of two Japanese climbers who had tried the Matterhorn shortly before had been killed and Lenkey decided to postpone the attempt. But he did not give it up and has offered to organize a group of Rutgers climbers to carry out his Matterhorn project in September of 1968.

Lenkey's flag-placing project is quixotic, but it is imagination catching and shares much of the spirit of adventure and derring-do which are part of the basic drive of intellectual pursuit. Only a few are privileged successfully to climb even symbolic mountains to plant their standards, but this questing for the Golden Fleece is the stuff of which scholarship and research are made. If mountains are climbed because they "are there," so the frontiers of knowledge are invaded and explored because they challenge the intellect.

Another Rutgers son had his own personal and professional reasons for a special observance of November 10, 1966. Dr. Richard P. McCormick, Rutgers' official historian, professor of American history and a member of the Class of 1938, was celebrating both the anniversary of a 200-year-old event and the official publication date of his new book, *Rutgers—A Bicentennial History*.

Appropriately and obviously, November 10 had been selected as the official publication date.

Scouting around for an unusual way to celebrate the Charter anniversary, Professor McCormick hit upon the idea of asking the 440 members of his sophomore class in American history to show up on November 10 in Early American costume.

Few of the students took this as literally as Dr. McCormick had wanted, but when class convened on the morning of November 10 there were many Rutgers ties on display and one group of four turned out in costumes allegedly copied from the famous fife-and-drum tableau of "The Spirit of '76."

Dr. McCormick himself stepped to the front of the class wearing a Rutgers tie, his Class of 1938 reunion jacket and cap, and proceeded to tell the students about early student pranks and other items of Rutgers history, noting that today's college students are far more serious, sedate, and quiescent than their predecessors of the early days of the college.

As he concluded his lecture that day Dr. McCormick said, "Gentlemen, I have enormously enjoyed this hour; it is the most enjoyable I have had in twenty-one years' teaching at Rutgers. I hope you will look back with mellowness and pride on this 200th birthday in years to come."

The standing ovation was concluded with the singing of "On the Banks of the Old Raritan."

Dr. McCormick and friends

A Stirring and Exciting View

A birthday usually calls for a celebration, but when it is the 200th anniversary of an institution it takes on much more importance than the party itself. The Rutgers Bicentennial was truly a celebration which had all the amenities including the customary many-tiered cake, but the pleasant task of recalling an illustrious and productive past was only a part of the observance. In the life of an institution a Bicentennial is, or should be, a time for looking forward. During the Rutgers Bicentennial the look forward was a stirring and exciting view of tremendous new beginnings and great potential for the service to state and nation to which Rutgers is dedicated.

The observance of Rutger's 200th anniversary came during a period of great change and exciting developments. It was widely recognized as one of the major universities in the nation; it had plans and programs under way which, if brought to their ultimate realization, would make it one of the great universities. Whether all of these were to come to the fullest realization of the fond hopes of its supporters is still unclear in the mists of the future. There were, however, as the Bicentennial Year became history, many bright spots on the horizon. As Rutgers started its third century it could count many evidences of future greatness.

Several events of the Bicentennial Year and just before it have cast strong light on the University's future. Two were particularly significant and both were enmeshed in politics. But politics in a democracy is the basic machinery of government and without government or the support of government a state university cannot survive.

The first of these was the affair involving a Professor Eugene D. Genovese, a history teacher and an admitted former Communist whose outspoken and well-publicized remarks about his "welcome" for a victory of the Vietcong whom American troops were fighting at the time precipitated a prolonged controversy over the basic question of academic freedom—there were many who argued that the issue was really over a basic constitutional right, in this case the right to dissent. The Genovese case became the major issue of the New Jersey gubernatorial campaign of 1965.

The Republican candidate, generally considered to be a friend of both Rutgers and higher education, took the position that Genovese's remarks transgressed academic freedom and said that, if elected, he would demand the professor's dismissal; the Democratic incumbent, running for re-election, said that he disagreed with what Genovese had said but that the matter was and would remain in the hands of the University's governing board.

That board* had said in a unanimous report to the Governor on August 6, 1965, that, while "every member of the Board is completely out of sympathy with the views expressed by Dr. Genovese, he has done nothing in the performance of his academic duties that would constitute grounds for preferring charges against him."

Governor Richard J. Hughes was re-elected by a decisive majority. While only the politically unsophisticated could claim that his victory was due solely to his defense of academic freedom, it was also evident that the voters of New Jersey did not consider the Genovese case a major political issue and that they did not believe it merited interference with the operations of their State University.

This was a new and, for Rutgers, a most welcome attitude on the part of the voters who not too many years before would have sat disinterestedly on the sidelines while the University was bombarded by whatever politician needed a target of opportunity.

---

*Appendix N—A Report on the Genovese Case—Prepared for Presentation to Governor Richard J. Hughes by the Board of Governors of Rutgers, The State University, August 6, 1965.

Rutgers had become in popular acceptance and support, as well as in name, New Jersey's State University.

Nationally, the University's stand in the Genovese case brought it new prominence as a center of intellectual life. It would be unrealistic to claim that the University went through the turmoil of the controversy without some cuts and bruises, but it is also clear that it gained new strength in some important areas. The academic world nodded in tribute to Rutgers' defense of this basic principle of academic integrity and applauded when the President of the University and its Board of Governors were presented the Ninth Annual Alexander Meiklejohn Award of the American Association of University Professors.

The other development which was deeply involved in New Jersey politics had great long-range financial significance. For some years prior to 1966 there had been a steady, but slowly growing, determination in New Jersey to do something about its long-standing deficit in public higher education. The will, however, was stronger than the means, for New Jersey, one of the few states which had not enacted a sales or an income tax, simply did not have the financial resources. It could not move toward a strengthening of its public colleges and the State University without new sources of revenue.

The 1966 state legislature, under strong prodding by the Governor, agreed to do something about the problem of finding new State revenues and after rejecting a proposal for a State income tax, enacted a 3 percent sales tax which became effective on July 1, 1966.

Whether this tax, only a little more than a year old, will provide enough revenue to finance the major expenditures needed to develop New Jersey's system of public higher education is still unclear—as this was written there were no proofs that it could provide the vast sums needed—but one of the telling arguments for the sales tax and one which received much popular support was that the State had too long lagged behind its neighbors in the field of higher education. The Governor, the Legislature, and much of the electorate recognized the necessity of raising more revenue for this important service of state government.

Attention had been brought to New Jersey's needs in public

higher education by the campaigns waged on behalf of the two College Bond Issues of 1959 and 1964, both of which were adopted by generous margins, and in the fall of 1965 a new and powerful champion entered the lists on behalf of a more adequate system of public higher education in New Jersey.

Dr. Robert F. Goheen, President of Princeton University, organized some of the most influential men in New Jersey into the Citizens Committee for Higher Education in New Jersey and started a campaign to make New Jersey aware of the need to bring higher education in the State up to the qualitative and quantitative needs of a highly complex and largely urbanized society.

The Committee had ample documentation for its position including two reports prepared for the State Department of Education and the report of the Governor's Committee on New Jersey Higher Education. All said that New Jersey must make major, early, and costly moves if it was to meet its responsibilities to New Jersey young people seeking education beyond high school.

The Citizens Committee in a "Call to Action" in December, 1965, had made twenty-two basic recommendations for a long-term plan to improve both the quality and the quantity of public higher education in the State. It called for early action by the State to provide the financing which would start the public institutions on a program of expansion enabling them to increase enrollments from 32,000 in 1965 to 134,000 by 1975. It also stressed the need for a reorganization of the educational establishment in New Jersey as a necessary step toward a long-range solution of the problems of higher education.

In a report submitted to the Governor in May of 1966, the Committee recommended the establishment of a separate Department of Higher Education and a separate Board of Higher Education. It argued that the existing State Department of Education and its board, concerned with education at all levels, could not be expected to devote enough of their time and effort to the complex and extensive problems of higher education in New Jersey.

Governor Hughes listened to the Committee, urged public dialogue on the question, and then backed the proposal with the full weight of his office. Finally, in the fall of 1966, the Legislature approved the reorganization plan to provide the separate Department and Board of Higher Education, the office of Chancellor to head up the new department, and new status for the public colleges.

Under the new setup the State University retained its autonomy as specified in the State University Act of 1956. It had welcomed the organizational change largely because it would provide the permanent machinery for statewide planning and coordination in public higher education so long lacking in New Jersey. President Gross had said in 1963 that New Jersey must have a master plan for its system of higher education if its development was to proceed on an orderly and logical basis and command the necessary wide public support.

Rutgers, however, had already been doing some planning of its own. In February of the Bicentennial Year it announced plans for an expansion over the next ten years which would more than double its enrollment, from a grand total of approximately 30,000 students—day and evening, undergraduate and graduate—to about 67,000.

This was not presented as a program which would take care of all the qualified young people who wanted to attend the State University. Rather, it was presented as what President Gross described as "a realistic and practical program within our capabilities and those of the State."

The expansion which this plan suggested would increase total enrollment in all divisions by more than 100 percent, would more than double the undergraduate daytime enrollment to about 27,000 by 1975, and would more than double full-time graduate enrollment to 6,600 by that same year. It also envisioned development of the two-year Medical School into a full four-year institution. The outline for Rutgers' long-range future had been prepared by Robert Heller Associates, Cleveland management consultants.

"We asked the Heller people," Dr. Gross said, "to develop a program for the University's expansion which would take into consideration not only the needs of the young people of the State but also our ability to plan and execute the needed physical facilities and our capabilities in recruiting faculty and staff within what we all must understand would be a relatively short period of time."

The program covered expansion on the campuses in New Brunswick, Newark, and Camden. It was estimated at that time that the total cost of this development would be in the neighborhood of $288,000,000.

This estimate included the physical facilities for a four-year medical school and its teaching hospital because by then it had become apparent that this development was no longer a question of whether but of when.

The new Rutgers Medical School in September of 1966 added its own historic touch to the Bicentennial celebration by admitting its first class. This was the culmination of an interest in medical education which was almost as old as the institution itself. Rutgers had actually granted medical degrees as early as 1792 and on three different occasions in its early history had been affiliated with medical schools for which its sole function was the granting of the M.D. degree. But none of these earlier efforts had survived.

Medical School under construction

The welcoming of the first class—a class of 16 carefully chosen from hundreds of applicants—had finally put Rutgers permanently in the field of medical education. A second class of 16 was admitted in the fall of 1967 and the school expected to welcome a full class of 64 in the fall of 1969.

A distinguished faculty of medical teachers and health scientists had been brought together by the first dean, Dr. DeWitt Stetten, Jr., M.D. Ph.D., and early in 1967 work was started on the large and complex building which eventually was to house the teaching and research units of this newest of Rutgers' educational programs.

The Rutgers Medical School had opened its doors in 1966 as a two-year school but even before it did so forces were moving to help speed it to its ultimate development.

The State of New Jersey, awakened to the need to remedy New Jersey's long-standing neglect of medical education, had committed itself to the construction of at least two full-year medical schools, one of which would be the Rutgers Medical School. While the Legislature could not formally commit future lawmakers, it voted legislation in the fall of 1967 which made it clear that the development of the school into a four-year institution was a matter of public policy.

Thus, as the Bicentennial Year closed, Rutgers and the State of New Jersey could look toward the day when a major medical center would be located on the University Heights campus in surroundings which would put it in proximity to a Science Center, which includes the Nelson Biological Laboratories, the Center of Alcohol Studies, the Wright Chemistry Laboratory, the Engineering Building, the complex of buildings for research and teaching of physics, and buildings planned for the future, including a Library of Science and Medicine, a Psychiatric Institute, and a new home for the College of Pharmacy.

No less exciting in the look toward Rutgers' future was a view directed only a short distance from the site of the Medical School to the latest addition to the Rutgers Campus. This is the Kilmer Area, a 540-acre tract which had formerly been a part of Camp Kilmer, World War II embarkation point for millions of American troops headed for European and African theaters of war.

Model of Livingston College

This new campus, within a short distance of the University Heights campus and contiguous with other Rutgers property in the area, is destined to become the site of at least three new colleges. As 1966 ended, the University was ready with the plans for the construction of the first of these, a college to be known as Livingston, in honor of William Livingston, the first Governor of New Jersey. The first units of Livingston College will be ready for use in the fall of 1969.

The physical and educational character of Livingston College has been planned most carefully as the University determined that it should offer to its students the advantages of both membership in a relatively small college with its own individuality and character and the variety of educational programs and strengths of a large university including those stemming from a strong graduate program.

Livingston College will be coeducational, will have its own dean, its own faculty, and its own campus with residence halls designed to maintain human dimensions. It will offer its students specialties unavailable elsewhere in the University, but they will also have the opportunity to benefit from the offerings of the entire University. At the same time the specialties—anthropology and urban planning are examples—offered at Livingston will be available to students in the other Rutgers colleges.

Rutgers' look to its future was equally impressive in Newark. There, on a tract cleared by municipal urban redevelopment, the Law School had moved into its handsome new building with appropriate ceremony. Nearby, in another redevelopment tract, work was well along on a new campus for the College of Arts and Sciences. Nearing completion by early 1967 and now in use were the first buildings the college that had been planned for academic use.

The new campus in Newark now covers more than 23 acres. The new student center was already in use and when the fall term of 1967 began, three more new buildings—Franklin Conklin Hall, a classroom building; Seth Boyden Hall, science building; and the John Cotton Dana Library—were opened for students. Contracts were signed early in 1967 for a second science building, a struc-

Groundbreaking for Livingston

Newark Campus

ture that will house, in addition to classrooms and faculty offices for physics and mathematics, the laboratories and office of Dr. Daniel S. Lehrman, director of the Institute of Animal Behavior, and the holder of a Research Career Award from the National Institutes of Health of the U.S. Public Health Service.

The University had in its planning a new classroom-office building for this Newark campus, it was conducting a drive for funds for a building for the Graduate School of Business Administration, and it planned the construction of a Fine Arts Building. Further in the future were a gymnasium-physical education building and a third science structure.

Thus, as the Bicentennial Year closed, Rutgers in Newark was emerging as one of the major urban universities of the nation.

In Camden, almost at the other end of the State, Rutgers by the end of 1966 was engaged in the development of another major educational institution. There, in an urban redevelopment area, it was building a new campus with an undergraduate enrollment in its four-year liberal arts college which will soon equal that of the parent institution of only a relatively short time ago. A library, a science building, and a student center had been constructed and space for growth had been acquired in the sixteen years since the former two-year College of South Jersey and its Law School became parts of the State University. Now under construction is a new classroom and faculty office building, planning is well along for a new structure to house the School of Law, and the University will soon start work on the programing of an addition to the Library.

The School of Law at Camden, formerly a branch of the Law School in Newark, has recently been given independent status and the University has pledged its resources to develop it as a full member of the Rutgers family of colleges—the eighteenth to be organized under the Rutgers banner.

In both Newark and Camden, the newly developing Rutgers campuses were part of the urban redevelopment of those cities and in both there was ample evidence that along with the physical improvement which they were bringing about there was recognition in both cities of the interdependence of university and community for the mutual benefit of both.

There was a lot more to the forward look of 1966 that is much harder to specify. It came from a growing feeling of intellectual depth among students and faculty. It was manifested in the awards and honors won by the faculty, in the books they wrote, in the art they created.

It came too from such an imaginative but quite logical step as the welcoming to Rutgers in Newark of the Institute of Jazz Studies, an organization dedicated to the preservation of the music and memorabilia of that peculiarly American musical form. It included such innovations as the appointment of a pianist in residence—an author in residence had been on campus for a number of years—and the establishment under a Rockefeller Foundation grant of a Contemporary Chamber Music Ensemble, comprising some of the finest musicians performing contemporary music, as a musical organization in residence.

This feeling of change and new purpose included such new ventures as the Water Resource Research Institute, the growing activity of the Center of Urban Studies, the renaming of the College of Agriculture to include "and Environmental Science" to indicate its changing role in an urban society, the creation of a Transportation Center within the Eagleton Institute of Politics, the organization of a Bureau of Community Affairs, and the decision that urban planning would be a special offering of the new college at Kilmer.

These were demonstrations of the changing nature of the institution as it underwent a voluntary evolution to meet the new demands of the society it seeks to serve.

Two of its strongest disciplines had been honored in May of 1965 when the Departments of Mathematics and Physics were chosen by the National Science Foundation for participation in the National Science Development Program. The Foundation's grant of $3,708,000 was designed to help the two departments, recognized as very good, achieve excellence—hence the name, "Center of Excellence," for units so designated under this nation-wide program.

Further impetus to the development of Rutgers' already impressive Physics Department was coming from another quarter. Negotiations were nearly complete by the end of 1966 for the University's acquisition of the Industrial Reactor Laboratories in Plainsboro, one of the largest privately owned nuclear reactors in the United States. The Plainsboro facilities consist of a five-million-watt reactor, laboratories, and related equipment located on a 300-acre site. It was completed in 1958 and since then has been operated by Columbia University as a research facility for the ten cooperating firms who built it. They offered it to Rutgers as the most logical future operator of this giant research tool. Rutgers has since accepted this gift.

Another event of the Bicentennial Year promises to be of significance far beyond its immediate effect. This was the reopening of Voorhees Hall, the former University library, as an art building. Handsomely rebuilt and redecorated, this structure was particularly adaptable to its new service—as an art museum and gallery, as the headquarters of the Rutgers College Art Department, and as the housing for the University's art reference books, a collection which includes some 3,000 items donated to Rutgers by the Louis E. Stern Foundation. Stern, a devoted collector of art and art books, had brought together some of the most authoritative research works on the major artists of the nineteenth and twentieth centuries.

Voorhees Art Gallery

There was great excitement and vitality on the several Rutgers campuses in 1966. Much of it was due to the celebration of the Bicentennial, but much of it was also due to the new vigor and health of an institution which had weathered many struggles and setbacks, was now facing new challenges and opportunities, and was determined that, having set a high standard of accomplishment over the past two centuries, it would do no less in the years to come.

Appendices

The Governor's Proclamation

Let it be remembered that on November 10, 1766, Governor Franklin of the Province of New Jersey granted in the name of King George the Third a Charter for the establishment in the Province of New Jersey of Queen's College, which came to be called in later years ˙Rutgers – The State University.

In the words of Benjamin Franklin, father of the Governor, "The good education of youth has been esteemed by wise men in all ages as the surest foundation of the happiness both of private families and of Commonwealth. Almost all governments have therefore made it a principal object of their attention to establish and endow with proper revenues such seminaries of learning as might supply the succeeding age with men qualified to serve the public with honor to themselves and to their country."

Almost a century after its founding Rutgers became the Land-Grant College of New Jersey, with a special relationship to the public interest. After World War II all units of the institution were designated as the State University of New Jersey.

As a colonial college, a land-grant college, and a state university Rutgers uniquely exemplifies the triple traditions of American higher education. Because it has constantly adapted itself to new tasks, it has been able to prepare men and women for a world characterized by rapid change. It has provided the technical knowledge demanded by an age of science. It has grounded its graduates in the enlarging vision of the liberal arts. As a public institution it has fostered democratic approaches to modern problems.

Over a two-century span Rutgers has earned the respect and gratitude of the citizens of this State and of many others beyond the borders of New Jersey. They have been attracted by the excellence of its curricula, the high esteem in which its faculty is held throughout the world, and the quality of its scholarship. It has met the various responsibilities of its triple tradition with imagination, foresight, vigor, intellectual honesty, and courage.

Now, therefore, I, Richard J. Hughes, Governor of the State of New Jersey, in view of the invaluable services which Rutgers – The State University has already performed for this State and the Nation and the greater services which it will fulfill in the future, do hereby proclaim 1966 to be a year for the observance of the Bicentennial of Rutgers – The State University and urge the people of New Jersey to join in this special tribute.

Given under my hand and the Great Seal of the State of New Jersey, this 4th day of January, in the year of Our Lord, one thousand, nine hundred and sixty-sixth, and in the independence of the United States, the one hundred and ninetieth.

/signed
Richard J. Hughes
Governor of the State of New Jersey

THE GLEE CLUB'S BICENTENNIAL TOUR

Our KLM jet buzzed with a giddy spirit of excitement and disbelief as we soared away from Kennedy Airport. May 30 had arrived, and a project for which many Rutgers men had worked was under way. Hearty shouts of congratulations went up for our business manager and president (who almost missed the flight); the Rutgers Glee Club had begun its European concert tour.

For a whirlwind twenty-six days the tour would take sixty-five Glee Club members, our director, Dr. F. Austin Walter '32, better known as "Soup," and our chaperons, Associate Dean of Men and Mrs. Barry M. Millett, through Holland, West Germany, Luxembourg, and France. In particular the Glee Club was traveling to Holland to present Bicentennial greetings from Rutgers to its forebear, the University of Utrecht. That observance was to take place later in the week.

On our arrival in Amsterdam's Schipol Airport we met a very gracious lady, Miss Wobbina Kwast, director of the Nederland-Amerika Instituut. She had been hard at work on our behalf long before we arrived in Europe, arranging concerts, sightseeing tours, and parties. One feature of her plans, that of accommodations, enhanced our stay in Holland immeasurably. Several Dutch families associated with the Instituut acted as hosts to the Rutgers visitors. We discovered that those who belong to this cultural organization have studied in the United States at some time. Communication with the younger set was easy because of their fluent English; they even were up on the latest slang. The opportunity for person-to-person contact, the warm hospitality, and the comfort of the beautiful Dutch homes are remembered with gratitude.

On Wednesday, June 1, the Glee Club embarked on an all-day bus tour in the northern provinces, circling the Zuider Zee. We saw the contrasting features of the Dutch landscape: ancient fishing villages, rolling farmlands, the Great Dike and new man-made polders—land reclaimed from the sea. At the same time, across the Atlantic, Professor Walter was receiving an honorary doctorate from his Alma Mater. Soup joined us on June 2 in time for our first concert.

The Glee Club's first performance was at the Heineken Brewery under the auspices of that firm and the Nederland-Amerika Instituut. After a day of touring the beautiful capital city we were primed for a good concert. There was some apprehension about the Rutgers brand of Dutch as we prepared to sing the national anthem, "William of Nassau." However, the enthusiastic response of the audience and the prospect of the brewery's postconcert party spurred the group on to a very fine show. This set the pace for the concerts before us.

Unlike most of their classmates who had received their degrees on June 1, eight members of the Class of '66 long will remember Friday, June 3, 1966. This was the date of the Rutgers European Commencement. These new graduates, the senior contingent of the Glee Club, are Thomas G. Christenson, Jr., William A. Dickinson, IV, David W. Hardy, David L. Heranney, G. Gregory Lozier (the club's business manager), Richard W. Matthes, John R. Parke, and Eric R. Riedel (club president). This unusual ceremony in Utrecht was a surprising climax to a day of colorful celebration.

As soon as we arrived at the University of Utrecht we took notice of tokens of the historic bond between that institution and Rutgers. One was a bronze plaque bearing Utrecht's motto, "Sol iustitiae nos illustra," the source of Rutgers' "Sol iustitiae et occidentem illustra." The University of Utrecht coat of arms is a bright scarlet. We also discovered a remarkable coincidence, one which involves our famous date of '66. Utrecht is now celebrating its sixty-sixth lustrum. The lustrum is an observance held every five years to commemorate its founding 330 years ago.

The Dutch students marked the occasion with the carnival spirit of American college homecomings, choosing as their lustrum theme New York's dapper mayor of the "Roaring Twenties," Jimmy Walker. The Rutgers group was escorted through the ancient streets by a boldly striped float. A reception committee was on hand, each man sporting a costume of the period, spats included. The Glee Club assembled in the square facing Utrecht's town hall with the Stars and Stripes waving overhead and, under the direction of Professor Walter, sang several selections for the mayor, city officials, and "Mayor Jimmy Walker," who was a student leader. The Rutgers delegation was welcomed officially at an elegant reception in the town hall. After the mayor's warm greeting, Eric Riedel, assisted by Soup and Dean Millett, presented a commemorative plaque of the 1966 European concert tour. The mayor remarked that this memento would receive a place of honor in his office.

That evening we presented a formal concert (white tie and tails). The site was the Aula, the university auditorium. This Gothic structure had served as the chapel house to the great thirteenth-century cathedral, and it was here that the Treaty of Utrecht was signed in 1713, ending the War of the Spanish Succession.

The audience responded to our singing with enthusiastic applause which prompted the club to repeat two selections, a spiritual and "Nobody Ever Died for Dear Old Rutgers," both arranged by Soup.

As the program was nearing completion, Professor Walter momentarily left the stage. With him when he returned was Professor Dr. H. M. J. Scheffer, the Rector Magnificus of the University of Utrecht. Both wore academic caps and gowns of the style traditional in the Netherlands. Reading a translation of the Latin text, Professor Walter presented a commemorative letter bearing greetings "from the President, Governors and Professors of Rutgers University to the Rector Magnificus, Senators and Professors at Utrecht . . ." Then, revealing a carefully kept secret, Soup announced that President Mason W. Gross had given him the diplomas for our seniors who were absent from the June 1 Commencement. He called the surprised students forward to receive their sheepskins from the Rector Magnificus of the University with the historic tie with Rutgers. A reception followed immediately in the Senate Chamber, an imposing room decorated with portraits of prominent scholars reminiscent of the portrait collection in Kirkpatrick Chapel. To make the unusual day complete a decidedly informal party was given in our honor afterwards by our student hosts at a social club.

Our time in Holland passed all too quickly. On Sunday evening the Glee Club participated in a church service in Amsterdam's Luthers Kerk before a congregation numbering over 2,000. The next day, June 6, found us at the United States Air Force Base at Soesterburg, near Queen Juliana's palace, where we entertained our servicemen with favorite spirituals and college songs.

The bustle of activity at Amsterdam's railroad station was shattered by the roar of a Rutgers football cheer, complete with Mark Shangold's ('69) bugle and pennant, as our train pulled out for Germany. This was to become the focus of our spirit for the rest of the tour, and it never failed to bring amazed smiles and friendly handwaving from our European friends.

Crossing West Germany to Munich, the club marveled at the great cathedrals at Köln and Ulm and the beautiful Rhine valley. The Bavarian capital itself had many attractions; few of the group missed the full-liter mugs of beer at Munich's Hofbrauhaus. Several of us spent a day exploring Mozart's birthplace, Salzburg, Austria, which was especially fascinating during a colorful religious festival. Rutgers appeared in Munich, June 10, at the Technische Hochschule, a renowned school of engineering. The performance was to reach beyond the Iron Curtain through Radio Free

Europe. The same recording was also to be used by the Armed Services Network for broadcasts to American bases all over the Continent.

Our train trip north to Hamburg brought us very near the East German border, with blockhouses and barbed wire in evidence. We reached the bustling port city in time to take in a bit of the night life of a Saturday evening. Amerika Haus, our sponsor, took us south to the ancient town of Lüneburg on Sunday, the 12th, where we presented an open-air concert in a beautiful park. Rutgers men were startled during this performance as, according to an old custom, a bouquet of flowers was presented to Soup. The University of Hamburg was the setting for our last appearance in Germany. As at our other performances in that country, Club President Riedel announced our selections in his best German, and, judging from the amused applause, the struggle was worth it.

We had observed the pride in punctuality of the German railways. Hamburg's stationmaster seemed concerned that there would be a serious delay when our large group arrived early on June 14 to board a train for Luxembourg. He was astounded to see the club load luggage, passengers, and even portable stage risers in barely forty-two seconds! For Merv Dickinson '68 and Bill Anderson '67, luck with the railway ran out when, stopping for a snack in the Essen station, they missed the train. The two caught up with us at Koblenz where we awaited an antique steam locomotive to take us through the Moselle River valley to Luxembourg.

The stopover in the picturesque town of Echternach in northeast Luxembourg was a pleasant change from the cities. Our open-air concert in the market place attracted a large crowd consisting of residents and of Belgian, French, and German vacationers. Once again Soup was presented flowers by a civic official, a man who had been rescued from a Nazi prison by American troops. He gave moving testimony of Luxembourg's gratitude for liberation in two wars and of his people's genuine affection for the people of the United States. The gift that followed caught us by surprise—two large dolls in eighteenth-century costume. The Rutgers delegation was honored by a gala reception given by the mayor of Echternach. We vividly remember the long table set with many glasses of Moselle wine in preparation for the toasts.

The concert tour soon would be completed. On Thursday, June 16, we arrived in France, where, during a ten-hour stop, the Rutgers Glee Club made its Paris debut. Continuing south late that night, we reached Orléans, where we were to give our final performance. The University of Orléans, where Rutgers is establishing the "Junior Year Abroad" program for French majors, provided tours of the new campus and of the beautiful Château de Chambord.

The concert was given in the city's opera house, which dates back to Mozart's era. Jeff Aaron '67 made program announcements in French, and the rendition of "Bow Wow Wow" presented a special challenge. The audience consisted largely of students—very excited students. They began to clap in unison after each song. The electrifying effect encouraged the Rutgers singers in their grand finale in Europe. After the concert we were invited to a reception at the château of M. Antoine, Rector of the University of Orléans. The exquisite affair was held in the gardens of the stately home, and we happily sampled the best French cuisine.

At this point the Glee Club split up to enjoy six days of travel. Several members remained in France, while others visited Scandinavia, Austria, Italy, Spain, and England. We all returned to Amsterdam on the eve of our return flight, enjoying our final night in Europe in a city which seemed almost like home.

The tour was over. Yet it could not stop. High over the Atlantic flying home, a group of Rutgers students, travel-worn but still full of spirit, gathered in the middle of the jet's cabin. With Soup directing from a makeshift podium in the aisle, we lifted our voices and an occasional bugle call in a farewell concert.

THE GONFALONS OF RUTGERS UNIVERSITY

The design of the gonfalons for the sixteen degree-granting schools of the University shows the "chief," or upper, compartment charged with the symbol of the school. The "field" beneath is set off by the school's name. Its center stripes, which extend through the streamers, carry the colors of the individual schools, white for liberal arts, yellow for science and so on, and are flanked by scarlet Rutgers. The date of each school's establishment is carried in the lower left scarlet stripe.

Rutgers College of Arts and Sciences

As the original Queen's College chartered in 1766, the Rutgers College of Arts and Sciences shows the official Rutgers seal: The motto "Sol Justitiae et Occidentem Illustra" (Sun of Righteousness illumine also the West) surrounds a sunburst. In the outer circle is the inscription "Sigillum Collegii Rutgersensia in Nova Caesarea" (Seal of Rutgers College in New Jersey). The colors of the degree stripes are white for arts and golden yellow for sciences.

College of Agriculture and Environmental Science

A book lies open before a plant and a beaker. The color of the degree stripe is maize for agriculture.

College of Engineering

A shield in three triangular sections carries symbols of the University's historical development: at the left, Q for the Colonial College founded in 1766, at the right, N.J. for the creation in 1864 of the College of Engineering under the Land-Grant Act; in the central position, the initial of the Rutgers of today. The color of the degree stripe is orange for engineering.

Graduate School

The mortarboard, lineal descendant of the heraldic lozenge which is said to represent a pane of glass, is the symbol of the candidate for as well as the holder of a degree. Upon it is the Q, having at each end a node signifying the motivating force of the University as it spreads the radiance of knowledge, represented by the surrounding red. The color of the degree stripe is dark blue for philosophy.

Douglass College

An evergreen pine tree, native to the Douglass campus and symbolic of the continuing generations of students, is centered in the emblem of the College with its founding date, 1918, near the top. Beneath is the college motto in Greek meaning Wisdom and Self-Control. The colors of the degree stripes are white for arts and golden yellow for sciences.

Graduate School of Education

The stylized sun of the Rutgers official seal surrounds a flame. Beneath are the words Veritas est Lux (Truth is Light). The color of the degree stripe is light blue for education.

University College

The emblem of University College, with its instructional centers in five areas of the State, shows a compass surrounding the lamp of learning. The colors of the degree stripes are white for arts and golden yellow for sciences.

College of Pharmacy

The insignia is the shield of the American Pharmaceutical Association: first quarter, the mortar and pestle; second quarter, the ℞ symbol, from the Latin word "recipe," indicating direction from physician to pharmacist to compound; third quarter, the bowl of Hygeia; fourth quarter, the alchemist's symbol from the Greek to compound a prescription. The green is the color for pharmacy, and is repeated in the degree stripe below, which is olive green.

School of Law

The scales of justice upheld by the torch of learning is the traditional emblem of schools of law. The color of the degree stripe is purple.

Newark College of Arts and Sciences

The circle represents the oneness of life within which the arts and the sciences interact. In turn the circle is within the rays of the sun, part of the University's official seal. The colors of the degree stripes are white for arts and golden yellow for sciences.

Graduate School of Business Administration

The emblem is a monogram. The color of the degree stripe is drab for commerce.

College of South Jersey

The lamp of learning upon a stack of books is the emblem of the College of South Jersey. The colors of the degree stripes are white for arts and golden yellow for sciences.

Graduate School of Library Service

The emblem is a shield: first quarter, two books; second quarter, an Egyptian scribe writing on a tablet; third quarter, the Gutenberg printing press; fourth quarter, a stripe of microfilm and a data card. The color of the degree stripe is lemon for library science.

Graduate School of Social Work

The basic philosophy of the School, hand outstretched to hand, is evident in the stylized symbol generally used by schools of social work. The color of the degree stripe is citron for social work.

College of Nursing

The College of Nursing shows the traditional symbol of nursing: Florence Nightingale's lamp. The color of the degree stripe is apricot for nursing.

College of Medicine

The insignia includes the Q representing the original Queen's College and the serpent climbing the staff of Aesculapius, the god of the healing arts. The two dates bringing out the fact that two hundred years elapsed between the founding of the college and the opening of the medical school. The color of the degree stripe is green for medicine.

PRESIDENT GROSS'S COMMENCEMENT ADDRESS

A university commencement is always an historic occasion in the lives of those who participate in it. It marks the satisfactory culmination of years of activity, and the beginning point of a whole new phase in one's life. Today each of you has the right to feel completely satisfied with himself and with what he has accomplished. We the faculty and the governing boards recognize that right by gathering you together with us to mark your achievement and to congratulate you. At the same time we, being your elders, know that even greater accomplishments and satisfactions lie ahead for you, and we wish you well in your pursuit of even greater happiness.

But if every commencement is an historic occasion, surely this must be pre-eminently true of a 200th anniversary commencement. Graduates of a university which is older than the nation itself, you the bicentennial class have special reasons for pride. And when you recall that the nation, 190 years old, has existed longer than any other nation on earth as a free, constitutional, democratic republic, you will recognize yourself as the inheritors of an extraordinarily vital and healthy tradition, upon whom we depend to carry that tradition forward.

Tradition can of course be a tricky thing. When the worship of tradition in and for itself becomes so blind as to destroy our flexibility and capacity for growth, then it is dangerous, for the very commitments which ensured our success in one period might render us incapable of adjusting to the new needs and demands of another generation. The devotion to classical modes of thought which characterized this University in its earliest years probably contributed an element of stability and solidity which were essential in the early years of the Republic. The philosophy of the Greeks, with its central concern for order, the civic virtues of the early Romans, the fear of God which characterized the Hebrews—all of these were reflected in the lives of our first great leaders. We named cities and towns after classical places, and our model of a military hero was Lucius Quinctius Cincinnatus.

This was a noble tradition, and significant elements of it are still important in our heritage. But had we frozen at that point much would have been lost. Fortunately from the very beginning one important part of the College's conception of itself was service to the community and the nation. Emphasis on this part of the tradition enabled Rutgers in 1864 to become a land-grant college, no matter how much that may have alarmed the classical purists. And again in 1945 the traditional concept of service led us to assume the responsibilities of a State University.

Tradition can thus either stifle or strengthen. If we become mere laudatores temporis acti, then we have to close our eyes to much that was reprehensible and mean. But if we recognize that our present vitality cannot possibly be entirely of our own making, then it would seem to be good to explore our past in order to tap again the sources of that vitality.

I wish that I were a historian capable of analyzing for you the main currents of the decade leading up to the Revolution, from 1766 to 1776, and of showing you the significance of the founding of this College in the light of those circumstances. There can be no doubt that there was a growing feeling both of independence and of the need for greater independence. The Stamp Act of 1765 was clearly seen as a move in the wrong direction and was rejected. Patrick Henry and Sam Adams were sounding off on the subject of tyranny. And the intent behind the founding of colleges in the colonies was to reduce the dependence on the mother countries for intellectual leadership. The notion of complete political independence was also growing during this period, but the sense of independence that comes from self-confidence was already manifest.

In 1766 Thomas Jefferson was twenty-three years old. He had studied law at the College of William and Mary, and his intellectual appetites were omnivorous. As he grew into a position of prestige in the Virginia legislature, he must also have been studying philosophy greedily, and using these philosophical ideas to interpret to himself and others the basic principles behind the move toward independence. Finally in 1766 he drafted the Declaration of Independence. As we all know, this Declaration includes a list of "repeated injuries" which would justify the separation of the colonies from the King's government. But what gives this document transcendent value is that in it Jefferson bases his argument for independence upon the philosophical concept of rights and the notion of liberty:

> We hold these truths to be self-evident, that all men are created equal, that they are endowed by their Creator with certain unalienable rights, that among these are life, liberty, and the pursuit of happiness.

Now, we all know these words and have felt their compelling power, but I doubt whether we have reflected enough about them to grasp their complexity or to follow their lead into difficult philosophical questions. There is the matter of having been created equal. To many people this is by no means self-evident. Only in recent years have we come to see that there is at least one sense in which these words are undeniably true, and that if we choose to neglect that truth our nation may indeed be in serious peril.

But I would draw your attention today to the affirmation of the three unalienable rights. Scholars, including our own Provost, have pointed out that, while Jefferson is here drawing on the *Essay on Civil Government* by the English philosopher John Locke, he has apparently chosen to deviate from Locke. The latter's triad is life, liberty, and property, while Jefferson substitutes the pursuit of happiness for property. Others complain that Jefferson calls a pursuit a right. Surely, they say, it has to be happiness which is the right, not the mere and perhaps futile, pursuit of happiness.

Some of these critics have not given Jefferson credit for having read more than one book. Their quotations come from Locke's *Essay on Civil Government*. But Locke wrote another book which was at least as well known in the colonies, his *Essay Concerning Human Understanding*. And in this book we find an extremely pertinent passage. It comes, significantly enough, from a chapter entitled "Idea of Power" and one sentence reads as follows:

> As therefore the highest perfection of intellectual nature lies in a careful and constant pursuit of true and solid happiness; so the care of ourselves, that we mistake not imaginary for true happiness, is the necessary foundation of our liberty.

This really is rather a remarkable statement. If Jefferson goes along with it, then he is not proclaiming for us three unalienable rights and using for the third a euphemism more palatable than the rather materialistic concept of property. If he is following Locke carefully, then in fact he is claiming, first of all, life as a right, which is obviously a necessary condition for any other rights, and then liberty and the pursuit of happiness, which in Locke's language are mutually interdependent. And Locke adds a further thought when he says that the pursuit of happiness is the highest perfection of our *intellectual* nature and that the intellectual power to distinguish between true and false happiness is the foundation of liberty.

What I am trying to say here is that what Jefferson accomplished in 1766 was to lift the whole argument about independence from the British crown to a higher level. Independence is in a sense a negative concept, and the mere establishment of independence would have no necessary corollaries so far as self-government was concerned. But liberty is a positive concept as Locke and Jefferson conceived it, and Jefferson's contemporaries seemed to have grasped that point. For you will recall that the most careful of them refused to support ratification of the Constitution until they were sure that there would be a set of amendments which would translate the essential elements of civil liberty into law. It was all very well to believe philosophically in these as natural rights; they wanted civil rights.

It thus seems clear that, whatever else was going on in the years from 1766 on, there was a great deal of concern over the concept of liberty. Philosophers like Locke, Hume, and Jonathan Edwards had taken this as one of their central themes. There were stirrings in France, and Rousseau was preaching the rights of man. In Germany Kant was proclaiming the irreducible dignity of man qua man.

There is one mystery in the history of ideas during this whole eighteenth century which has always fascinated me. The Jewish philosopher Spinoza died in the Netherlands in 1677. Prior to his death he corresponded with most of the learned men of Europe, but after his death his philosophy drops out of history until it is revived by the German philosopher Jacobi, in 1785. Except for one reference in Hume to his "hideous hypothesis," he seems to have been ignored altogether. And yet this seems impossible. There are, for example, passages in Jonathan Edwards which are so close to Spinoza that it seems impossible to believe that he had not read him.

It is the phrase "the highest perfection of our intellectual nature," which I quoted from Locke, which leads me to mention Spinoza. For it is Spinoza more than any other philosopher who reiterates the essential interdependence of knowledge and freedom. You all know the title to the fourth part of his great work, the *Ethics* "Of Human Bondage, or the Strength of the Emotions." The title to the fifth and last part corresponds to it: "Of Human Liberty, or the Power of the Intellect."

Spinoza was a combination of scientist, philosopher, political theorist, scholar, and theologian. He would gladly have adopted Bacon's aphorism that "Knowledge is power," but his real concern was the discovery of human liberty. Like Locke, he writes on civil government in an effort to establish the conditions for political freedom within an organized society. But he realizes that all the political freedom in the world will not produce one free man unless he also has the kind of control over his emotions which is unattainable by an ignorant man. He would have agreed with Locke that liberty and the pursuit of happiness were indispensable to each other—in fact he would have gone further and found them one and the same thing, and he would agree that they constituted the highest perfection possible for us as beings capable of intellectual strength.

I wish there were evidence to believe that those men who labored so long to establish their college in New Brunswick had known and read Spinoza. With their background in the Netherlands, the country which had extended freedom from persecution to him and his people, and with their knowledge of Latin, the language in which he wrote, they could easily have become familiar with him and have found in his books a clear expression of the goals which they sought and which were beginning to receive public acceptance in their day. However, in establishing a college they were moving in what he would have considered the right direction, for the road to knowledge must also be the necessary road to freedom and to happiness. We today are the beneficiaries of their wisdom and their foresight.

There is a passage in Washington's Farewell Address which receives less attention than the passages on foreign policy, but it is significant again as indicating the temper of the times. Washington writes:

> Promote, then, as an object of primary importance, institutions for the general diffusion of knowledge. In proportion as the structure of a government gives force to public opinion, it is essential that public opinion should be enlightened.

Thus in 1766, in 1776, and with Washington in 1796, the recurring theme of the times was the interdependence of knowledge, freedom, and happiness.

At Gettysburg President Lincoln referred to this country as "a new nation, conceived in liberty." I believe that the same spirit of liberty presided over the beginnings of this University, the same faith and the same dedication. We have now endured for two hundred years. May the spirit of liberty continue to be our principal source of strength.

MAJOR SPECIAL EVENTS OF THE BICENTENNIAL YEAR

January 1 — Start of the Bicentennial Year was heralded by the pealing of the Henry Rutgers bell in the tower of Queen's Building.

January 4	Bicentennial Proclamation signed by Governor Richard J. Hughes on a visit to the campus. Portraits of Governor William Franklin, signer of the charter of Queen's College in 1766, and his wife placed on display in Kirkpatrick Chapel, on loan from Mrs. J. Manderson Castle, a descendant of Benjamin Franklin, William's father.
January 22	Midwinter Alumni Day.
January 27	Award to Rutgers by the New Jersey Agricultural Society accepted by President Gross.
February 20	French Culture Day, College of South Jersey.
February 23	Spanish Culture Day, College of South Jersey.
March 1	Physics Day, College of South Jersey.
March 4	Bicentennial Lecture, *The Viet Nam War, Tran Van Dinh*, College of South Jersey.
March 10	Award by the Salmagundi Club of New York to President Gross for his devotion to advancement of the arts.
March 11	Russian Culture Day, College of South Jersey.
March 16-18	Bicentennial Drama Festival, College of South Jersey.
March 17	Conference: *Tackling Planning Problems with University Resources.*
March 18-20	Intercollegiate Student Conference: *Ethics in Our Time.*
March 26	All-Alumni Dinner, honoring all the presidents of Rutgers.
April 13	Conference: *Is the Soviet Economy Moving Towards Capitalism?*
April 16	Annual Conference, Intercollegiate Broadcasting Systems, WRSU.
April 17-24	Bicentennial Week, each major undergraduate group sponsoring one day's program: April 17—Traditional Dutch service in Kirkpatrick Chapel April 18—Douglass College April 19—College of South Jersey April 20—Newark Colleges April 22—Formal Dinner Dances April 23—Rutgers College April 24—University College
April 18	Bicentennial Lecture: *United States Foreign Policy Today and Tomorrow*, Dr. Richard N. Gardner, College of Arts and Sciences, Newark.

April 25	Bicentennial Lecture: *The Washington Underground Lobby and the Consumer*, James Ridgeway, College of Arts and Sciences, Newark.
April 29	Bicentennial meeting: Rutgers Engineering Society and College of Engineering.
April 29	Bicentennial Lecture: *Sex and the College Student*, Dr. Albert Ellis, College of South Jersey.
May 2	Bicentennial Lecture: *Theology Today—Winds of Change*, Msgr. Henry C. J. Beck.
May 9	Bicentennial Lecture: *Creative Evolution*, Dr. Harlow Shapley, College of Arts and Sciences, Newark.
May 30- June 24	The Glee Club on tour in Europe; eight members of the Class of 1966 receiving their diplomas at the University of Utrecht, academic and spiritual godmother of Queen's College.
June 1	200th Anniversary Commencement.
June 2-3	Douglass College Alumnae
June 2-4	Rutgers College Reunion Week End. Douglass Reunion Day.
June 8-10	Fulbright Conference on Higher Education.
June 12-16	Annual convention: American Association of University Presses.
June 19-22	Annual meeting: American Society of Agronomy.
July 12-13	Conference on Water Resources.
July 31- August 4	Annual meeting: American Society of Animal Science.
August 26- Sept. 2	Fourth Triennial Congress: International Society of Bio-meteorology.
August 29- Sept. 2	Annual meetings: American Mathematical Society, Mathematical Association of America, Society for Industrial and Applied Mathematics, Pi Mu Epsilon, Mu Alpha Theta, and Institute of Mathematical Statistics.
September 8-10	Bicentennial Symposium of the Rutgers Institute of Microbiology—Subject: Organizational Biosynthesis.
September 9-10	Dedication of the Law Center, Newark.
September 21	President's reception for Convocation delegates.
September 22	The Bicentennial Convocation.
September 25- Oct. 2	Rutgers Open House.

October 1	Open House, Medical School.
October 5	Open House, College of Pharmacy.
October 7	Conference: *The Environment, the University and the Welfare of Man.*
October 7-8	Conference: *Early American History.*
October 10-11	Conference: *What's New on Earth?*
October 14	First of nine lectures on *The Urban Frontier: 1966-1986.*
October 17	Bicentennial Lecture: *Theology Today—Winds of Change*, Dr. Samuel J. Miller.
October 21	Reunion of Cap and Skull alumni.
October 22	Alumni Homecoming.
October 25	Citation to Rutgers by New Jersey Conference of Mayors for "outstanding and meritorious services in the advancement of good government."
October 27	Bicentennial Career Day, College of South Jersey.
October 29	Conference: *Changing Patterns in Health and Professional Education*, College of Nursing, Newark.
November 7	The medal of The Holland Society of New York to President Gross for "distinguished achievement in academic leadership."
November 10	Charter Day; Rutgers Night Around the World.
November 12	Business-Industry Annual Dinner.
November 14	Bicentennial Lecture: *Theology Today—Winds of Change*, Rabbi Abraham Joshua Heschel.
November 16	First awards of the Graduate School of Library Service for contributions by New Jersey residents to literature for children.
November 21	Bicentennial Lecture: *The Strange Death of President Kennedy*, Herbert A. Philbrick, College of South Jersey.
December 8	Bicentennial Lecture: *The Political and Military Transition in Europe*, Professor Aldin Z. Rubinstein, College of South Jersey.
December 13	International Business Conference, Newark.
March 2, 1967	Performance of Bicentennial choral works, "Et Occidentem Illustra," by Robert Moevs, Rutgers University Choir, F. Austin Walter, director, and the Boston Symphony Orchestra, Erich Leinsdorf, conductor.
April 26-28	Japan Conference.

Article written by William Sloane for the
July 4, 1966, issue of *Publishers Weekly*.

At 30 College Avenue, New Brunswick, the Rutgers University Press is celebrating an anniversary of its own concurrently with the University's 200th.

Thirty years ago, in 1936, the Trustees of Rutgers voted to establish a scholarly press as a necessary part of the University, charging it to assist in the stimulation and publication of faculty and scholarly research in general, and in particular to provide a publishing outlet for the scholarship fostered by the University's Research Council. Further, the new Press was to serve as a means of broadening the educational purposes of the University as a whole.

The decision to establish the Press may conceivably have been reinforced by the initiative of a professor at the Rutgers College of Agriculture, Jacob S. Joffe. A soil scientist with a missionary zeal for his subject, he had pressed for the establishment of his specialty on a worldwide basis and had long been preparing a massive volume, entitled *Pedology*. In 1936 he printed and distributed his magnum opus himself over the name Rutgers University Press, thus boldly reminding the authorities that, though the University had no official press, it ought to have one.

As a first stage in its development, the new official Press was temporarily to operate as part of the Department of Alumni and Public Relations, of which Professor Earl Reed Silvers was director. Silvers was a popular and inspiring teacher with a national background of successful writing and editing. He was fortunate in having on his first staff Earl Schenck Miers, a recent Rutgers graduate with a notable career of writing and publishing ahead of him. Donald Cameron, currently the retiring (June 30, 1966) university librarian, was to serve as editor.

Professor Silvers and his staff launched the Press vigorously. By the spring of 1938 the first group of new titles was edited and printed, and before the end of the year five volumes had been published.

As was to be expected, the authors of all five were Rutgers teachers. Four of those original books are today out of print, but the fifth is still very much alive. Written by Professor Richard C. Reager and Ernest E. McMahon, who today is dean of the University Extension Division, it bore the optimistic title *Speech Is Easy*. The latest revision, completed after Professor Reager's death by two of his pupils, Norman P. Crawford and Edwin L. Stevens, is more conservatively entitled *You Can Talk Well*.

Professor Silvers was followed in the directorship by Earl Schenck Miers. Mr. Miers had a special enthusiasm for American history. Under his leadership, and with the sponsoring and editorial cooperation of the Abraham Lincoln Association, the Press undertook to publish a nine-volume set, *The Collected Works of Abraham Lincoln*, edited by Roy Basler, a scholarly publishing achievement which brought the Press national and international distinction when it appeared in 1953.

Even before the publication of this major contribution to the Press and to national scholarship, Earl Miers had found and brought out a group of lively books which found readerships outside the normal academic pattern. The most famous, *The Lincoln Reader*, became a Book-of-the-Month Club selection for February, 1946. This volume, the result of the collaboration between Miers as publisher and his historian friend Paul Angle as compiler and editor, sold almost half a million copies through the Club and the Press in the first ninety days after publication. Its success marked the emergence of the Rutgers Press from comparative obscurity—many of the early titles had been issued in printings of 750 copies or even fewer.

The changes induced by growth and success resulted in a number of alterations in the Press's formal structure. Although there had been a Press Council under the chairmanship of President Robert Clothier established after the founding of the Press itself but before World War II, the University trustees, in 1949, created a more clearly defined Rutgers Press Council. The Council was headed by the provost, Mason Gross, who continued in that post until he became President of Rutgers and was succeeded by the new Provost, Richard Schlatter.

The 1949 reorganization spelled out the relationship of the Press to the University and defined its operations and purposes. Meantime, Earl Miers had joined the publishing staff of Alfred A. Knopf, Inc., as editor, and after a brief interlude Harold Munger became the next director of the Press.

The new appointment continued the policy of entrusting the direction of the Press to experienced hands. Mr. Munger's background in university press work had been gained as a colleague of Datus Smith, Princeton University Press director at the time.

Harold Munger believed profoundly in a publishing philosophy of service to scholarship, and the lists he brought out at Rutgers reflected and enhanced the University's growing stature in many academic fields— among them microbiology, engineering, biology, history, and geology. Under his supervision the publishing of *The Collected Works of Abraham Lincoln* set a high standard of university press accomplishment.

Personal considerations resulted in Mr. Munger's resignation from the Press in 1953, and for a time its affairs were administered by Alan James, a long-time member of the staff who today is serving as book officer of the United States Information Service in Brazil. After some months the Council secured as the new director Roger W. Shugg, a scholar, historian, and editor with Alfred A. Knopf. Mr. Shugg's tenure of office was brief; in 1954 he resigned to become director of the University of Chicago Press.

The present Press director, William Sloane, came officially to the post on April 1, 1955, after twenty-six years of experience in various areas of commercial publishing. He had been a founder and the president of William Sloane Associates and had represented American publishing abroad on a wartime mission to China and a postwar one to Germany and Austria.

In the decade that followed, the Press has brought out approximately 250 new titles.

In those thirty years since 1936, the Rutgers Press has published some 460 titles. Today the Press is bringing out new books at a rate of 30 or more new titles each year.

More than half the volumes the Press published are still in print. Many of them have been republished abroad in British editions and foreign language translations and are to be found in the great libraries of the entire world. Their authors are, more often than not, scholars on other campuses and professional writers. A number are citizens of foreign countries. The publishing scope of the Press today is international, and Rutgers books are known and read throughout the world.

Some 30 percent of the Press's book sales come from one special area of publishing—its widely known New Jersey books, many of them issued in paperback form. The Press serves about 200 outlets, only a few of them regular bookstores, where the long list of Rutgers New Jersey titles can be secured by the residents of the State. Probably there isn't a single New Jerseyan who lives more than ten miles from the nearest Rutgers Press book rack. So successful has this part of the Press's publishing program been that it is now employing a full-time New Jersey book salesman, and he daily operates a panel truck loaded to capacity with regional volumes.

Although the regional publishing program at the Press is a continuing one, with many lively and important New Jersey books scheduled for 1966, 1967, and later, the present Rutgers list and the valuable "Tercentenary Historical Series" volumes combine to make New Jersey one of the most extensively and usefully published states in the nation.

The Rutgers Press is still developing. Its publishing plans for the next thirty years include many major projects, including a 20-volume *World History of the Jewish People* and a series of books designed to introduce new and important American artists to a wider public. It does not plan on any leveling off.

John K. Hutchens' article, "One Thing and
Another: Report from Rutgers," appeared
in the June 11, 1966, issue of *Saturday Review*

To the Delegates to the forthcoming Annual Meeting of the Association of American University Presses:

Dutiful as ever on your behalf, your advance field agent in charge of scouting the locale of your next convention—the one that begins tomorrow, June 12, on Douglass Campus of Rutgers University—is ready with his report. He doesn't mind telling you that this called for a bit of work, his acquaintanceship with Rutgers having been hitherto on the vague side. Indeed, it was limited to that ancient legend of the local football hero who, felled on the field of glory in combat with Princeton in 1891, remained conscious long enough to exclaim, "I'd die for dear old Rutgers!" and thus found his way to immortality.

The trouble is, it seems that this never really happened (although another Rutgers warrior of a later vintage was to claim that he uttered those deathless words, even if his forerunner did not). The authoritative rejection of this tale gave me a bad turn, I must say, shortly after I arrived on the banks of the pretty if polluted Raritan River. But presently, this disenchantment having subsided, I was learning that you will have rather more to occupy you here during your four-day session than a stricken quarterback's bugle call.

"Rutgers – The State University," they call the institution that was born on November 10, 1766, as Queen's College and now, as a quick bit of arithmetic suggests, is celebrating its bicentennial.

As it happens, your host, Rutgers University Press, also is marking an anniversary: its thirtieth. The coincidence of these twin occasions doubtless has something to do with your presence in this largely industrial city, which hasn't much to recommend it aesthetically but a good deal intellectually, thanks to a charter granted so long ago by our old enemy, George III, at the request of his Colonial subjects in the Dutch Reformed Church.

Just at first, if you have bothered to look up the Rutgers enrollment figures before you came here, you may well wonder, as you look out across old Queen's Campus from the 126-year-old building that houses the Press, exactly where the 25,5554 students are. They surely aren't visible in any such numbers on this venerable and leafy campus, and they could hardly be strolling around in subterranean corridors. The explanation is that Rutgers University is actually a number of places. There is Rutgers College for men, right here, with an undergraduate body of 5,871. Across town is its coordinate college for women, Douglass, with 2,766 students. Beyond the Raritan, on the University Heights Campus, you can see the walls of the new medical school rising in a nexus that includes microbiology, engineering, chemistry and physics, the biological sciences, and a nuclear research center. Other major campuses, all coeducational, are in Newark (the College of Arts and Sciences, with affiliated schools of nursing, pharmacy, business, law) and in Camden (the College of South Jersey, offering the liberal arts, dentistry, and nursing, and the South Jersey division of the Law School). There are research branches and "teaching stations" in Jersey City, Paterson, Sussex, Pemberton, Adelphia, Cream Ridge, and Bivalve.

Bivalve? It's the site of a laboratory where scientists are looking for whatever it is that is afflicting the oyster population along the Atlantic seaboard.

Naturally all this was a good bit of time coming together under, so to speak, a single administrative umbrella. In 1825 Queen's College was re-named in honor of Colonel Henry Rutgers, a Revolutionary War soldier and perhaps the leading philanthropist of New York City in the 1820's. In 1864 the New Jersey Legislature designated the then Rutgers Scientific School as New Jersey's Land-Grant College in accordance with the pro-visions of the federal Morrill Act of 1862.

In due course a school or college here and there around the State having been added to the original one, what had been the privately en-dowed Rutgers College became today's Rutgers – The State University. Its annual operating budget is $58,000,000, which includes a state appropriation of $26,000,000. Tuition, endowment income, research grants, and so on make up the rest. Rutgers alumni total 43,000, about three-fourths of whom have gone right on living in New Jersey.

Under an administration generally recognized as brilliantly creative and imaginative—i.e., the presidency of Mason Welch Gross, who took office in 1959—the University has grown at an all but incredible rate. In terms of its budget at the operating level it has expanded 300 percent in the last decade. The structural growth has been even greater. Fortunately for the reason that brings you here, President Gross, professor of philosophy and a combat intelligence officer in World War II, is also a deeply dedi-cated bookman.

So too is William Sloane, director of Rutgers University Press, who came to this post in 1955 after a distinguished publishing career in New York. Miss Helen Stewart, who had been associated with him at Henry Holt & Company, William Sloane Associates, and Funk & Wagnalls, joined the Press as executive editor at the same time.

Before Mr. Sloane's arrival the Press had had its success under one or another of his five predecessors as full-time director. Notable among them were *The Lincoln Reader*, edited and compiled by Paul M. Angle (still the Press's all-time best seller); *The Life Records of John Milton*, edited by Professor J. Milton (the late Dr. J. Milton French, professor of English 1940-1960) of Rutgers; a monumental work of scholarship; and the begin-nings of a fine regional series in John Cunningham's *This Is New Jersey* and *Made in New Jersey* and Henry Beck's *Jersey Genesis*. Still, there was work to be done.

As of 1955, through nobody's fault in particular, the Press's backlist contained no more than four or five titles selling as many as 200 copies a year. Only a handful of future books were under contract. Total sales came to something like $70,000 annually. Today, of the 450 titles Rutgers University Press has published in its thirty years (230 of them in the last eleven years), 70 percent are available. First printings run from 2,000 to 3,500 copies. Gross sales average from $250,000 to $300,000 annually. Thirty books will be published this year, the director hopes; five of them will be in the "New Jersey Books Series," and of the remaining twenty-five most will be scholarly, as becomes a university press—learned studies, contributions to knowledge, with libraries as their principal market—but some will be for the general reader.

As things go in the university press world, where thanks to subsidies and tax exemptions books don't have to pay their way, Rutgers Press certainly seems to be operating on a sound basis. But Mr. Sloane is too old a hand at this profession to be rushing down to the footlights, taking bows as he goes. "I think our Press in thirty years has made a good beginning," he said without false humility to this visitor. The visitor believed him. Big projects are ahead at the Press—the 20-volume *History of the Jewish People*, of which Volume I appeared last year; the complete letters of Dostoevsky; a series on American painters and sculptors; definitive one-volume surveys of the Asiatic heartland and Islam. No, Mr. Sloane is anything but complacent or given to looking over his shoulder at the past.

"I believe that we should have fewer books merely representing the orthodox academic disciplines," he will tell you. "I want to have more that have an interdisciplinary synthesis—psychologists writing about the social sciences, historians writing about the arts." But the unhappy fact is that most academicians don't write very well. At the end of his freshman year as director Mr. Sloane went on record as saying, in *SR*:

> The commercial writer is continuously exposed to the sharpening and educative influence of public acceptance or rejection. He stands or falls by the extent to which he can attract and interest readers. The scholar in his writing is not shaped and tempered on this anvil. Instead he starts off his writing career with a doctoral thesis. Now, doctoral theses are valuable in many ways. Each one presumably adds to the barrier reef against the sea of ignorance . . . They accomplish much good, but they do not make trained writers out of the men who produce them.

He still, regretfully, holds to this. "Too many of them disregard the reader as a buyer or a listening ear," he finds. Editors with the patience and skill to make their manuscripts readable for the general public—editors able to "reduce sentences of jargon to a simulacrum of the English language"—are hard to come by, at university press salaries. There are other frustrations, such as what a university press publisher would most like to publish and what he can publish, because in their higher reaches universities tend to be conservative and certainly to stop well this side of the avant-garde. And there is what Mr. Sloane calls "a big difference between commercial and academic publishing—that is, the lack of public exposure. Outside an occasional review in the popular press, you can't tell whether anybody gives a damn. You just can't tell."

There are gratifying exceptions, notably in the "New Jersey Books Series" of fifty volumes. Bookstores being scarce in New Jersey, the Press takes them by truck to gift shops, department stores, and the like, some 200 outlets in all. They represent about 30 percent of the Press's book sales.

Whatever is finally selected for publication by the Press must survive readings by two or more outside authorities and then meet with the approval of the Rutgers University Press Council, headed by Dr. Richard Schlatter, vice-president and provost of the University. If it makes the grade there, it is on its way to production. The manufacturing cost of a book will average $6,500, plus the cost of editing, distribution, etc. Its first home will be one of the quartermaster's warehouses assigned to the Press across the Raritan at the otherwise ghostly remains of Camp Kilmer, where two employees stand ready to fill orders on a twenty-four-hour basis for any book in stock.

Will a book sell? Rutgers Press doesn't lie awake at night worrying about it. The author, of course, cares, and he gets the usual royalty, generally beginning at 10 percent. Most of the Press's profit or loss usually is $2,000 or $3,000, one way or the other, on the basis of that annual $250,000 to $350,000 sales volume.

In the course of your New Brunswick stay you almost certainly will be dropping in at the old house at 30 College Avenue, once a private home, and then for fifty years the Rutgers preparatory elementary school. It still is a home, in a way, because you get a distinct notion that the director and his staff of twenty are a family. The homelike air is enhanced by the paneled Book Room, a wing attached several years ago to the old house, where students come to browse along shelves of books donated by alumni and friends, play chess, talk, or sit around in a small adjoining garden enclosed by a privet hedge.

Student interest in the Press is, in fact, a source of much satisfaction to the director. They are proud of it, he says, perhaps not in quite the same way they are proud of a football team that once in a great while beats Princeton, but proud nonetheless. Three recognition awards of different sorts are awarded by Rutgers students to faculty and staff. The director of the Press has received all three.

Indeed, it struck your field agent that the fifty-nine-year-old Mr. Sloane must be one of the busiest people on Queen's Campus—so busy that he has not in the last twelve years had time to add to the four books that he wrote or edited between 1937 and 1954. Besides presiding over the Press, he is adviser to the student literary magazine, *The Anthologist;* teaches a creative writing course for Rutgers College and Douglass upperclassmen; serves on the New Jersey State Commission on the Arts (its report on the arts at all levels in the State will soon be published), and serves on the Publishing Committee of the Association Press. In summer he teaches, as he has for the last twenty-five years, at the Bread Loaf Writers' Conference at Middlebury College, Vermont.

But, then, he was a busy man too in his New York publishing years, always available for services outside his regular publishing duties—director of the Council on Books in Wartime, chairman of the Editorial Committee for the Armed Services Editions, and representative of the Book Publishers Committee sent to Germany in 1948.

Does he miss those days and that New York scene where he made the reputation that brought him to Rutgers? He does not. He pulled on a pipe and said, "I am happier here, in the good sense of the word, than I have ever been in my life." It isn't that academic publishing is quieter, softer than the frenzy of Publishers' Row in Manhattan. "The phone rings as often in New Brunswick as in New York," he once observed. His day begins at 8:30 A.M., and ends with the afternoon's last appointment. The rewards are many.

"I can't understand," he said, "why more people can't see the joy of small publishing, the kind of publishing where the publisher plays a real part, accepts a book, works on it. It's a good life, the best life going. A man ought to be willing to work himself to death to have so good a life as this."

The rewards further include the company of a knowledgeable college community, he added, quoting Dr. Johnson's aphorism to the effect that life holds few pleasures comparable to the conversation of enlightened men.

Three hundred and fifty of you ladies and gentlemen are expected at the assembly that begins tomorrow with a buffet lunch at Neilson Dining Room and opening remarks by Earl Schenck Miers, perhaps Rutgers' most widely published living alumnus-author and Rutgers Press's first full-time director. Among other speakers during the convention will be David Horne, assistant director for editorial affairs at Harvard University Press; Dan Lacy, managing director of the American Book Publishers Council; Ben Shahn, the artist; August Heckscher, and Rutgers' own Mary V. Gaver, a professor in its much-acclaimed Graduate School of Library Service and currently president of the American Library Association. There will be a cookout in a park beside the Raritan, a tour to the garden and home of the Governor's Mansion at Princeton, and, as a finale, dancing for those who are still up to it after four days of talking and listening.

So have a good time, and try not to fret too much about that football player who never said what the legend says he said.

The text of Mr. Justice Warren's address of September 10, 1966

Anniversaries such as those you are celebrating this year at Rutgers and in your home city are, it is true, joyful events in themselves. They are tokens of accomplishments over the years, the satisfaction of building, and a general sense of well-being. But occasions of this sort serve another purpose. They embolden us to project our thoughts into the future. They encourage us to use past successes as steppingstones to further accomplishments. At the same time they constitute useful reminders of the guidelines of our predecessors which we sometimes overlook in our preoccupation with the more immediate demands of the day. We need to remind ourselves not only by means of anniversary functions such as this but in our classrooms and elsewhere of the fundamental principles which guided our Founding Fathers.

There is an old saying which I feel is very appropriate to occasions such as this: "Men more frequently require to be reminded than informed." By means of this process of reminding ourselves, of re-evaluating attitudes in terms of our great heritage of democratic freedom, and in rededicating ourselves to the enduring standards by which our forefathers set their sights, we can combat the erosion of our fundamental values which comes from indifference and self-satisfaction.

In this process of self-reminder generated by such anniversary occasions as we observe today, we must be sure that we do not merely give lip service to precepts. The Golden Rule can only be tarnished by being invoked instead of practiced. And the Constitution, particularly its Bill of Rights, cannot fulfill its function of being our nation's beacon light unless we see to it that it is not just a document but a vibrant code of daily conduct. Its words mean very little indeed unless they are implemented in our lives. It has been sadly noted that "Too many approach the Bill of Rights . . . as they do the New Testament: in Samuel Butler's words they 'would be equally horrified to hear [it] . . . doubted or to see it practiced.'"

If I were asked to name the outstanding characteristic of the period in which we live I believe that I would say that it is the attribute of change. That is not to say that other eras have not known change. It is not to say that all things are different now from the way they were before, even long ago. Indeed, I once read somewhere that when one of the most ancient writings discovered was finally deciphered it read: "What times are these when children won't obey their parents and everyone wants to write a book!"

I do not for a moment regret the fact of change, though there are some who view it as an annoyance rather than as a challenge. No, much is to be said for change. Indeed, as Washington Irving once wrote "[t]here is a certain relief in change, even though it be from bad to worse; as I have found in traveling in a stage-coach; that it is often a comfort to shift one's position and be bruised in a new place."

A rather dramatic recital of the developments which have occurred during the lifetime of those who are now of university age came to my attention in an article which appeared not long ago. Just some of the events which have taken place since this generation was born were listed by the writer in random fashion. He started by mentioning the atom bomb. He then commented that when those now at the University were four years old the giant computers began commercial operation. "When they were eight," he continued, "men climbed Mount Everest. When they were ten, they were immunized against polio. When they were twelve, Sputnik went up and the first civilian nuclear reactor went into operation. When they were thirteen, the atomic submarine *Nautilus* crossed from the Pacific to the Atlantic under the north-polar ice. When they were fourteen, a Russian rocket photographed the far side of the moon and returned to earth. When they were fifteen, the bathyscaphe took men down to photograph the bottom of the Pacific Ocean's deepest hole. When they were sixteen, a Russian orbited the earth in a rocket. When they were seventeen, the DNA genetic code for the control of the design of all life was discovered." This list of events which have occurred during the lifetime of those now at Rutgers and other universities can impressively be supplemented in many ways. Recent developments in space alone make the fanciful tales of Jules Verne and H. G. Wells almost tame by comparison.

In the field of science one miraculous achievement has followed another as our full resources have been applied to research and development of the physical sciences. The speed of travel, the conquest of space, and the ability to bring the atom within control have placed overwhelming power in the possession of man. Translated into physical potential, the men of science have made it possible to add to the well-being of all of humanity. This possibility can become reality through a corresponding advancement of law and the social sciences.

The dramatic discoveries of our time have produced equally dramatic changes in our social, economic, and political structures. Medical science has reduced infant fatalities and has extended the life expectancy of man. The population of the world has increased and continues to increase to a point far beyond any previous expectation. This trend itself is now recognized as constituting one of the most serious problems of the day. The pattern of living has shifted from the rural areas to gigantic metropolitan centers. Universal education has spread and all of man's energies are being released in his struggle for a share of the earth's material goods. Every aspect of living in this society has taken on greater proportions and has increased in complexity. Goods are produced and distributed on a mass scale. Labor has become highly organized in an effort to deal on an equal footing with business. And government has increased in size and function in order to preserve a balance of power among the competing groups.

The greatest problem of today is that of adapting our democratic institutions to these precedent-shattering changes without disturbing the basic fundamentals of a free society. To a very large extent this adaptation falls upon the legal institutions of our nation, for it is there that the framework of business and society should be equated with the constitutional safeguards of our government.

The legal profession has contributed greatly to such leadership in the past, and I am confident that it will rise to meet these new challenges of public service. It is through this leadership that scientific knowledge can be fully employed in a free society for the advancement of the dignity and well-being of all mankind.

There have already been visible changes in the teaching and practice of law which represent the adaptation of law to economic, social, and political changes of this age. Forward-looking law schools now recognize that their function is not just to contribute men and women trained in law. As the late Chief Justice Arthur T. Vanderbilt of New Jersey once said: "If we are ever to modernize our judicial procedure, we must teach the lawyers of tomorrow while they are still in law school not only what the practice in their state is, but what it should be." Our law schools must produce men and women who are trained in relating the law to the needs of a free, democratic society. The democratic ends of our society must be served by professional lawyers educated to achieve clearly defined, democratic values.

The lawyer is an important factor in policy formation. He is frequently an active participant in the political and civic life around him, but even more important is the cumulative effect of his multiple thousands of daily presentations of fact and expressions of opinion.

Lawyers must always be among the most influential leaders of opinion in modern society. In this position it is the responsibility of lawyers to call upon the experiences of the past and to correlate law with history, economics, and all of the social sciences available in the solution of human problems. Many law schools are now recognizing this important relationship of law and social science, and the laws enacted by our legislators have drawn heavily on this area. This is reflected in the statutes which regulate labor relations, unemployment compensation acts, and in legislation designed to provide housing for lower income groups.

The law school of today carries an important responsibility for leadership not only in the training of lawyers, but in the actual development of the operation of our democratic system. This calls for new types of research consisting of programs of critical and analytical examination of the operation and impact of our laws on business and society. The law schools can provide leadership in the development of law itself through unbiased and objective examination of our legal system with long-range planning and perspectives. It is in the environment of the law school that extensive factual inquiry can be conducted and where the troublesome areas of the law can be analyzed.

There is a pressing need for creative research projects designed to bring insight to the solution of new and difficult problems of the substantive and procedural law. It is through this type of activity that the law schools can contribute to the growth of law which must accompany the changes in our social and economic institutions. It is the type of development which Jefferson must have had in mind when he wrote, "But I know also, that laws and institutions must go hand-in-hand with the progress of the human mind. As that becomes more developed, more enlightened, as new discoveries are made, new truths disclosed, and manners and opinions change with the change of circumstances, institutions must change also, and keep pace with the times."

Now, I realize that three years is a short time for any law school to teach students the objectives and the fundamentals for a legal career. I know also that the curricula of necessity must be rather strictly controlled, but this new institution is more than a law school. It is Rutgers Law Center, which implies much more. It is a center for research, for exciting seminars on the problems of state and nation. It is a place for an inspirational faculty to arouse young men and women to a realization of the problems confronting them. It is a place where men of government, lawyers in private practice, scholars, and citizens can meet and in a scholarly atmosphere fashion law to meet the challenges of the times. I think that the great enemy of this dynamic concept of the growth of the law as well as the growth of the democracy which law serves is complacency. We must never forget that free government is the most difficult to achieve and the most difficult to maintain. It is never so much a form of government as it is the spirit of a people. Every generation must breathe new life into it. There is no such thing as the permanence of free government. Free governments rise, they decline, they erode, and they fall as other governments do. They never stand still. They are either on their way up or they are on their way out. That has been true throughout the ages.

Ours is not the first republic to be established. Ours is not the first to recognize the dignity of the individual and personal freedoms. Such governments existed before the birth of Christ. But they fell as did monarchies and authoritarian governments of many kinds. They fell when the people no longer had the will to preserve them.

Free government is being tested today, as it will always be tested, in comparison with other forms of government. But the supreme test of free government will be what it has always been in the past, whether it serves ideals and the best interests of the people for whom it was created.

And the very essence of a free government is the Rule of Law. If we who are privileged to be servants of the law—whether as judges, lawyers, law professors, or students—can successfully concentrate upon establishing and upholding the Rule of Law here and throughout the world we can be assured that there can be no finer commitment of our talents and energies. In this connection, I like to think of the law as a shining, concentrated light.

In all countries and from the beginning of literature it has been traditional to express our ideas about education, the pursuit of knowledge, and progress towards ideals by analogy to the sun and to the mysteries of light.

Perhaps such analogies are no less useful today. Recently the physical scientists have produced a most extraordinary invention which will produce a beam of what they call "coherent" light, a kind of light never found in nature and never before seen in the world. The device is called "optical maser." The principle was discovered here in America and the word "maser" derives from the key letters in the phrase "microwave amplification by stimulated emission of radiation."

In this fascinating device, by the application of electrical power, atoms are reflected and bounced back and forth within a tube reaching a crescendo from which a cascade of photons emerges in a beam of light in which each wave is in step with its predecessor, each wave thus adding to the power of the wave which has gone before. Because these waves are all in step, each adding to the force of the other, a beam of light of incredible power can be produced. The optical maser has actually flashed a spot of red light on the surface of the moon which could be observed with telescopes on earth. At present not even the scientists can estimate the potential usefulness of this device.

How wonderful it would be if we could develop a kind of maser for the Rule of Law—if the elementary principles of law and justice could be broken down and reflected and re-reflected, striking sparks from all who want freedom under law, and if the mixture could produce a beam of coherent legal light of immense power capable of revealing the Rule of Law in its full glory to any and every part of the earth.

In the past several years I have been privileged to take part in a number of ceremonies of this kind, and am always impressed with the solemnity of the occasion. I like to think of these fine buildings as more than a school where young people are taught how to make a living by advising people what the law is, or solving their problems when they are having legal difficulties. I like to think of them as Temples of Justice.

I am sure your President and faculty who envisioned the project, your Governor who has made such a great fight for higher education in New Jersey, and your Legislature that appropriated the money, all expect it to be just that—a Temple of Justice.

It is my hope that the Center will serve as the hospitable abode of a challenging faculty and challenged students for generations to come, and that new ideas will be generated here which will help to solve the problems not only of your local community, the state and the nation, but of the international community as well. May the hopes and aspirations of those who have made this day possible be realized in the searching and the finding which will go on here for the solution to the age-old problem of living together.

To each of you connected with the Rutgers School of Law I wish Godspeed and every success for the future.

COLLEGES, UNIVERSITIES, LEARNED SOCIETIES, AND FOUNDATIONS WHO SENT GREETINGS OR OTHER TRIBUTES TO RUTGERS

Academy of Sciences—Göttingen
  (greetings)

University of Adelaide
  (greetings)

Adelphi University
(greetings)
Agnes Scott College
(greetings)
Ain Shams University
(greetings)
Universitatea "Al. I. Cuza" Din Iasi
(greetings)
University of Alberta
(greetings)
Albright College
(greetings)
University of Allahabad
(greetings)
Alma College
(greetings)
American Academy of Arts and
Sciences
(greetings)
American Institute of Physics
(greetings)
American Philological Association
(greetings)
American Society for Aesthetics
(greetings)
American Society for
Microbiology
(greetings)
American University
(greetings)
Appalachian State Teachers College
(greetings)
Assumption College for Sisters
(letter of appreciation)
Australian National University
(greetings)
Babson Institute of Business
Administration
(greetings)
Ball State University
(greetings)
Bergakademie
Clausthal—Technische
Hochschule
(greetings)

University of Bergen
(greetings)
Bethany College
(greetings)
University of Birmingham
(greetings)
Universite di Bologna
(greetings)
Brandeis University
(greetings)
University of British Columbia
(greetings)
Brown University
(greetings)
Bryant College
(greetings)
Bryn Mawr College
(greetings)
Bucknell University
(greetings)
Institutul Politehnic Bucuresti
(greetings)
California Institute of Technology
(greetings)
California Lutheran College
(greetings)
California State College at Long
Beach
(greetings)
California State College at Los
Angeles
(greetings)
University of California
(greetings)
University of Cambridge
(greetings)
Case Institute of Technology
(greetings)
Catholic University of Puerto Rico
(greetings)
Central Organization for Applied
Scientific Research in the
Netherlands
(greetings)

Centro Escolar University
(greetings)
University of Chicago
(greetings)
Chung Chi College
(greetings)
Clarkson College of Technology
(greetings)
Cleveland State University
(greetings)
College Entrance Examination
Board
(greetings)
Colorado State College
(greetings)
Columbia University
(greetings)
Connecticut Agricultural
Experiment Station
(greetings)
University of Connecticut
(greetings)
The Cooper Union
(greetings)
Council on Social Work
Education
(greetings)
Dakota Wesleyan University
(greetings)
Dana College
(greetings)
Danmarks Tekniske Hojskole
(greetings)
Dartmouth College
(greetings)
University of Delhi
(greetings)
University of Denver
(greetings)
Université de Dijon
(greetings)
Doshisha Women's College of
Liberal Arts
(greetings)

Drake University
(greetings)
Dropsie College
(greetings)
Drury College
(greetings)
East Texas Baptist College
(greetings)
University of the East
(greetings)
Ecole Centrale des Arts et
Manufactures
(bronze medallion)
Electrochemical Society
(letter of congratulation)
Emmanuel College
(greetings)
Ethnikon Metsovion
Polytechneion
(greetings)
Fourah Bay College
(greetings)
Collège de France
(greetings)
L'Institut de France
(greetings)
Freie Universitat Berlin
(greetings)
Geneva College
(greetings)
Georgetown University
(greetings)
Georgia Institute of Technology
(greetings)
Georgian Court College
(greetings)
State University of Ghent
(greetings)
University of Glasgow
(greetings)
Goucher College
(greetings)
Hampden-Sydney College
(greetings)

Harvard University
(greetings)
University of Hawaii
(greetings)
Hebrew Union College
(greetings)
Hebrew University
(greetings)
College of the Holy Cross
(greetings)
Holy Family College
(greetings)
Hosei University
(greetings)
University of Houston
(greetings)
Howard University
(greetings)
Humboldt-Universitat zu Berlin
(3 volumes and medal)
Immaculate Heart College
(greetings)
Imperial College of Science and
Technology
(greetings)
Indiana University
(greetings)
Institute of Food Technologists
(greetings)
Institut National Agronomique
(greetings)
International Christian University
(greetings)
Iowa State University
(greetings)
Technical University of Istanbul
(books and pamphlets)
Judson College
(greetings)
Universita Karlova
(greetings)
University of Kentucky
(greetings)

University of Kerala
(greetings)
Knox College
(greetings)
Kyoto University
(greetings)
La Verne College
(greetings)
Université Laval
(greetings)
Lebanon Valley College
(greetings)
University of Leiden
(greetings)
Lexington Theological Seminary
(greetings)
Université de Liège
(greetings)
Facultés Catholiques de Lille
(greetings)
Accademia Nazionale dei Lincei
(greetings)
Long Island University
(greetings)
Loretto Heights College
(greetings)
Louisiana State University
(greetings)
Louisville Presbyterian Seminary
(greetings)
University of Macerata
(greetings)
Malone College
(greetings)
Manhattan College
(greetings)
University of Manitoba
(greetings)
Martin-Luther-Universitat
Halle-Wittenberg
(scroll and pamphlets)
Mary Baldwin College
(greetings)

Mary Mount College
(greetings)

Mary Washington College—
University of Virginia
(greetings)

Massachusetts Institute of
Technology
(greetings)

McPherson College
(greetings)

Meadville Theological School of
Lombard College
(greetings)

Medical Research Council
(greetings)

Medical Society of New Jersey
(greetings)

University of Melbourne
(greetings)

Memorial University of
Newfoundland
(greetings)

Mercer University
(greetings)

Michigan Technological
University
(greetings)

University of Michigan
(greetings)

University of Minnesota
(greetings)

University of Mississippi
(greetings)

University of Missouri
(greetings)

University of Modena
(greetings)

Mysore University
(greetings)

Nanyang University
(greetings)

National University
(greetings)

Nebraska Wesleyan University
(greetings)

New England Conservatory of
Music
(greetings)

New Jersey Agricultural Society
(greetings)

New Jersey Society of Certified
Public Accountants
(greetings)

New Orleans Baptist Theological
Seminary
(greetings)

New York University
(greetings)

Public Library of Newark, New
Jersey
(greetings)

Universidad Nacional de
Nicaragua
(greetings)

Nippon Gakushiin
(greetings)

Northeastern University
(greetings)

Northwestern University
(greetings)

College of Notre Dame of
Maryland
(greetings)

Oak Ridge Associated Universities
(greetings)

Oberlin College
(greetings)

Ohio State University
(greetings)

Ohio University
(greetings)

Oklahoma City University
(greetings)

Osaka University
(greetings)

Universitetet I Oslo
(greetings)

University of Oxford
  (greetings)
Paleontological Research Institution
  (greetings)
Panjab University
  (greetings)
Université de Paris à la Sorbonne
  (greetings)
Pasadena College
  (greetings)
University of Pennsylvania
  (greetings)
Peru State College
  (greetings)
Philadelphia College of Textiles
  and Science
  (greetings)
University of Philippines
  (greetings)
Philipps Universitat
  (greetings)
Polytechnic Institute of Brooklyn
  (greetings)
Princeton University
  (greetings)
University of Puget Sound
  (greetings)
University of Queensland
  (greetings)
Reed College
  (greetings)
Rhodes University
  (greetings)
Rider College
  (greetings)
Ripon College
  (greetings)
Rockefeller University
  (greetings)
Universitat Rostock
  (greetings)
Royal Academy of Sciences,
  Letters, and Arts of Belgium
  (greetings)

Royal Danish Academy of
  Sciences and Letters
  (greetings)
Royal Dutch Academy of
  Sciences
  (greetings)
Royal Society of London
  (greetings)
Royal University of Malta
  (greetings)
Sacred Heart Dominican College
  (greetings)
Saint Augustine's College
  (greetings)
College of Saint Elizabeth
  (greetings)
College of St. Francis
  (greetings)
Saint Joseph's College
  (greetings)
St. Martin's College
  (greetings)
Saint Mary's College of California
  (greetings)
Saint Peter's College
  (greetings)
Salve Regina College
  (greetings)
Sam Houston State College
  (greetings)
Samford University
  (greetings)
Universidad Nacional de San
  Antonio Abad del Cuzco
  (greetings)
San Fernando Valley State College
  (greetings)
Universidad de Santiago de
  Compostela
  (greetings)
University of Sassari
  (greetings)
Shorter College
  (greetings)

Slovenska Vysoka Skola
Technicka, Bratislava
(crystal paper weight)
Smithsonian Institution
(greetings)
Southern California School of
Technology
(greetings)
Southern Illinois University
(greetings)
Southwestern at Memphis
(greetings)
Speech Association of America
(greetings)
Springfield College
(greetings)
Stanford University
(greetings)
University of Strathclyde
(hand painted shield)
Suomalainen Tiedeakatemia
(greetings)
University of Sydney
(greetings)
Syracuse University
(greetings)
Politechnika Szczecinska
(greetings)
University of Tasmania
(greetings)
Texas A & M University
(greetings)
University of Texas
(greetings)
Texas Western College
(greetings)
University of Toronto
(greetings)
Tufts University
(greetings)
Tulane University
(greetings)
Union College, Kentucky
(greetings)

Union College, New York
(greetings)
U.S. Coast Guard Academy
(greetings)
U.S. Military Academy
(greetings)
University of Utah
(greetings)
Utkal University
(greetings)
University of Utrecht
(greetings)
Vassar College
(greetings)
Victoria University of Wellington
(greetings)
University of Virginia
(greetings)
Viterbo College
(greetings)
Vysoka Skola Technicka
Kosiciach
(greetings)
State Agricultural University of
Wageningen
(greetings)
University of Wales
(greetings)
Washington and Lee University
(greetings)
Washington University
(greetings)
University of Washington
(greetings)
Wayne State University
(greetings)
Wells College
(greetings)
University of Western Australia
(greetings)
Wheaton College, Illinois
(greetings)
Wheaton College, Massachusetts
(greetings)

Universitat Wien
(greetings)
College of William and Mary
(greetings)
William Carey College
(greetings)
Wilson College
(greetings)
Worcester Polytechnic Institute
(greetings)

Wyzsza Szkola Rolnicza
(greetings)
Yale University
(greetings)
Universidad Nacional del Zulia
(greetings)
Universitat Zurich
(greetings)

Address by Dr. Mason W. Gross on receipt of the Gold Medal of The Holland Society of New York, November 7, 1966

I am not in any sense a historian, but I am a devoted reader of history. I must confess, however, that one of my main motives in reading history may be plain escapism. It is a relief to escape to some great historical periods, when everything seems to have been so much simpler and clearer than things are today—the Golden Age of Pericles, for example. Conversely, other periods seem clearly to have been so much worse than today that one can almost be optimistic—if you challenge me on this, I invite you to refresh your memory of the Crusades. This year, which from many points of view has been the most complex and confusing year any university president has had to endure, has also, by virtue of its being our Bicentennial Year, provided me with an excuse for escaping back into colonial America, to study the history of our founding, and from that vantage point to gain some perspective on what we in American higher education are trying to do today.

One cliché that we always use in connection with founders is to say that they were men of vision and of dedicated purpose, and in saying this we usually mean to imply that we are what they envisaged and that our purposes are the same. Obviously this cannot be literally true, since it strains our imagination to suppose that Theodorus Frelinghuysen could have had even the remotest idea of what America would be like in the year 1966. But we can examine what they said, and thus discover what their hopes were; and historical curiosity need not be our only justification for doing so. Educators, like other professional people, are at their weakest when they step out of their professional activities and try to state in simple language what they think they are up to. Perhaps a review of what our founders said they were up to can help us out.

Harvard's charter of 1650 states its aim as the education of young people "in knowledge and godliness" and in "good literature Artes and

Sciences." Columbia undertook "to set up a Course of Tuition in the learned Languages, and in the liberal Arts and Sciences" as well as in religious knowledge and piety. Benjamin Franklin, in laying out the design for his Academy in Philadelphia, emphasized the utility of knowledge, but also supported the ornamental aspects of learning. And the founders of Queen's College in 1766 hoped for "the education of youth in the learned languages, liberal and useful arts and sciences and especially in divinity, preparing them for the ministry and other good offices."

It is clear that the conception of the role of college education changed little from Harvard's founding in 1636 to ours one hundred and thirty years later. Only Franklin's University of Pennsylvania had no explicit church orientation, which the others all shared with William and Mary, Yale, Princeton, Brown, and Dartmouth. With all of these it is clear that their founders felt keenly the need for an adequately educated supply of clergymen. And it is further clear that with changing times this part of the original purpose of our colonial colleges no longer plays the role it once did. Some of the original nine still include schools of divinity within their general complex, like Harvard and Yale, while others, Princeton, Columbia, and Rutgers, maintain cordial relations with neighboring seminaries, but no official connections. Conversely theological seminaries hopefully look to these colleges for their graduates, but expect to assume the full responsibility for theological education.

If we then discount the explicit and immediate purpose of these colonial colleges to come to the aid of the various churches, what shall we say of their more general aims? Of our six first Presidents, five were college graduates—the two Adamses of Harvard, Jefferson and Monroe of William and Mary, and Madison of Princeton. Washington left a bequest for the purpose of helping to found a national or federal college, gave his name to Washington College in Maryland, and wrote forcefully of the need for an educated public in his Farewell Address. Jefferson as Governor of Virginia revised and modernized the curriculum at William and Mary, and then, of course, later founded the University of Virginia. And while the Constitution of the United States has nothing to say on the subject of education, thereby reserving that area for the responsibility of the states, the Northwest Ordinance of 1787 anticipates later federal legislation by stating, "Religion, morality and knowledge being necessary to good government and the happiness of mankind, schools and the means of education shall forever be encouraged."

From all this I draw the conclusion that while in the years between the Stamp Act and the inauguration of President Washington the attention of our national leaders may have been focused primarily on such matters as national defense, political organization, taxation and survival, they were all fully conscious of the fact that an educated citizenry was an essential element in the success of their dreams for an enduring free country.

From that I draw the still further conclusion that the college men of those exciting days, over and above their special concern for the continuing health of their churches, believed that they were engaged in preparing the future leaders of their country. We must remember that our colleges inherit far less from the European universities, with their devotion to scholastic and Aristotelian scholarship, than from the schools founded in the Renaissance by such men as Vittorino da Feltre and Guarino, whose objective was the preparation of the future rulers of the Italian duchies and principalities. And they shared with these Renaissance teachers a confidence that the best materials for such an educational program were the humanistic and liberal arts and letters to be found in the learned languages, namely, Greek and Latin, to which they added some mathematics and some Hebrew. A few graduates—and Simeon DeWitt* of Rutgers seems to have been one of them—caught the spirit of the advancement of knowledge and became scientific almost in the contemporary sense of that word. But for the rest it was not knowledge in the sense of an ever-moving, ever-changing world of discovery that they sought, but rather what was called learning. In short, they sought to become learned men, masters of Cicero and Plutarch and Blackstone. As such they would take their place among the leaders of our new Republic.

Thus, I think that in order to understand the vision and the purpose of the leaders of American education in the pre- and post-Revolutionary days, we must set over against the specific aims of the founders of the colleges, which I have already quoted, another set of explicit aims, namely, those quoted in the preamble to the Constitution, "to form a more perfect Union, establish justice, insure domestic tranquillity, provide for the common defense, promote the general welfare, and secure the blessings of liberty to ourselves and our posterity."

Now, I am not arguing that these were in any sense the objectives which Queen's College or any other college had in mind, but I do suggest that with these as the express objectives of our national government, the colleges did believe that they were going to turn out the kind of men who would preserve and promote that sort of government. And I believe that to a remarkable degree they did just that. Professor McCormick has pointed out that the Class of 1836 at Rutgers, small though it was, produced a Secretary of State, a Justice of the U.S. Supreme Court, a critically important federal commissioner, a Governor, and a congressman. And while it was Woodrow Wilson who coined the phrase "Princeton in the nation's service," John Witherspoon, signer of the Declaration of Independence, would have found nothing strange about it. And this also accounts for at least two-thirds of the cry, "For God, for country, and for Yale."

*DeWitt, a graduate of Queen's College in 1776, served as Geographer General to Washington, and subsequently served for fifty years as Surveyor General of New York State.

The fascinating thing about the Constitution of the United States has been its flexibility and adaptability. There have been only twenty-three amendments since its original adoption, and ten of these came about almost at once and are really thought of as parts of the original document. Three came as the direct result of the Civil War and one canceled another one out. The substance of the Constitution has remained basically unchanged.

Much of this has been due to the interpretation which both the Congress and the Supreme Court have put upon the wording of the preamble. For example, as I have already mentioned, the Constitution apparently reserves educational matters to the states. But in 1862, Congress passed the Morrill Act which led to the establishment of the so-called land-grant colleges, of which Rutgers was designated later as one. It avoided direct interference with the states' prerogatives by simply authorizing the states to use federal resources for this purpose, but still it did prescribe the purpose, namely, to promote teaching in agriculture and the mechanic arts, and this could be justified under the general welfare phrase in the preamble. It went on to require the offering of instruction in these colleges of military science, but this too could be justified under the phrase about providing for the national defense, which would be all the more readily justified because the nation was then in the middle of a war.

In our own day this same gimmick was used when massive federal aid to education got under way under the name of the National Defense Education Act, although previous aid to education has been justified under the general welfare clause. The very name of the department of the federal government—Health, Education, and Welfare—as established by President Eisenhower, indicates how far this phrase has been stretched, since there is obviously nothing else in the Constitution which would authorize such a department.

But if the changing times have warranted a change in the interpretation of the Constitution, they have also brought about a change in the educator's conception of his responsibilities. The new concept which the land-grant act introduced has been vastly extended. For a while federal aid was confined to agriculturalists and engineers. It now explicitly includes aid for instruction and research in the natural and social sciences, with even a pittance for the arts and the humanities, in foreign languages, the medical and paramedical sciences, social work, librarianship, teacher education, with doubtless more to come. And the justification can always be found in the preamble to the Constitution.

Oddly enough, however, the educator himself, while flexible enough to adapt to all these changes in the conception of his role, still has not abandoned his conception of the greatest contribution which his college can make towards carrying out his duty to the ideals of the Constitution. To make our nation prosper, all kinds of trained people are needed, and all kinds of professions. In other words, there are all kinds of slots that have to be filled—so many M.D.'s, so many lawyers, pharmacists, translators, nuclear physicists, computer technicians, and so on. This corresponds to the situation which disturbed the leaders of the church in colonial days, when there were so many pulpits to be filled and not enough people to fill them.

This is what I call the objective element in education. Our society objectively needs people for so many different positions. These people qualify for those positions if they have mastery over a certain amount of skills and knowledge, together with a comprehension of how those skills and that knowledge can be constantly advanced. All of this at any moment is objective and relatively clear. We may not know exactly how many aviation mechanics we need right now, but we can make a good guess, and we can tell what kind of training they should have for at least the short-range future.

But we also need 100 senators, 435 congressmen, 50 state governors, nine Supreme Court justices, one vice-president, and one president. And here there is no objective blueprint. Here we look vaguely for some objective qualifications, especially in the case of Supreme Court justices, but what we are really after are what I call subjective qualifications. We look, for example, to the successful military man or the successful business-man, because we believe that, even though his objective qualifications may be largely irrelevant, there must be some factors which have contributed to his eminence in his previous career which will give us hope for success in the field of statesmanship. And sometimes this works.

My point here is that it is these subjective qualifications that the colonial educators, like their Renaissance forebears, were aiming at. Maybe Cicero and Plutarch were the wrong formulae; at least they were chosen for their contribution to the development of character.

Some of the goals which the founders of our colleges set for them-selves I find quite difficult. When they spoke of the learned languages I think we could emulate them quite successfully, but when they chose piety and godliness, I would find it difficult to prescribe the elements in the curriculum which would produce those desirable results, and I would find it equally hard to point to those graduates with whom we had been successful in these areas. The point is that when we confine our aims to those which I have called objective we can usually claim a high degree of success, but when we are concerned with the subjective qualities, the qualities of character, then we have a real problem. The only agreed-upon formula that I know of for character building is an unsuccessful football season, and no college president ever plans for this, however much he may value it.

However, let us consider again the objectives presented in the preamble to the Constitution, in the belief that the aims of an education system in any country derive their validity from the aims of the country itself.

"A perfect Union"—the writers of the preamble were obviously think-ing of a union more perfect than could be achieved under the Articles of

Confederation. Here the aim is objective and without definite limitation. Our colleges can turn out graduates who can contribute to an increasingly perfect union.

"Establish justice"—here again the program is objective, and while the definition of justice may be difficult, it is still not difficult to identify approximations to it, and this is what our social scientists and our students of law can help to effectuate.

"Insure domestic tranquillity"—here is obviously one of the most complicated areas. From the Whisky Rebellion to the Police Review Board, this has been one of the more troublesome problems. However, the intent of the framers of the Constitution was obviously to provide the means by which such disputes could be resolved. Those today who are motivated by the same concern tend to follow the lead of the founders and to set up the kinds of democratic machinery which will attempt to achieve the same objective. Colleges and universities can and should help here too.

So far as providing for the common defense and promoting the general welfare are concerned, again there is no theoretical difficulty at all. The colleges are the major source of leadership for our armed forces, and in times of war their research laboratories are a main source for devising the means of victory. And it is generally agreed that over and above all the other means of promoting welfare, education itself still remains the sine qua non of any positive program.

It is when we come to the final objective of the preamble that our task becomes interesting—"secure the blessings of liberty to ourselves and our posterity." Here again, to understand what education should aim at, we must distinguish between objective and subjective. Objectively, liberty means many of the things which the Constitution and the Bill of Rights set forth. It means freedom from foreign domination, from taxation without representation, from the billeting of foreign or alien troops. It means freedom of speech, of the press, of assembly, and of religion. Even more specific freedoms are spelled out, but in each case they are objectively recognizable and can be secured. But there are many more aspects to freedom which the Bill of Rights cannot touch. In his listing of the Four Freedoms, Mr. Roosevelt hit upon one of them—freedom from fear. If one's fear is only the fear of foreign invasion, then perhaps this can be dealt with objectively, but man is subject to many more kinds of fear than that. To insure the blessings of liberty in the sense of freeing people from the most enslaving of all their emotions is a task which requires more than an amendment to the Constitution or a resolve by statesmen. Let us examine this a bit more fully.

Near the beginning of the sixteenth century a colony of Jews, who had been previously driven from Spain into Portugal, were again driven out of Portugal in order to make perfect a wedding present. The Netherlands provided them with a refuge, because the Dutch had a clearer conception of civil liberty at that time than any other nation in Europe. They settled in the Netherlands, but remained very much a community to themselves, observing their own religious customs and laws, and taking little part in the general affairs of their new homeland. Towards the middle of the seventeenth century they were confronted by a challenge from within, in the person of a young man who took seriously the concept of freedom and began to think for himself. He was convicted of heresy and excommunicated from the already self-isolated community. He must as a result have been one of the most solitary people the Western world had ever known, relying only upon his intellect and his strength of character to survive.

This man, of course, was Benedict Spinoza, one of the very few really great intellects the Western world has known. His best-known work is called the *Ethics*, a philosophical treatise in five parts, the fourth of which has the familiar title, "Of Human Bondage, or the Strength of the Emotions," while the fifth and final part is called "Of Human Liberty, or the Power of the Intellect." The *Ethics* as a whole is an extremely difficult book and probably so influenced by the logic and the science of his day as to be unacceptable in general today. But his insights and often his reasonings have a cogency which force their attention upon anyone who is concerned with the blessings of liberty.

Spinoza's conception of the prerequisites of human liberty demand the attention of all who are concerned with the over-all objectives of education. To him the great threat to human liberty was the power of the emotions, which he defined as inadequate ideas—inadequate knowledge of the true state of things, which led to fear and general impotence. Knowledge of the true situation, or adequate and true ideas, was the only remedy. The emotions were subjective, personal, and confining. Knowledge was objective and liberating. I cannot here go into a full account of Spinoza's reasoning. But I will say that I find it both the most compelling account of human liberty that I know and at the same time the most complete definition of the aims of education.

I have already said that we professionals are at our worst when we are called upon to state and defend the aims of education. We assume that everyone agrees with us that education is the sine qua non of a free society, and we are caught off base when, not infrequently, our presuppositions are challenged. I suggest that we have a ready answer to all such challenges if we will recall the objective of the Constitution "to secure the blessings of liberty to ourselves and our posterity," and when we think of Spinoza's title, "Of Human Liberty, or the Power of the Intellect."

The simplest objective of education at all levels is to prepare the young newcomer to society to develop such native skills and talents as he may possess, to the end that he may carve out for himself a position in society and win economic freedom. This is the specific aim of all vocational and technical programs, but no less of most professional schools.

An almost equally well-understood objective is the contribution which educated men make to their society. Thus, for example, a military man not only wins economic freedom for himself, but he presumably makes a vital contribution to the independence of our nation. The same is true of a medical man, whose contribution strengthens society while also winning for himself freedom from want and need. This conception was certainly uppermost in the minds of those who founded the early colleges in this country.

A third level of freedom comes about through the mastery of the secrets of nature. Here what Spinoza calls the power of the intellect comes into play. Scientific understanding of the forces of nature not only brings about freedom by increasing our power, but it also decreases the nameless fears which cripple our spirit. Certainly no one will question the advancement of knowledge as one of the main objectives of education and of the modern university.

A more difficult level of freedom is that which we both achieve and contribute to through the gradual understanding of people of other races, religions, and colors than ourselves. If the kind of political slavery which we knew in this country until the close of the Civil War was a hideous phase of history that we had to grow out of, it was, in my opinion, far less hideous than the defenses that are put up nowadays against recognizing the just claims of our fellow human beings. On the election eve, 1966, we can only contemplate with horror and shame the political cries which are being used to justify downgrading and maltreating our fellow citizens of this free Republic. But if the damage to these minorities is great, how much greater is the damage to the spokesmen for the oppressors. They have willfully turned their backs on the power of the intellect and have sold out to those evil, lying, and prejudicial emotions whose domination constitutes human bondage. The shoe is now on the other foot, and the oppressors are now, in the fullest sense of the word, the slaves.

But the final freedom which I would mention is one which a college teacher learns to recognize and to cherish. We all know the student in our classes who is competent and intelligent, but unconcerned. Then the great moment occasionally comes when suddenly the student catches fire and is off on his own in a glow of wild excitement. It makes little or no difference what his subject is—mathematics or literature, physics or the arts. Suddenly his creative energies are summoned into action, and he probably experiences the greatest freedom he can ever know. The basic materials to which he has been introduced are instantly transformed by a new spiritual glow, and he is off to the clouds. This is the man who is consciously experiencing the greatest blessings of liberty, and Spinoza would salute him as the free man who through the power of his intellect is feeling the greatest joy that man can experience.

You may now see why I have coupled the explicit and possibly narrow objectives set forth by the founders of our early colleges with the aims which the new Constitution of the new United States set forth. The years from 1766 to 1787 were years in which the concept of freedom was the dominant theme in our emerging country. But no man or group of men ever exhausted the full meaning of this concept. The founders of the colleges, the founders of the Republic, together with the great intellects to whom they so often turned, Spinoza, Locke, yes, and Plutarch, were all reaching in this direction. We today in our colleges and universities must recognize these same goals—the freedom of the individual, the freedom of our society; because of the freedom of its members, the freedom from fear which comes about through knowledge, and most of all the creative freedom of the human spirit. These are the goals to which—once every two hundred years at least—we must rededicate ourselves.

Rutgers Night Around the World Gatherings

New Jersey

Atlantic County: Smithville Inn, Absecon; 64. Songleader, Dr. Wilbert B. Hitchner '22. Speakers, Bonnie A. Conover D'68 and Jan K. Astin '67. Cochairmen, Elizabeth Jones Barker D'29 and Walter W. Clark '22.

Bergen-Passaic-Hudson-Rockland (N.Y.) Counties: Marriott Motor Hotel, Saddle Brook; 175. Toastmaster, Robert R. Comstock '52. Songleader, John F. Gordon, Jr. '37. Cochairmen, Patricia Mate Knox D'57 and John A. Behrend '51.

Bergen-Passaic Counties (Douglass): Robin Hood Inn, Clifton; 17. Speaker, Margaret Denton Wagner D'24, member of State University Bicentennial Commission. Chairman, Catherine Palmer Ballantine D'45.

Camden-Philadelphia: College Center, College of South Jersey; 170. Toastmaster, Assistant Dean Walter W. Herkness, Jr. Speakers, Arthur E. Armitage, chairman, Council of the College of South Jersey, Hon. Thomas A. Madden L'30, and trustees, A. Paul Burton '32, Allan G. Mitchell '27, Rosamond Sawyer Moxon D'29, and Frederick O. Ziegler. Chairman, Harry A. Brown '49.

Essex County: The Manor, West Orange; 150. Master of ceremonies, Frank P. Travisano '43. Toastmaster, Newark Dean Emeritus Herbert P. Woodward. Speaker, Newark Vice-President Malcolm D. Talbott. Cochairmen, Muriel DeRose Irwin D'46 and Frank S. Robinson '48.

Hunterdon County: Coach 'n' Paddock Restaurant, Hampton. Cochairmen, Elizabeth Smedley Wettstein D'49 and William G. McIntyre '40.

Mercer County: Geneva Inn, Trenton; 100. Cochairmen, Diane Daly Rogers D'54, Bruce T. Tretheway '51, and Francis G. Mendrey UC'41.

Monmouth County: American Hotel, Freehold; 150. Toastmaster, Arthur Z. Kamin '54. Speaker, Professor Emeritus Houston Peterson, also Trustee Peter Cartmell '43, Joseph C. Irwin '29, Arthur C. Swift '08, Howard Newman L'66, Football Coach John F. Bateman, Baseball Coach Matthew J. Bolger. Cochairmen, Mary Lou Farry Van Iderstine D'51 and Ridgeway V. C. Moon '38.

Morris County: Florham Park Country Club; 40. Speaker, Donald J. Taylor '58, assistant director of admissions. Cochairmen, Helen Stratton Neidhart D'49 and Donald W. Braly '50.

Ocean County: 5. Alumni who are members of the Toms River Kiwanis Club toasted the University. Chairman, Sidney L. Harris '48.

Sussex County: Perona Farms, Andover; 44. Cochairmen, Susan Gahs Luthman D'41 and Rev. Carl A. Luthman '40.

Tri-County (Union, Somerset, Middlesex): Somerville Inn; 150. Toastmaster and speaker, Harvey J. Hauptman '51. Cochairmen, Rita Farrer Taub D'46 and Robert Linder '55.

Warren County: Lanark Inn, Phillipsburg; 12. Cochairmen, Joyce Houghtaling Anderson D'57 and Brevoort C. Conover '52.

Out of State

Phoenix, Arizona: Villa Monterey Golf Club, Scottsdale; 20. Speaker, Former Athletic Coach Arthur A. Matsu. Cochairmen, Marshall G. Rothen '39 and Kenneth Ross '42.

Tucson, Arizona: Old Pueblo Club; 16. Chairman, Stephen M. Kreyns '53.

Los Angeles, California: Biltmore Hotel: 106. Speaker, former professor Samuel C. McCulloch, now dean of humanities at University of California at Irvine. Chairman, Robert H. McBride '55.

San Diego, California: Vacation Village, Mission Bay; 41. Master of ceremonies, Donald Thomas '52. Cochairmen, John F. Borchers '32 and Otto C. Jahnke '50.

San Francisco, California: Fairmont Hotel; 150. Cochairmen, Judith Ann Cox D'65, and Edwin J. Schwartz '55.

Denver, Colorado: Continental Denver Motor-Hotel; 18. Chairman, Richard D. Holt '29.

Washington, D.C.: Twin Bridge Marriott Motor Hotel; 170. Speakers, David L. Kreeger '29, Samuel Zagoria '41, Dr. Franklyn A. Johnson '47, Edward E. Cubberley '61, L'64, Louise Rovner D'34, Carolyn Grosse Gawarecki D'53, Helen Eldridge Vogel D'41, Marilyn Raitano D'63. Chairman, Caspar H. Nannes '31.

Wilmington, Delaware: DuPont Country Club; 26. Cochairmen, Harriet Winarsky Berson D'58, Abbott Shilling '54, and Dale E. Wolf Ph.D. '49.

East Coast, Florida: Home of Julian A. Siegel UC'49, Miami Beach; 51. Speakers, Jay Lombardy UC'53, Harold Heller L'29, and A. L. Plager L'26. Songleader, Dr. N. Ralph Frankel '53. Chairman, Julian A. Siegel UC'49.

Central Florida (Douglass): Officers Club, Orlando Air Force Base; 12. Chairman, Ardis Guice Brenner D'46.

West Coast, Florida: Sheraton Inn, St. Petersburg; 51. Cochairmen, Naomi Stern Jaffer D'51 and Daniel T. Winter '36.

Atlanta, Georgia: Yohannan's Across the Street Restaurant; 12. Cochairmen, Evelyn Rauch Chesnutt D'55 and Will G. Atwood, Jr. '39.

Honolulu, Hawaii: Queen's Surf; 16. Alumni attending were conferees at National Association of County Agricultural Agents conference. Chairman, Robert R. Windeler '38.

Chicago, Illinois: The Germania Club; 55. Toastmaster, Rees E. Davies '32. Speaker, Albert W. Twitchell '35, director of athletics. Cochairmen, Rosemary Honecker Anderson D'51 and Joseph E. Orlick '50.

Indianapolis, Indiana: Greentree Country Club; 14. Chairman, Robert G. Busse SB'39.

Portland, Maine: Cumberland Club; 22. Speaker, Edith McEwen Dorian, author and former Douglass professor. Cochairmen, Doris Libby Lindquist D'24 and Stanley W. Letson '35.

Baltimore, Maryland: Center Club; 77. Speakers, Leon Rose '47, John D. Hackett '44, Wallace S. Moreland, Jr. '53, Samuel B. Temple '35. Cochairmen, Helen Platt Hollingsworth D'46 and Fred L. Dechowitz '49.

Boston, Massachusetts: Maugus Club, Wellesley; 110. Speakers, Frederick E. Gruninger '53, assistant to the director of athletics, and Leslie H. Unger '52, director of sports information. Cochairmen, Lucille DeAngelis Bicknell D'50 and Donald A. Millard '35.

Detroit, Michigan: Pontchartrain Hotel; 40. Chairman, James G. Periale '55.

St. Paul, Minnesota: Hilton Hotel; 26. Cochairmen, Lois Brown Ennis D'57 and Roger N. Ennis '57.

St. Louis, Missouri: University Club; 28. Cochairmen, Anne Schnepel Ross D'26 and Robert D. Seeley '40.

New Mexico: La Posta, Old Mesilla; 4. Dr. and Mrs. David W. Francis '41 and Dr. and Mrs. Allen Van Heuvelen '60 dined and spent the evening together.

Buffalo, New York: Buffalo Athletic Club; 40. Toastmaster, L. Nelson Hopkins, Jr. '39. Speakers, Philip M. B. Boocock '26, headmaster of the Nichols School, and Salvatore J. Sedita '63. Chairman, John C. Adourian '31.

Ithaca, New York: 7. C. Lyman Hatfield '50.

Long Island, New York: Felice's Restaurant, Westbury; 40. Speaker, Albina Martin D'33. Chairman, Robert Goodwin '43.

Mid-Hudson Area, New York: Talbot's Inn, Pleasant Valley; 13. Chairman, Richard A. Lowenstein '58.

New York, New York: Hilton Hotel; 318. Master of ceremonies, David A. Werblin '31. Speakers, Charles H. Brower '25, chairman of Board of Governors, Senator Clifford P. Case '25, President Gross. Chairman, I. Robert Kriendler '36.

Rochester, New York: Town House Motor Inn; 35. Master of ceremonies, Robert P. Hoffman '41. Chairman, Rudolph F. Illig '21.

Walden, New York: A gathering was held at the home of Earle Houghtaling '39.

Westchester, New York, and Fairfield, Connecticut, Counties: Sloan-Kettering Institute, Rye, New York Cochairmen, Sara Holtzman Glick D'50, Ann Priory Laraja D'46 and E. Gaynor Brennan '25.

Chapel Hill, North Carolina: Blair House; 33. Cochairmen, Mary Elizabeth Goslin Adams D'46 and George V. Taylor '41.

Cincinnati, Ohio: Wishing Well Restaurant; 29. Chairman, Paul J. Jansak '52.

Cleveland, Ohio: Shaker House Hotel, Shaker Heights; 28. Chairman, Jerome M. Friedlander '57.

Columbus, Ohio: The King's Inn; 41. Speaker, Professor Robert B. Sutton of Ohio State University. Guests, Bruce Harding, Ohio State archivist, and Sue Giffen, former Douglass counselor in residence. Cochairmen, Marie Lou Lindemann Dagnall D'43 and Donald R. Edmonds '60.

Toledo, Ohio: Northwood Inn; 20. Speakers, Robert L. Knight '29 and Doris Johnson Clevenger D'56. Chairman, Allen I. Gordon '50.

Pittsburgh, Pennsylvania: Press Club; 34. Speakers, John N. Meury '31 and Chester Ward '66. Cochairmen, Catherine McElligott Anderson D'59 and Stanley R. March H'33.

Columbia, South Carolina: 30. Guests, Professor Emeritus and Mrs. Paul S. Creager; also widow of Clemson University President Robert F. Poole M.S. '18, Ph.D. '21. Chairman, Dr. Victor Hurst '38.

Houston, Texas: Ye Ole College Inn; 26. Speakers, Jerome R. Epstein '27 and Miriam Feinsod Epstein D'29. Chairman, Robert E. Applegate NAS '56.

Burlington, Vermont: Victorian Inn; 12. Cochairmen, Agnes T. Powell D'35 and Theodore R. Flanagan '48.

Richmond, Virginia: Hotel Jefferson; 14. Cochairmen, Ruth Mann Wurtzel D'28 and Carl L. Kempf '31.

Seattle, Washington: Norselander Restaurant; 25. Cochairmen, Diane Brod Hoffman D'64, Barnett E. Hoffman '62, L'65, and Harold F. Vhugen '48, L'50.

Overseas

Tucumán, Argentina: Professor Emeritus James J. Slade of the College of

Engineering and Mrs. Slade "enjoyed a little banquet." Professor Slade now teaches mathematics at Universidad Nacional de Tucumán.

Cochabamba, Bolivia: Home of W. Douglas Smith '54; 4. The Smiths and Rev. and Mrs. C. Peter Wagner '52 had a full-fledged celebration.

Santiago, Chile: 4. Robert N. Repp '35 and Mrs. Repp, Javier Zaldivar M.S. '60, and Mrs. Zaldivar toasted Rutgers.

London, England: English-Speaking Union; 9. Speaker, Professor Emeritus Raymond M. Bennett of Douglass. Chairman, Richard A. Powell '60.

Milan, Italy: Home of Eloise Degenring Finardi D'41; 6. The group talked of old times and former faculty members.

Kingston, Jamaica: Home of Gladstone W. Morgan M.S. '61; 16. Chairman, Basil E. Collins '64.

Tokyo, Japan: Gakushi-Kaikan (graduate house of University of Tokyo); 37. Speakers, William Logan, Jr. '23, Kokichi Kunishima '24, Dr. Toru Imura. Cochairmen, Bernadette Terango D'56 and Professor Imura.

Nairobi, Kenya: Dr. Ordway Starnes, on leave as director of the East African Agriculture and Forestry Research Organization, held a party for the senior officers of the organization.

Seoul, Korea: Korea House; 5. An informal reunion was organized by William F. Kingsbury '58.

Lima, Peru: David E. Bennett, Jr. '59 and Gerald J. Nagel UC'54 and their wives had dinner together.

Madrid, Spain: Air Force Captain Alan G. Schreihofer '59 invited his Seton Hall alumnus neighbor to join him in a toast to Rutgers.

Bangkok, Thailand: Star Dust Club; 9, mostly Library School alumnae. Chairman, Hsin-min W. Brohm LS'62.

Caracas, Venezuela: Lee Hamilton's Famous Steak House; 9. Chairman, Frank Bor, Jr. UC'49.

Belgrade, Yugoslavia: Hunters' Club; 2. Consul General Robert I. Owen '41 and Embassy Political Officer Frank G. Trinka '50 toasted Rutgers at luncheon.

Special Groups

Air Force Academy: Officers' Club, Colorado Springs, Colorado; 25. Alumni on the Academy faculty and staff, with their wives. Chairman, Lieutenant Colonel Arthur S. Knies '49.

Pennsylvania State University: The Tavern, State College, Pennsylvania; 5. Alumni currently or formerly on the Penn State faculty. Cochairmen, Robert E. Galbraith '24 and Martin S. Hanopole '60.

Law School Alumni Association: The Chanticleer, Millburn; 300. Speaker, legal humorist Carl F. Conway. Awards presented to Judge William F. Smith L'29 and Professor Thomas A. Cowan, Chairman, Martin J. Loftus L'33.

College of Pharmacy Alumni Association: Hotel Robert Treat, Newark; 300. Toastmaster, William Levine P'26. Honored were deans of the college Robert P. Fischelis, Ernest E. Little, Thomas D. Rowe, and Roy A. Bowers. Chairman, Amalia S. Ricciardi P'36.

Class of '27 (Rutgers College): Charnor Lodge, South Bound Brook; 22. Songs, stories, and toasts. Chairman, F. Richard Cass '27.

Class of '35 (Rutgers College): Old Times Inn, New York; 7. Luncheon get-together of classmates.

Class of '63 (Pharmacy): Luchow's Restaurant, New York; 6. Friends gathered for "an evening of wining and dining." Chairman, Frank W. Dederbeck P'63.

Faculty and Staff: University Commons, New Brunswick; 300. Speakers, President Gross, Paul H. G. Wright of British Information Service, and Princeton University President Robert F. Goheen. Chairman, Ernest E. McMahon '30.

Address by President Robert F. Goheen of Princeton University at the New Brunswick Charter Night Dinner, November 10, 1966.

To be with you this evening on this 200th anniversary of the conferring of Rutgers' Charter is a pleasure and an honor. Over the two centuries, Rutgers and Princeton have shared New Jersey's history, first as Colonial Province and then as State. During these same two hundred years relations between the two institutions have been close and sometimes curiously intermingled.

Both our universities sprang from a common seed, the religious and emotional ferment of the mid-eighteenth century known as the "Great Awakening." From the "New Light" evangelical movement of the Presbyterian Church came the College of New Jersey. Twenty years later evangelical leaders in the Dutch Reform Church brought Queen's College into being as the eighth institution of higher learning in the then English colonies.

These young colleges, founded as they were by men of uncommon religious zeal, demonstrated from the beginning great tolerance and liberality of mind. The purpose of each, as stated in similar language in the Charter of each, was "the education of youth in the learned languages and the liberal arts and science," and sectarian constraints on students and on faculty were deliberately omitted. The freedom of conscience sought and protected in these youthful colleges is direct antecedent of that freedom of inquiry which is so indispensable to the modern university, as represented by both Rutgers and Princeton.

But for a moment more I want to remain with early links in the association that binds us. As is well known, Nassau Hall—I call it that because the title "College of New Jersey" was less used during the eighteenth century—gave Queen's College its first tutor, Frederick Frelinghuysen, of the Princeton Class of 1770. After a distinguished career in the service of his country as a member of the Constitutional Convention, Officer in the Continental Army, twice Member of the New Jersey Assembly, and United States Senator from New Jersey, this first member of the Rutgers faculty returned to Nassau Hall as Trustee and so served until his untimely death in 1804. As far as I can discover, this was the first exercise in two-way lend-lease between our institutions—and a most profitable one.

The War of Independence put the resources and morale of both Queen's and Nassau Hall to severe test. For the next forty years both institutions (as did others in New England) suffered recurring periods of financial strain and doubt about their futures. At one ebb period, in 1795, a proposal for merger was defeated by the Trustees of Queen's by the slim majority of a single vote!

After the desperate years, consolidation and slow growth appear to mark the history of both institutions in the period from about 1825 to the Civil War. Queen's became Rutgers, the vicissitudes of the War Between the States were survived, the famous football match of 1869 was played, and a quickening pace of development was apparent in the closing years of the nineteenth century and the beginning of the twentieth.

In due course, but not quite on the same schedule, each institution acknowledged its expanded scope and aspirations by taking on the title of university. Princeton did this first—perhaps even prematurely, as some have held—in 1896. In New Brunswick, Rutgers delayed to assume the name of university until 1924, and by this delay, so far as I know, she avoided all challenge to her right to that title.

So we stand today, no longer two provincial colleges but universities, with national and international responsibilities. And while for two hundred years we have shared New Jersey's history and contributed much to the enlightenment and progress of the people of this State, I do not hesitate to predict that these two universities will contribute more, and be of greater influence, within the State of New Jersey in the decades ahead than ever in the decades past. This follows from the critical, deep-reaching role which universities, both public and private, occupy in these later years of the twentieth century. Sir Richard Livingston once put it this way:

> If you wished to destroy modern civilization, the most effective way to do it would be to abolish universities. They stand as its center.
> . . . Their discoveries and thought penetrate almost every activity

of life. . . . On their health and vigour the well-being of the whole modern world depends. They add nothing to the amount of natural intelligence now existing, but they refine and perfect what exists and fit it to serve purposes and take stresses which in its raw form it could not meet. Their influence is increasing and will increase unless there is a collapse of modern civilization. [*Some Thoughts on a University Education* pp. 5-6.]

Beyond question, never has there been as much ready and fruitful intercourse between the realms of scholarship and instruction, on the one hand, and those of production and affairs, on the other hand, as there is today in this country. Both Rutgers and Princeton are deeply involved in this interchange, in a considerable variety of ways, and they will become more so.

Schematically conceived, it is the mission of the modern university to teach, to perform research, and to engage in public service. In a recent series of lectures, published as *The University in Transition*, President Perkins of Cornell observed that these three missions correspond to three prime attributes of knowledge: its acquisition, transmission, and application. He further observed that "the explosive power of knowledge" in our day may be traceable to interaction among these three activities, and he suggested that the university has its great importance in the modern world because it alone of institutions fully embraces these three ways of handling knowledge and seeks to put them into interaction.

If the imaginative and persevering search for new knowledge, the effective passing on of that already known, and a deliberate application of learning (both new and old) to the public benefit constitute the mark of the powerful university, then clearly Rutgers is powerful. Indeed, those of us who are concerned with such things find it hard to exaggerate the accomplishments of Rutgers and its most recent presidents. They are the more remarkable because the great powerhouse which is current-day Rutgers—with lines that extend near and far, generating, conveying, and putting to use ideas and skills—this great power-system has been brought into being despite very great budgetary limitations and with all too little understanding and encouragement from the people of New Jersey and their representatives.

Recently, of course, the long-standing parsimony of the State toward public higher education has been fading—fading quite fast. Now the people, the Legislature, and the Governor are in process of reassessing the status of public higher education in New Jersey and ways in which it may best be advanced. There is an awakening to the great educational needs which confront the State and to the opportunities within reach. A bill introduced in the New Jersey Senate (S. 434) provides for reorganization of the structure of public higher education, and extensive hearings were held on it this past summer. There is reason to hope that New Jersey will no longer appear high on the list of states which lag the most in opportunities for higher education. And there is hope that New Jersey will not so commonly be cited as one of those states which still has no effective statewide system for the planning, coordination, and encouragement of public higher education, from the community college and technical institute through to advanced forms of professional training.

It is useful to consider the role of the state university in a quality *system* of higher education. There are those, I know, who fear that, if the structure of higher education in New Jersey is reorganized, if a genuine, coordinated system is developed, then the relatively developed condition of the University and its prestige will relegate the two- and four-year institutions to subservient positions and reduce their faculties to the rank of second-class educational citizens. These fearful voices raise predictions that Rutgers will carry such disproportionate weight in a coordinated system that it will grab more than its due share of the funds available for higher education and thus work to hold down and deprive the smaller institutions.

All this really is nonsense! Consider any of the states which has a truly great state university in it. If that university were wiped out, the other institutions would become not stronger but weaker. They would be severely weakened, because they would lack the intellectual nurture, the force of example, and the supply of able faculty which a strong and vigorous state university provides to all of the institutions in a statewide system.

The worth to society of a well-organized and balanced system of public higher education in a state is a whole greater than the sum of its parts, just as the university itself has a usefulness and a power far beyond that of its component academic departments. This is to say that within the proposed system the state university must play a major pivotal role; but it will be a role of leadership by example and intellectual nurture, not one of repression and self-aggrandizement. The correct image is not the octopus but the flowing spring. Experience in many states bears this out, as it also makes clear that in higher education leveling is unproductive.

Operating within a coordinated system, the every action of the state university, but especially the standards which it sets and achieves—standards of academic excellence, standards of faculty status, standards of institutional integrity, standards in a dozen interrelated areas—should have effect throughout the educational hierarchy and help to lift (which does not mean to equate) standards throughout the system.

And there is one critical aspect of this on which I want to pause. To date Rutgers has enjoyed a very large measure of independence, and this is as it should be. A university may combine many curricula and divisions, it may offer professional and nonprofessional studies in profusion, it may feature a host of service activities; but if it is not free in its teaching and research, it is not fully a university. By free, I mean not subject to dictation from external sources—from government, from political pressure groups, from factions of the right or the left. To the extent that an institution is subservient in how it pursues, transmits, and applies knowledge it is the less a university, whatever its name. The business of a university is not dogma, but truth; not indoctrination, but inquiry; not slogans, but sanity.

While Rutgers has been able to live and grow true to this idea of a university, New Jersey's State Colleges have, unfortunately, enjoyed relatively little freedom. They have been kept on a tight rein to Trenton, hamstrung by niggling administrative particles, allowed little initiative or vigor of their own. Both that condition and its consequences seem to me deplorable.

As we look ahead toward a coordinated system of higher education in this State, one of the important tasks for Rutgers will be to function with a heightened sense of relationship and responsibility to the other elements of the system—and to the system as a whole. At the same time, one of Rutgers' major contributions must be helping to infuse and uphold within the system a healthy sense of institutional independence, integrity, and enterprise. Inevitably, in the period of transition and growth which seems to lie just ahead, the need for coordinated planning and effort, on the one hand, and the desire for autonomy, on the other, will produce strains and stresses. Let's not fool ourselves about that. But it is my belief—and there is ample evidence for it—that genuine progress is won out of just such tensions as these.

Within the statewide system for public higher education conceived in New Jersey Senate Bill 434 and under the sort of forward-looking master plan that we need, much room will be left open for institutional initiative and autonomy. And in any comprehensive system which develops in New Jersey, I am confident that Rutgers will continue to be living witness to the importance and efficacy of these prerogatives of vital educational institutions. In doing so, she will assist the State and County Colleges to achieve —and dare display—their proper vitality and vigor as individual members of the pluralistic whole.

And so, as Rutgers moves into her third century, I am proud to hail her and declare myself in favor of all efforts that will contribute to her advance. Rutgers is important, critically important, in her own right, and she is important because of the pivotal point she must occupy in any coordinated system of higher education in this State. Two hundred years of history declare her mission—past, present, and future!

John Lenkey III's letter to Colonel Vincent Kramer describing the climbing of Mt. Fujiyama, Japan, to place the Rutgers flag on its summit.

On arriving in Tokyo, I contacted Professor Toru Imura, chairman of the Rutgers University Club—the man to whom President Mason Gross telegramed good wishes on being the first to celebrate Rutgers Night Around the World (due to International Date Line). Professor Imura had lined up the assistance of three agencies: the Japan Meteorological Agency, Japan Alpine Club, and the Waseda University Alpine Club Old Boys Corporation (alumni to you and me).

Professor Imura took much personal time off to escort me, first to the Meteorological Agency where I was fully briefed on equipment required, temperatures and wind velocities expected, and invited to join the Weather Station Climb on March 9. I accepted their offer to accompany me to any equipment store and buy the eight-pointed crampons necessary, and head and face protection. They also presented to me contour maps and official drawings. Many thanks to them.

However, there were other plans afoot. Having appealed to three groups for assistance, we still had two others scrambling to lend it. On Thursday, March 2, Professor Imura presented me to a special meeting of the Japan Alpine Club and to Seiji Yamamoto, a 27-year-old electrical engineer and climber, who would then become climb organizer. The officers of the Alpine Club signed our spare Rutgers flag, presented me a Japan Alpine Club wall pennant, and a JAC lapel button, which I have worn ever since. I was made an honorary member. Yamamoto would be assisted by Kenji Shiratori, also 27 years old, and a member of the Waseda Alpine Club. The date was set for March 7.

On March 6 we left Tokyo by train for Lake Kawaguchi, some 140 km away, where we took Japanese lodgings in a youth hostel near the mountain. It was snowing. The next morning at breakfast weather still looked dim, but near 8:30 A.M. the clouds parted and we saw the brilliantly-lit white cone of Fuji-san and it seemed to say to us, "Rutgers, Fuji awaits." Yamamoto said, "Let's go."

We took an automobile up the toll road (officially closed except in July and August only) as far as he dared to go before the road became too ice-covered; when he gave up we started walking further, but luckily caught a ride with a carpenter who was repairing the fifth station. So we rode to the 2,000 meter altitude and there were only 1,776 left; but what a last mile that was!

The snow and ice was so thick we had to put on our crampons immediately at the 2,000-meter level and we started out looking for the trail upward. We walked about one mile clockwise around the base to locate the trail, and then started up. It was cloudy and snowing lightly. Shiratori set the pace with me second and Yamamoto third. I clung two steps behind Shiratori throughout the entire ascent. The trail zigzagged up from the fifth station to about the seventh entirely on sheet ice covered with a thin veil of snow. The new crampons bit in well and I had no trouble; Shiratori loaned me a French ice ax which also worked very well. At the seventh station the trail quit zigzagging and buried under the snow and ice pointed straight up. We met a few practice climbers between seven and eight stations, but none were going higher. The stations are summer huts where climbers can rest; they were buried in ice but their roofs gave us a flat surface to pause for breath. After the eighth station we were above 10,000 feet altitude and now really climbing in earnest. We started out at 11:00 A.M. from the south and the mountain angle was now steeper, over 30 degrees. Because it is an extinct volcano, unlike many mountains which level out nearer the top, Fuji gets steeper and steeper. The altitude began having its effects and our rate of climb slowed. At station eight and a half we broke out above the clouds (about 3,200 meters) and the sun seemed straight up the hill in front of us. But it was sinking rapidly over Fuji's rim. At station nine we could see the top and its gate. It was only about 300 meters altitude above us. Yamamoto said it would take us one hour and 20 minutes to climb that last 300 meters. I was sure he was wrong. He was right.

At station nine and a half, about 120 meters from the top (I could throw a rock that high, I thought), the sun had passed over the rim and the temperature, which was −22° C., really felt it. We paused on the roof of the last hut and threw on every last piece of clothing and gloves and woollies we had in our packs. The wind blew down the slope into our faces trying to pry us away from the ice slope. One slip or one patch of rotten ice and you would fall about 4,000 feet. Eight climbers had been killed so far this winter on this same face. Dead slow, Shiratori led us up about one step every five seconds for breath and safety. A U.S. Air Force F-102 flew past, banked and came around inverted to look us over. His jet nozzle thunder was the last thing in the world we wanted—it could loosen the ice we were climbing on. We waved him away. I doubt if he saw—but he went away. Suppose he were a Rutgers ROTC pilot and I had pulled out our flag.

At long last we reached the crest of that great hollow, icy volcano, pulling ourselves hand-over-hand through the top gate and we rested a few minutes. I had been able to snap a few pictures of the climb up to station eight, but it was too dangerous above that. Now we broke out our Rutgers flag and snapped one picture. It was 5:30 P.M. and we were again in sunlight. But the official hoisting was to be postponed for the Rising Sun, of course. Now we found we were on the wrong side of the crater—far away from the weather station house where we were to spend the night. We started around the crater. The snow was too deep to go down and up. The wind blew in 60-mile bursts. It was the Spirit of Fuji's last challenge, the Japanese said. We stood legs spread and leaning on our ice axes until it subsided. Not fifty feet from the station the final problem stood. It was a huge lava boulder which blocked our way. Shiratori, still leader, chose to go around the outside. Huge fingers and sheets of rotten ice blocked the way, but he chopped our path of about 23 steps. As each 50 to 100 lb. piece of ice sailed down the steep slope for some 4,500 feet, we stepped ever more carefully. Finally we were at the wooden platform and hailed the weather station keeper. He opened the door and we were safe. He was Yoshishige Kobayashi and he and some four others manned this, the highest weather outpost in the world. They stay up two months at a time, twice a year. All the supplies are towed up or dropped during the summer. He provided us bunk beds and a supper, and after supper we had an hour and a half signing ceremony. I entered Rutgers thanks for the honor of showing our flag from Mt. Fuji, and he signed and stamped the Japanese flag we were carrying, and presented me a souvenir certificate officially signed and stamped describing the event. On noting Rutgers was two hundred years old and duly respectful, Mr. Kobayashi presented me a 300-year-old coin and "Suzu," a bell to bring us luck for the descent. He insisted we descend the eastern path to Gotemba because the southern steep route was too dangerous. Shiratori and Yamamoto agreed, much to my relief. It was only then that Shiratori showed that in his pack he had nylon rope to be used in event I faltered while climbing. I am pleased to say that in Rutgers' honor I did not.

The next morning at 7:30, March 8, 1967, year of Showa 42, the Scarlet flag greeted the rising sun with the American and Nippon flags at 12,535 feet, held squarely on the marker showing the highest point in Japan. Many pictures were taken. The day was gloriously clear. We could see the Pacific Ocean, the Japanese alps, and many lakes and smaller volcanoes surrounding the mighty Fuji.

After the ceremony, we re-entered the weather house and Mr. Kobayashi insisted I sign and inscribe the Rutgers flag with the moment and date. It will be hung inside the station on the wall as a permanent exhibit for station visitors in the summer. It was very rare to have a non-Japanese visitor climb Fuji in winter.

We started down at 9:15 A.M. by a gentler route; it was ten km longer to walk, however. The descent, steep at first and gradually slackening, was uneventful and extremely wearing on the legs as we walked directly down the fall line due to our good crampons. After descending 7,000 feet we entered the clouds and lost forever the most beautiful view in Japan. After 1,000 feet of groping for trail markers, the visibility improved and we walked (wobbily for my legs—the Japanese stoutly as ever) toward Gotemba. Around station one, down 11,500 feet, we encountered a group of weather bureau skiers and a four-wheeled-drive truck. They made excuses that they were just on exercises, but when we gladly accepted a ride the remaining five km to Gotemba, all the skiers doffed their slats and piled in, too. It developed Mr. Kobayashi had radioed Tokyo (his only contact point) and the Meteorological Agency telephoned Gotemba that the Rutgers expedition was descending, and they were all out looking for us. After a final interview by the Gotemba Station boss who wanted all the details as his climbing days were in the past, we returned to Lake Kawaguchi, to Japanese baths, and a hilarious party hosted by Mrs. Mary L. Lenkey, my staunchest supporter and occasional Geisha. Only then would Yamamoto and Shiratori sign the Rutgers flag—now that success was here. An official welcome home and reception for the climbers and Mrs. Lenkey will be held by the Japan Alpine Club March 14, at which time the honorary membership will be solidified.

A Report on the Genovese Case—Prepared for Presentation to Governor Richard J. Hughes by the Board of Governors of Rutgers – The State University, August 6, 1965

At the request of Governor Hughes, the Board of Governors of Rutgers – The State University has again reviewed the case of Dr. Eugene Genovese and remarks he made at the so-called "teach-in" on the campus on April 23, 1965.

Every member of the Board is completely out of sympathy with the views expressed by Dr. Genovese and believes that the expression of some of these views evidenced a lack of good judgment.* But they also believe that his statement, however offensive it may be to individual members of the Board, does not constitute grounds for dismissal.

The following paragraphs present the essential facts in the case:

1. Professor Genovese came to Rutgers on his current appointment as Assistant Professor in the College of Arts and Sciences, July 1, 1963. His B.A. was from Brooklyn College; his M.A. and Ph.D. from Columbia.

2. In December, 1964, the Chairman of the History Department recommended to the Dean of the College of Arts and Sciences that Dr. Genovese be promoted to Associate Professor with tenure, effective July 1, 1965. The recommendation had been approved by the History Department's Committee on Personnel which gave Dr. Genovese a high rating as a teacher, scholar, and member of the college community. The College Committee on Appointments and Promotions also approved the promotion. The Dean of the College of Arts and Sciences approved. The promotion was approved by the University History Section, which includes the tenure members of all the History Departments of the University. The final reviewing authority, which at that time was the Acting President, together with the Dean of the University, concurred.

It is common practice at the University, where a promotion to a tenure position is under consideration, to seek the advice of experts in

---

*Although the report was unanimously accepted by the Board members for presentation to Governor Hughes, four members—Messrs. Alexander, Jacobson, Jurgensen, and Muccilli—dissented from that part of the second paragraph which states: "and believes that the expression of some of these views evidenced a lack of good judgment." Messrs. Alexander, Jacobson, Jurgensen, and Muccilli wished instead that the following words, which had been in the original draft of the report, be retained: "and with the way they were expressed."

the field outside the University. The replies by two of the most respected American historians were high in their praise of Professor Genovese.

At the regular meeting of the Board of Governors on April 9, the promotion was approved.

There was no evidence that would have made Dr. Genovese's promotion questionable.

On his original appointment he had taken the following loyalty oath which is given to all members of the Rutgers University faculty:

"I, ..., do solemnly swear (or affirm) that I will support the Constitution of the United States and the Constitution of the State of New Jersey, and that I will bear true faith and allegiance to the same and to the Governments established in the United States and in this State, under the authority of the people; and will defend them against all enemies, foreign and domestic; that I do not believe in, advocate or advise the use of force, or violence, or other unlawful or unconstitutional means, to overthrow or make any change in the Government established in the United States or in this State; and that I am not a member of or affiliated with any organization, association, party, group or combination of persons, which approves, advocates, advises or practices the use of force, or violence, or other unlawful or unconstitutional means, to overthrow or make any change in either of the Governments so established; and that I am not bound by an allegiance to any foreign prince, potentate, state or sovereignty whatever. So help me God."

There was not then—and is not now—any reason to suspect that he had used the classroom to win students over to his political views.

3. On April 23, 1965, an all-night open discussion was held on American foreign policy with respect to Vietnam, similar to the "teach-ins" previously held at many other universities. The "teach-in" was organized by members of the Rutgers faculty. Tapes of Dr. Genovese's remarks at the "teach-in" show that he said in part:

"As I understand the 'teach-in,' it is not in any sense an enlarged classroom, but a place where professors and students can speak their minds on vital questions in a manner not ordinarily proper in class.

"I ought to make my framework clear at the outset and, in any case, I have no wish to hide any of my private intellectual or political commitments. But let me emphasize that in telling you where I stand on certain fundamental questions, it is first to put you on guard against my prejudices as you should be on guard against everyone's, especially your own, and secondly to suggest that no matter how deep the ideological and political divisions among us, that it is vital to our country's survival that we find a common basis on which to defend the peace. Those of you who know me know that I am a Marxist and a Socialist. Therefore, unlike most of my distinguished colleagues here this morning, I do not fear or regret the impending Vietcong victory in Vietnam. I welcome it."

In reporting the "teach-in" the student newspaper *Targum* condensed Professor Genovese's remarks to:

"I am a Marxist and a Socialist, and I would welcome a victory by the Vietcong." This statement in the *Targum* was picked up by the press, generally, and stimulated the present controversy.

The Board points out that the "teach-in" took place over three months ago. At that time the question of our next move in Vietnam was generally thought to be a much more open question than it is today. There was considerable confusion in the public mind about our role in Vietnam, and many people advocated the withdrawal of American troops, then still in the role of advisers. The meaning of "a victory of the Vietcong" today is interpreted as a victory over the American troops. Subsequent to the "teach-in," Professor Genovese denied ever favoring such a victory, but rather, said he had hoped for withdrawal of American troops, even though this would have permitted a victory of the Vietcong over the South Vietnam governmental troops.

4. On June 28 a report was made to the General Assembly of the State of New Jersey by a committee consisting of Assemblyman William V. Musto and Assemblyman Douglas E. Gimson on the Genovese case. The report pointed out that "the concern of our citizens is real and legitimate and should not be ignored." It disagreed completely with Dr. Genovese's views. It recommended that the Assembly ask the University Board of Governors and administration to re-examine its regulations, practices and procedures relating to personnel. It questioned Dr. Genovese's judgment and his sensitivity to the responsibility inherent in being a Rutgers professor.

And it included among its conclusions: "The inquiry of the undersigned disclosed no violation of the laws of this State, nor any infraction of the University regulations."

The question that has come before the Board divides itself into two parts:

1. Has Dr. Genovese in any way abused the privilege of academic freedom or violated professional ethics by his behavior as a scholar and as a teacher?
2. Were Dr. Genovese's actions or utterances at the time of the "teach-in" "both reprehensible and detrimental to the University" within the meaning of the University Regulations?

The Board of Governors concludes that Professor Genovese has done nothing in the performance of his academic duties that would constitute grounds for preferring charges against him.

The Board also concludes that his actions and utterances at the time of the "teach-in" were not "both reprehensible and detrimental to the University" within the meaning of the University Regulations.

The Board has also reviewed the University Regulations having to do with academic freedom. They are as follows:

3.91 The faculty are members of a great and honored profession; their conduct should be in accordance with standards dictated by law, professional ethics, and good morals, especially as members of the student body may be influenced by their example, and the opinion of the public with respect to the University may depend in considerable measure on their acts and utterances.

3.92 Since the very nature of a university and its value to society depend upon the free pursuit and dissemination of knowledge, every member of the faculty of this University is entitled, in the classroom and in research and in publication, freely to discuss subjects with which he is competent to deal, to pursue inquiry therein, and to present and endeavor to maintain his opinion and conclusions relevant thereto. While free to express those ideas which seem to him justified by the facts, he is expected to maintain standards of sound scholarship and competent teaching.

3.93 Outside the fields of instruction, research, and publication which are the subject of Section 3.92, the faculty member shall be free from institutional discipline unless his actions or utterances are both reprehensible and detrimental to the University.

The Board sees no present reason for revising these regulations.

The Board has re-examined its methods of judging candidates for promotions that carry tenure. The Board, being made up principally of laymen, feels that it must depend primarily upon the administration to judge a candidate's worthiness. The practice has been for the administration to present at each Board meeting a printed summary of the merits of each candidate whose promotion would involve tenure. Beyond this, the administration has been asked to call to the attention of the Board of Governors any unusual situations that might not appear in a printed résumé. This appears to the Board to be appropriate procedure.

Adopted unanimously by the following members of the Board of Governors of Rutgers – The State University in special meeting, August 6, 1965:

Charles H. Brower
Chairman, Board of Governors

Archibald S. Alexander
Mrs. Bessie Nelms Hill
Joel R. Jacobson
Charles A. Jurgensen
Mrs. John Moxon

Philip C. Muccilli
Roy F. Nichols
Roy M. D. Richardson

Dr. Mason W. Gross, President of the University, an ex-officio and nonvoting member of the Board, was also present.

The above-named voting members constituted a quorum.

The following letter was submitted to the Board of Governors and made a part of the record of the August 6 meeting:

RUTGERS – THE STATE UNIVERSITY
INTERDEPARTMENT COMMUNICATION

August 5, 1965

Dr. Mason W. Gross
President's Office
Old Queens

Dear Dr. Gross:

It has occurred to us that at the special meeting of the Board of Governors this Friday, there may possibly be some discussion of Professor Eugene Genovese's performance as a teacher. Although we feel that this aspect of a professor's conduct should not be called into question other than on the basis of very specific charges and that a proper determination of the weight of such charges must rest with his academic peers, we should like to offer some observations based on our acquaintance with Professor Genovese over the past two years.

Before appointing anyone in our department we conduct a wide canvass of the eligible scholars in the field, examine professional credentials, secure letters of reference from respected authorities, and interview candidates personally. In addition, in the instance of Professor Genovese, we read all of his published works. We assured ourselves as best we could that he was a well-trained scholar of considerable promise. During the two years he had been in our department he has more than justified our expectations of him as a teacher, scholar, and colleague. Some of us have heard him lecture, all of us have heard him read scholarly papers. We have observed that he is conscientious in meeting his teaching responsibilities and that his teaching has elicited favorable response from both undergraduate and graduate students. He has willingly and effectively served on departmental committees and has proved to be an agreeable and cooperative colleague in every way.

From all we know of Professor Genovese as a colleague we have never had any reason to believe that he has acted in an unprofessional manner in the classroom. As you know, it is not customary for us to monitor one another's classes, nor do we interrogate students about the performance of our colleagues. But we should expect to learn of any singular behavior by a member of our staff, and no such reports have come to our attention regarding Professor Genovese. His own introductory remarks at the "teach-in," in which he clearly stated his concept of his role in the classroom, would seem to be thoroughly in character.

Some may assert that because he has described his intellectual position as Marxist, Professor Genovese cannot therefore perform acceptably as a scholar. The test here, we believe, would be the professional evaluation of the articles that he has published and the book that will appear within the next few months. Members of our department hold widely varying beliefs in religion, in ethics, and in social and political philosophy, but we do feel strongly that none of these beliefs in itself disqualifies a man as a teacher or a scholar.

As historians we are all too well aware of the fact that in times of national crisis—as at present—a mood of hysteria usually develops and that those who stand apart in their public utterances from the popular senti- ments may become the victims of repressive persecution. We hope most fervently that sanity will prevail in the situation that now confronts us and that Professor Genovese will not be unjustly harassed for what are to him matters of conscience.

Sincerely yours,

Peter Charanis, Chairman
Department of History

Henry R. Winkler
Professor of History
Chairman 1960-64

Richard P. McCormick
Professor of History
Acting Chairman, March-June, 1965

BICENTENNIAL COMMITTEES
Student Committee

John G. LeVeck R'66, chairman
Susan E. Carlozzo, D'67, secretary

Elliot Abrutyn N'64	Elena M. Caruso D'67
Constance J. Allen D'66	Maureen F. Connelly SJ'66
Robert Baskin UC	Richard J. Countess SJ'66
John R. Baxendale R'66	Edward J. Dauber R'66
Sally Jo Beddoe D'67	James R. Dvorin R'66
Larry Benjamin R'66	Gary L. Falkin R'67
Jill M. Best SJ'66	Michael Feltman R'66
Robert J. Bluestone R'68	Stuart B. Finifter R'66
Craig Burlington R'66	Barbara L. Fisk D'66
Susan Canter N'67	Stephen J. Fritzsche SJ'66

Janice L. Goldsmith N'67
Joan F. Gorlin N'67
Margo S. Greenebaum N'66
Charles J. Hallahan, Jr. SJ'68
Carole A. Halsey SJ'66
Ted Hardies R'66
Wilma M. Harris D'66
Edward R. Hearn SJ'67
Lynn A. Holopigian N'66
Kenneth B. Hurdle N'66
Andrew Jacobs
Benjamin Kagan SJ
George Kandravy R'66
Edmond Klinger SJ'66
David P. Lefever SJ'65
Henry J. Leis SJ'66
L. James Lentz SJ'66
Edward Liston R'66
Jeffrey D. Lukowsky R'66
Leo Masciulli N'67
Marilyn Mason SJ'66
Keith E. McDermott R'66
Stanley Menker R'66
Joel Migdal R'66
Randolph J. Miller SJ'64
Sidney G. Nusbaum N'66

Thomas M. Palmieri N'64
Robert Peckar
Mary Polascik UC
Anne E. Roach D'67
Dorothy Robinson UC
Gene Rosen R'66
Joel Rosenberg
Rolf C. Rudestam R'66
Lawrence M. Rotgun R'67
Barry J. Sagotsky R'67
Susan E. Schnefel N'66
Morton S. Simon N'68
Charles F. Simpkins SJ'67
Thomas G. Sitzmann R'66
Terry Slater
Stanley Sorkin R'66
Peter D. Spear R'66
Dickson Spencer R'66
Barrie S. Stern N'66
Thomas J. Venables SJ'67
David R. Wasserman N'66
Neil S. Webber N'66
James W. Welsh N'67
John J. Woloszyn R'66
Barbara E. Wright D'68

Steering Committee

Dr. Richard Schlatter
Dr. Donald F. Cameron
Ernest T. Gardner
George H. Holsten, Jr.

Karl E. Metzger
Dr. Roy F. Nichols
John L. Swink
Dr. James A. Johnston

Camden Committee

W. Layton Hall
Dr. James B. Durand
J. Fredrik Ekstrom

M. Donald Kepner
Ralph L. Taylor

Newark Committee

Malcolm D. Talbott
Dr. John M. Cross
Marvin W. Greenberg

Irving Pawa
Herbert P. Woodward

Charter Day Committee

Dr. Marvin L. Granstrom
Van Wie Ingham
Dr. Charles F. Main, Jr.
Mr. John F. McDonald

Prof. Remigio U. Pane
Dr. Harry F. Stark
Dr. Thomas Weber
Dr. Ernest E. McMahon

Publications Committee

William Sloane
A. Paul Burton
Elizabeth Jessen
George J. Lukac

Dr. Richard P. McCormick
Earl S. Miers
Donald A. Sinclair
Jose A. Steinbock

Concerts and Lectures Committee

Mr. Julius Bloom, Chairman
Dr. Erwin R. Biel
Dr. Elizabeth Boyd

Dr. Houston Peterson
Dr. Richard Schlatter
Dr. F. Austin Walter

Convocation Committee

Mrs. Mason Gross
George H. Holsten, Jr.
Dr. Albert E. Meder, Jr.

Mr. Karl E. Metzger
Dr. Ernest R. Zimmerman

Alumni Committee

Ernest T. Gardner
John F. Anderson
William O. Barnes
Floyd H. Bragg
Dorothy Q. Cost
Herman Crystal
Thomas M. Geisler

William H. Hess
Robert Kaplan
William Levine
Richard Levis
George J. Lukac
Edgar L. Ropke
Barbara Smith

Alumni Relations Committee

Mrs. Alma G. Cap
Mrs. Marian G. Ewing
Mr. Ernest T. Gardner
Col. Vincent R. Kramer
Mrs. Grace M. Liefeld
Mr. George J. Lukac

Mr. Robert G. Lusardi
Miss Frances E. Riche
Mr. Walter C. Sibley
Miss Barbara M. Smith
Mr. Donald E. Stevens
Mr. George H. Holsten, Jr.

THE RUTGERS FACT BOOK OF 1966

The following has been reprinted—with some updating—from the Rutgers Fact Book of 1966 to provide a factual benchmark of the University in the year of its Bicentennial. It includes such information as the officers of the University, the educational and research units, course offerings, enrollment, degrees awarded at the 200th Anniversary Commencement, and, what may prove to be of especial value in the years ahead, the maps of the several campuses as they were in 1966.

THE RUTGERS SEAL

The Seal of Rutgers is an adaptation of that of the University of Utrecht in The Netherlands, an ancient seat of learning whose late Latin motto, surrounding a sunburst, is "Sol iustitiae nos illustra"—"Sun of righteousness, shine upon us"—based on two Biblical texts, "unto you . . . shall the Sun of righteousness arise," Malachi 4:2 and "then shall the righteous shine forth as the sun," Matthew 13:43. Rutgers, with its early connections with Dutch culture, asked a like boon for the Western world in this modification of the Utrecht seal: a stylized sunburst surrounded by the motto, "Sol iustitiae et occidentem illustra"—"Sun of righteousness, shine upon the West also."

THE OFFICERS OF THE UNIVERSITY

MASON W. GROSS .... *President*
RICHARD SCHLATTER .... *Provost and Vice President*
JOHN L. SWINK .... *Vice President and Treasurer*
MALCOLM D. TALBOTT .... *Vice President for Newark*
ALBERT E. MEDER, JR. .... *Vice Provost and Dean of the University*
KARL E. METZGER .... *Secretary of the University*
MAURICE T. AYERS .... *Assistant to the President*
DAVID D. DENKER .... *Director of the Greater University Fund
and Assistant to the President*
NORMAN D. STEVENS .... *Acting Librarian*
EARLE W. CLIFFORD, JR. .... *Dean of Student Affairs*
IRVING PAWA .... *Director of Alumni Relations*
GEORGE H. HOLSTEN, JR. .... *Director of Public Relations*
GEORGE A. KRAMER .... *Director of Admissions*

THE UNITS OF RUTGERS

New Brunswick

College of Arts and Sciences
    School of Chemistry
    School of Journalism
    Bureau of Biological Research
    Bureau of Mineral Research
    Bureau of Government Research

College of Agriculture and Environmental Science
    Division of Resident Instruction
    New Jersey Agricultural Experiment Station
    Co-operative Extension Service in Agriculture,
       Home Economics and 4-H
    Bureau of Conservation and Environmental Science
    Water Resources Research Institute
College of Engineering
    Bureau of Engineering Research
Graduate School of Education
    Division of Field Studies and Research
    New Jersey School Development Council
Douglass College
Graduate School
    Bureau of Economic Research
    Interdisciplinary Research Center
    Statistics Center
    Center of Alcohol Studies
Graduate School of Library Service
    Bureau of Information Sciences Research
Graduate School of Social Work
University College
Medical School
Library
University Extension Division
    Stonier Graduate School of Banking
    Institute of Management and Labor Relations
    Institute for Continuing Legal Education
    Bureau of Conferences
    Bureau of Community Services
    Bureau of Special Services
    Bureau of Social Work
    Bureau of Management Services
    Reading Center
    Government Services Training Program
Institute of Microbiology
Summer Session
Eagleton Institute of Politics
Urban Studies Center
Division of Physical Education
Division of Military Education
Rutgers University Press
Radiation Science Center
Center for Information Processing

Newark

Newark College of Arts and Sciences
    Institute of Animal Behavior
Graduate School of Business Administration
    Division of Public Accounting
College of Pharmacy
    Pharmaceutical Extension Service
School of Law
College of Nursing

Camden

College of South Jersey
School of Law, South Jersey Division

THE GOVERNING BOARDS

The Board of Governors, established under the New Jersey Legislature's reorganization act of 1956, has general supervision over and is vested with the conduct of the University. The Board is composed of eleven voting members and two ex officio: The Commissioner of Education and the President of the University. Six of the eleven voting members are named by the Governor of New Jersey with the consent of the Senate, while five are appointed from among its own members by the Board of Trustees. Governors serve six-year terms and may be reappointed once. They are unsalaried.

The Board of Trustees was designated under the reorganization act of 1956 to serve in an over-all advisory capacity to the University. The Trustees review the use of properties acquired prior to that act and invest funds under their control. The Trustees may exercise a veto on a selection for the University presidency.

Under a 1962 New Jersey statute, the Board of Trustees is authorized a maximum of 59 members. Of these, 25 are charter trustees who are elected by the Board. Eleven are public trustees appointed by the Governor with the advice and consent of the State Senate. (The six public trustees named by the Governor to the Board of Governors are automatically appointed trustees.) Not less than 12 or more than 20 are alumni trustees nominated by all 12 Rutgers alumni associations and elected by the Board. The President of the University and the State Commissioner of Education serve ex officio.

THE BOARD OF GOVERNORS

Archibald S. Alexander,
    Bernardsville

Charles H. Brower,
    Brielle

Philip J. Levin,
Mt. Bethel

William Levine,
Paterson

V. D. Mattia,
Essex Fells

Leslie G. McDouall,
Short Hills

Donald A. Millard,
Lincoln, Mass.

William C. Miller,
Englewood

Allan G. Mitchell,
Philadelphia, Pa.

Mrs. William A. Mitchell,
Lincoln Park

Mrs. John Moxon,
Berks County, Pa.

Philip C. Muccilli,
South Plainfield

Claire W. Nagle,
Bound Brook

Roy F. Nichols,
Philadelphia, Pa.

Frederick W. Pfister,
Saddle River

Norman Reitman,
Highland Park

Roy M. D. Richardson,
Brooklyn, N.Y.

Willard A. Sahloff,
Bridgeport, Conn.

Edgar T. Savidge,
New Brunswick

Irwin W. Sizer,
Lexington, Mass.

Frederic W. Smith,
Madison

Herbert H. Tate,
Newark

Mrs. S. Herbert Taylor,
Cherry Hill

George B. Underwood,
Short Hills

Tracy S. Voorhees,
Brooklyn, N.Y.

David A. Werblin,
Elberon

Grace M. Winterling,
Highland Park

Benjamin Wolfson,
Merchantville

Frederick O. Ziegler,
Merchantville

Hon. Frederick M. Raubinger,
ex officio, Princeton

Mason W. Gross,
ex officio, Piscataway

Officers

Chairman .... William C. Miller, Englewood
Vice Chairman .... Allan G. Mitchell, Philadelphia, Pa.
Vice Chairman .... Frederick O. Ziegler, Merchantville
Treasurer .... John L. Swink, Westfield
Secretary .... Karl E. Metzger, Piscataway

THE RUTGERS BICENTENNIAL

This fact book has a special purpose and interest since it is published in the year that Rutgers – The State University is celebrating its 200th anniversary.

As a vigorous and growing institution, Rutgers hopes that side by side with the celebration of its past, its plans for the future will be noted by all members of the Rutgers family and by friends of higher education everywhere.

The birthday festivities started with the proclamation of the Bicentennial Year by New Jersey's Governor Richard J. Hughes on January 4, but the high point of the celebration will be reached on September 22, date of the Bicentennial Convocation.

Universities throughout the world and the leading learned societies will be represented at this traditional event in the Rutgers Stadium. Thousands of delegates, guests and faculty, students and alumni are expected to attend.

The procession for this affair will be splashed with the color of academic gowns from hundreds of universities throughout this country and abroad.

Beyond the Bicentennial Convocation, the entire Rutgers calendar for 1966 will be enlivened by special programs or by enlargements of customary programs.

The Bicentennial Rutgers Concert Series in New Brunswick undoubtedly was the finest musical presentation in New Jersey of all time. Vladimir Horowitz, generally considered the world's foremost pianist, made his first appearance outside New York City in 14 years when he presented a special concert before an overflow audience as a special tribute to the Bicentennial. The concert series included appearances of such musical notables as the American pianist Abbey Simon, the Philadelphia Orchestra (with the University Choir), the Norwegian Festival Orchestra, the London Symphony (with the University Choir) and American basso Jerome Hines.

An Intercollegiate Student Conference, with the theme, "Ethics in Our Time," was held March 18-20.

Highlight of the Bicentennial from the standpoint of student participation was the Student Bicentennial Week, April 17-23, when undergraduates on each of the university's campuses were responsible for one day's program.

The Bicentennial Commencement on June 1 was an especially colorful event with some 4,000 graduates following in the footsteps of the single first graduate of Queen's College.

The football season of 1966 will also be of unusual interest. The game with Army on October 15 will be the first for which the entire Cadet Corps has appeared in Rutgers Stadium. The game with Columbia on October 22 will not only be the traditional Homecoming Game but also part of a day-long program which includes a demonstration crew race with Columbia on the Raritan River, an evening picnic and a fireworks display.

On November 10, the day the University's charter was signed by Royal Governor William Franklin, Rutgers men throughout the world are expected to gather together wherever they are to give a toast to Alma

Mater. A specially-prepared film strip will be shown by Rutgers Clubs on that day and the Rutgers family will gather on the campus to join in this concluding event of the Bicentennial Year.

ADMISSION TO THE UNIVERSITY

By Dr. George A. Kramer
Director of Admissions

Rutgers – The State University consists of a number of colleges in different locations throughout the State. The curricula, size, and historical development of these colleges differ considerably.

Each year an increasingly larger number of prospective freshmen seek admission to each college of the University. Since it has not been possible to construct facilities to meet the demands of students seeking acceptance, admission is both selective and competitive.

Admission is selective because freshmen must be able to meet the academic demands placed upon them by the faculties of the colleges of the University. Strong preparation in such disciplines as reading, writing, mathematics, the sciences, and foreign languages is required of each candidate. In addition to this, a prospective freshman is expected to be sufficiently interested in one or all of these basic disciplines to have a strong desire to pursue work at the college level. Selective admission attempts to identify those prospective students who have had strong training in these disciplines and who possess that degree of curiosity which indicates they are ready and prepared to pursue college work.

Admission becomes competitive when there are more qualified students seeking admission than existing facilities can accommodate. A program of competitive admissions attempts to choose the best qualified students from those who have met standards of the selective process. Each undergraduate college of the University is both selective and competitive in admission.

The University follows certain priorities in administering its admissions program:

1. Full consideration is given all applications received prior to February 15 of the year in which the candidate seeks admission.

2. Rutgers, as The State University, gives priority to students who are residents of the State of New Jersey. Out-of-state students are admitted, but this number in any particular class is a limited one. As a result, admission for out-of-state students is even more competitive than for State residents.

3. Sons and daughters of alumni of Rutgers are considered in the same competitive category as residents of New Jersey.

For the semester beginning in September, 1965, 15,000 prospective freshmen made application for admission to the University. Of this number

6,800 were granted admission, and 3,500 of the 6,800 elected to attend a division of the University. It is evident that during the next several years, the number of applicants for admission will far exceed the ability of the University to supply the facilities needed for the qualified candidates.

THE PROGRAMS OF STUDY AVAILABLE AT VARIOUS UNITS

Rutgers College

The men's resident division was founded in 1766 as Queen's College. Located in New Brunswick, Rutgers College offers programs through the College of Arts and Sciences, College of Engineering, and College of Agriculture and Environmental Science. Most of the student body of 5600 reside in the University's modern dormitories.

Agriculture
  Agricultural Business
  Animal Science
    (including Pre-Veterinary)
  General Agricultural Science
  Plant Science
  Preparation for Research
Engineering (four and five year)
  Agricultural Engineering
  Ceramic Engineering
  Ceramics
  Chemical Engineering
  Civil Engineering
  Electrical Engineering
  Industrial Engineering
  Mechanical Engineering
  Planning Engineering
Arts and Sciences
  American Civilization
  Art
  Biological Sciences
  Business Administration
  Chemistry
  Classics
  Dramatic Art
  Economics

English
Geography
Geology
German
History
Journalism
Latin-American Civilization
Mathematics
Music
Philosophy
Physics
Political Science
Psychology
Romance Languages
Russian
Russian-Area Program
Sanitary Science
Sociology
Statistics
Physical Education
Pre-Dentistry
Pre-Law
Pre-Medicine
Pre-Pharmacy (one year)
Pre-Veterinary (see Agriculture)

Douglass

The University's coordinate women's college has a student body of 2700. The majority of these students live in dormitory or cottage units on campus; about 20 per cent commute from their parents' homes. The academic programs lie primarily in the liberal arts; in addition, many pre-professional and professional courses are offered.

Agriculture (see Rutgers College)
Chemistry, Foods and Nutrition
  Engineering
  (four and five year)
  (see Rutgers College)
Home Economics
Journalism
  Arts
  Bacteriology
  Biological Sciences
  Chemistry
  Civilization in the United
    States
  Classical Civilization
  Dramatic Art
  Economics
  English
  French
  Geography
  German
  History

Latin-American Studies
Mathematics
Music
Philosophy
Physics
Political Science
Psychology
Religion
Russian
Russian Studies
Sociology
Spanish
Speech Therapy
Statistics
Medical Technology
Physical Education
Pre-Law
Pre-Medicine
Pre-Nursing
Pre-Pharmacy

Rutgers-Newark

Is coeducational, and most students commute daily. The College of Arts and Sciences offers majors in liberal arts and pre-professional programs. The College of Nursing, the College of Pharmacy, the School of Business Administration, and the School of Law provide professional training. The enrollment of the undergraduate college in Newark is 3,200.

Five-year Engineering
  (first two years)
Arts and Sciences
  Art
  Biology
  Business Administration
  Chemistry
  Classics
  Comparative Literature
  Dramatic Arts
  Economics
  English
  French
  Geology

German
History
Mathematics
Music
Philosophy
Physics
Physiology and Biochemistry
Political Science
Psychology
Sociology
Spanish
Statistics
Zoology
Medical Technology

Nursing
Pharmacy
Pre-Dentistry
Pre-Law

Pre-Medicine
Pre-Pharmacy (one year)
Pre-Veterinary (one year)

College of South Jersey

In Camden offers pre-professional, business, and liberal arts programs. A division of the School of Law is located in Camden. As at Rutgers in Newark, the great majority of the men and women students commute. The undergraduate enrollment at Camden is 950.

Five-year Engineering
  (first two years)
Arts and Sciences
  Biology
  Business
  Chemistry
  Economics and Business
    Administration
  English
  Foreign Languages
  Geology
  History

Mathematics
Political Science
Psychology
Sociology
Statistics
Medical Technology
Pre-Agriculture (one year)
Pre-Dentistry
Pre-Law
Pre-Medicine
Pre-Pharmacy (one year)
Pre-Veterinary (one year)

University College

Offers the mature part-time student the opportunity to pursue a college degree in evening study. Currently, 7,700 men and women study at University College centers in Camden, Jersey City, Newark, New Brunswick, and Paterson.

Accounting
Home Economics
Arts and Sciences
  Chemistry
  Economics
  English
  History
  Mathematics
  Political Science

Psychology
Sociology
Statistics
Management
Marketing

Preparation for secondary school teaching is available at each of the University's liberal arts colleges.

STUDENT ENROLLMENT

In the fall of 1966 Rutgers University enrolled 26,116 college credit students. Naturally the bulk of the student body (about 90 percent) came from the State of New Jersey but there also were representatives from forty-six of the states, the District of Columbia, and Puerto Rico in the student mix and there were 172 students from foreign lands.

The annual geographic tabulation (made each fall by the University Registrar) shows that every county and virtually every community in New Jersey have students enrolled in the State University.

Student delegations are roughly proportional to the population of the counties, although proximity to University units is also an important factor. Thus Middlesex County, of which New Brunswick is the county seat, has the largest delegation. Other large delegations are from Essex, Bergen, Camden, Hudson, and Union counties.

University College was the largest single unit within the University, enrolling 7,868 students working toward degrees in evening courses, almost all of them part-time students. Rutgers College enrolled 6,246 students; Douglass, the coordinate women's college, 2,840; the undergraduate colleges in Newark, 2,743; the College of South Jersey at Camden, 1,035; and the graduate and professional schools, 5,384.

Enrollment by New Jersey Counties*

Atlantic County	210	Middlesex County	4,152
Bergen County	2,276	Monmouth County	1,023
Burlington County	659	Morris County	723
Camden County	1,807	Ocean County	274
Cape May County	52	Passaic County	1,299
Cumberland County	166	Salem County	97
Essex County	3,601	Somerset County	1,302
Gloucester County	378	Sussex County	90
Hudson County	1,809	Union County	2,561
Hunterdon County	183	Warren County	103
Mercer County	715	Total	23,480

Student Enrollment by State*

Alabama	6	Indiana	8
Alaska	2	Iowa	10
Arizona	4	Kansas	5
California	39	Kentucky	7
Colorado	6	Louisiana	2
Connecticut	114	Maine	23
Delaware	17	Maryland	122
District of Columbia	20	Massachusetts	130
Florida	27	Michigan	19
Georgia	11	Minnesota	13
Hawaii	9	Mississippi	2
Illinois	42	Missouri	7

*As of October 14, 1966.

Montana	1	Texas	7
Nebraska	3	Utah	6
Nevada	1	Vermont	8
New Hampshire	15	Virginia	53
New Mexico	2	Washington	6
New York	1,028	West Virginia	6
North Carolina	13	Wisconsin	11
North Dakota	2	Wyoming	2
Ohio	88	Canal Zone	2
Oregon	9	Puerto Rico	8
Pennsylvania	507	Total	2,464
Rhode Island	29		
South Carolina	10	Foreign	172
Tennessee	3	Grand Total	26,116

DEGREES AWARDED

Advanced Degrees   *1966**

Doctor of Philosophy	122
Doctor of Education	38
Specialist in Education	6
Master of Arts	158
Master of Arts (sst)	31
Master of Fine Arts	9
Master of Science	220
Master of Science for Teachers	1
Master of Education	268
Master of Library Service	177
Master of Social Work	70
Master of Business Administration	99
Bachelor of Laws—Newark	98
Bachelor of Laws—Camden	29
	1326

sst: Special Curriculum for Secondary School
     Teachers (Graduate School and Graduate
     School of Education)

Douglass College   Bachelor Degrees   *1966*

Bachelor of Arts	505
Bachelor of Science (Chemistry, Foods and Nutrition)	2
Bachelor of Science (Home Economics)	24
Bachelor of Science (Medical Technology)	1
Bachelor of Science (Physical Education)	8
	540

*Includes degrees dated October, 1965, January, 1966, and June, 1966.

College of Agriculture and Environmental Science	*1966*
Bachelor of Science	99
College of Arts and Sciences	
Bachelor of Arts	816
Bachelor of Science (Chemistry)	7
Bachelor of Science (Physical Education)	10
	833
Graduate School of Education	
Bachelor of Science, In-Service Teachers	12
College of Engineering	
Bachelor of Science (Ceramics)	10
Bachelor of Science (Ceramic Engineering)	7
Bachelor of Science (Chemical Engineering)	11
Bachelor of Science (Civil Engineering)	11
Bachelor of Science (Electrical Engineering)	50
Bachelor of Science (Industrial Engineering)	14
Bachelor of Science (Mechanical Engineering)	27
Bachelor of Science (Planning Engineering)	1
Bachelor of Science (Sanitary Engineering)	1
	132
Newark Colleges of Arts and Sciences	
Bachelor of Arts	415
Bachelor of Science (Medical Technology)	9
Bachelor of Science (Pharmacy)	45
	469
Graduate School of Business Administration	
Bachelor of Science	1
College of Agriculture and Engineering	
Bachelor of Science	
College of Nursing	
Bachelor of Science	25
College of Pharmacy	
Bachelor of Pharmacy	47
College of South Jersey	
Bachelor of Arts	165
Bachelor of Science (Medical Technology)	1
	166

University College	*1966*
Bachelor of Arts	125
Bachelor of Science	164
Bachelor of Science (Home Economics)	3
	292

Associate Degrees

College of Nursing	*1966*
Associate in Science	1

University College	
Associate in Science (Business Science)	39
Associate in Science (Chemistry)	1
	40

TOTAL	3,983

The Cost of a Rutgers Education

The annual appropriation by the State to Rutgers makes it possible to hold tuition costs substantially below those of private institutions offering educational services of comparable quality.

The tuition for full-time undergraduates who are legal residents of New Jersey is $400 annually. The cost of fees and books varies from campus to campus depending on course work.

Nonresidents of New Jersey pay an additional $118 per term in tuition.

On-campus students at Rutgers, Douglass, and University Heights pay $900 a school year for room and board. Commuting students at all colleges may purchase meals through University dining halls or snack bars.

Total costs for resident students amounts to between $1,400 and $1,500 annually, exclusive of personal expenditures. Commuting students' costs annually are between $600 and $700, but this is exclusive of personal expenditures, food, and transportation.

Full-time day students at the School of Law and Graduate School of Business Administration have a basic tuition of $500 annually. Tuition at the Medical School when it admits its first class in the fall of 1966 will be $750 annually for New Jersey residents and $1,000 for out-of-state students.

Part-time undergraduate students are charged $13.50 per credit hour. Graduate part-time tuition is $16 per credit hour except in the Graduate School of Business Administration, where the charge is $20 per hour.

Financial assistance to students at the State University is considerable and growing. About one third of the undergraduates in the University's day colleges in New Brunswick, Newark and Camden during the year 1964-65 held scholarships with a total value of $1,581,300.

Some 1,200 undergraduates received about $720,000 in loans and more than 2,400 students were placed in part-time jobs with a total wage of more than $1,082,000.

Financial assistance is offered principally through the State University Office of Financial Aid, which functions on the various campuses as a service to students in the solution of problems accompanying college financing.

However, a new and major form of assistance began in November, 1965, with enactment of the Federal Higher Education Aid Act.

Assistance through the Rutgers Office of Financial Aid is available in three basic forms:

1. Scholarships—awarded annually on a competitive basis to incoming freshmen. Academic performance in the secondary school, financial need, scholastic aptitude test scores, character and extra-curricular contributions to secondary school and community are major factors in scholarship competition. Undergraduates may continue to apply for scholarship assistance throughout their collegiate career, depending on financial need and satisfactory personal and academic record. More than half the scholarships held by undergraduates are granted by the State. State scholarships provide $400 annually and application for them is made to the State Scholarship Commission. The University has no part in the award.

2. Loan Funds—The main source of financial assistance through higher education loans is through the National Defense Student Loan Program. Each aid office is equipped to offer information and applications to procure a loan through the various state loan programs such as the New Jersey Higher Education Assistance Authority and the New York Higher Education Assistance Authority. Finally, there are University loans available to cover short term emergency situations that cannot be handled through federal or state plans.

3. Student Employment—is available on a part-time basis to undergraduates in all colleges of the University. Every effort is made to assist the student in finding employment which most nearly meets his needs, interest, and abilities. Summer employment is an important source of income in meeting college expenses and financial aid offices on all campuses are prepared to help undergraduates find summer employment.

Under the Federal Higher Education Aid Act it is expected that nationally about 140,000 men and women will be eligible for scholarships of from $200-$1,000 per year. Under the same act, colleges may provide federally financed work-while-you-learn jobs paying up to $500 per year.

The exact impact of this new act, the first such legislation in support of higher education in U.S. history, at Rutgers and other universities cannot be measured at the present time but it is expected to be enormous.

In addition to the Higher Education Aid Act, two other forms of Federal assistance are of importance. Under the Student Employment College Work Study Program (part of the Economic Opportunity Act of

1964) underprivileged students are allowed to work up to 15 hours a week in an area related to their studies or future profession.

Finally, there is the federal long-term, low-interest loan program. More than 1,000 Rutgers students took advantage of this assistance opportunity during the 1964-65 academic year.

Many scholarships and fellowships are available at the graduate level, a substantial number of them from industrial concerns seeking to advance careers of outstanding students.

THE COLLEGES OF THE UNIVERSITY

Colleges and Divisions	Founded	Location	Dean or Director	No. Students	Degrees Granted—1966
College of Arts and Sciences (Rutgers)	1766	New Brunswick	Arnold B. Grobman	4,623	833
College of Agriculture and Environmental Science	1864	New Brunswick	Leland G. Merrill, Jr.	614	99
College of Engineering	1864	New Brunswick	Elmer C. Easton	1,009	132
Graduate School of Education	1923	New Brunswick	John J. O'Neill	1,114	356
Douglass College	1918	New Brunswick	Margaret A. Judson (Acting)	2,840	540
Graduate School	1876	New Brunswick	Henry C. Torrey	2,659	509
Graduate School of Library Service	1953	New Brunswick	Neal Harlow	367	177
Graduate School of Social Work	1953	New Brunswick	Werner W. Boehm	219	70
University College (Evening School)	1934	New Brunswick, Camden, Newark, Jersey City and Paterson	G. Stuart Demarest	7,868	332
University Extension[1]	1925	New Brunswick, Camden, Newark, Jersey City and Paterson (and off campus)	Ernest E. McMahon	3,781	...
Medical School[2]	1961	New Brunswick	DeWitt Stetten, Jr.	16	...
Newark College of Arts and Sciences[4]	1946	Newark	William N. Gilliland	2,346	469
Graduate School of Business Administration	1946	Newark	Horace J. De Podvin	429	100
College of Pharmacy	1927	Newark	Roy A. Bowers	207	47
School of Law[4]	1927	Newark, Camden	C. Willard Heckel	580	127
College of Nursing	1956	Newark	Laura B. Chapman	190	26
College of South Jersey[3]	1950	Camden	W. Layton Hall	1,035	166
Livingston College[3]	1965	New Brunswick	Ernest A. Lynton	...	...

[1] Does not grant degrees.
[2] First class entered in fall of 1966.
[3] On drawing board.
[4] Founding date is of inclusion within University system.

Rank and Scale of the Faculty

Faculty Distribution by Rank

Deans	19
Directors	14
Professors	377
Associate Professors	343
Assistant Professors	450
Instructors	306
Assistant Instructors	250
Professors of Law	21
Associate Professors of Law	4
Assistant Professors of Law	7

Medical—Basic Sciences

Professors	5
Associate Professors	4
Assistant Professors	5

Medical—Pathology and Clinical Sciences

Professors	5
Associate Professors	4
Assistant Professors	2
Military and Air Sciences	12
Total Academic Full-Time Equivalent	2,083

Faculty Salary Scale, July 1, 1966

General

Professor, 10 month appointment	$11,431-24,080
Professor, 12 month appointment	12,603-26,538
Associate Professor, 10 month appointment	9,405-15,515
Associate Professor, 12 month appointment	10,369-17,103
Assistant Professor, 10 month appointment	7,737-11,607
Assistant Professor, 12 month appointment	8,530-12,800
Instructor, 10 month appointment	6,684- 9,356
Instructor, 12 month appointment	7,369-10,313

School of Law

Distinguished Professor of Law	16,890-25,340
Professor of Law	13,895-20,845
Associate Professor of Law	12,003-18,003
Assistant Professor of Law	9,875-14,815

Medical School (All 12 Month Appt.)

Basic Sciences

Distinguished Professor	20,531-28,747
Professor	17,735-26,605
Associate Professor	14,590-20,430
Assistant Professor	12,003-16,803

Pathology and Clinical Sciences

Professor	20,531-28,747
Associate Professor	17,735-26,605
Assistant Professor	14,590-20,430

FROM COLONIAL COLLEGE TO STATE UNIVERSITY . . .

A BRIEF RUTGERS HISTORY

Only one university in the United States can claim a colonial background, designation as a land-grant college and the status of a state university. Rutgers, New Jersey's State University, has this distinction.

Rutgers, now one of the major universities in this country with more than 25,000 students enrolled in college credit courses in the fall of 1965, had its beginnings when clergymen of the Dutch Reformed Church in America launched a movement for a new college in the Province of New Jersey in the mid-eighteenth century.

As a result of their efforts, Royal Governor William Franklin granted a charter for the college in the name of King George III of England on Nov. 10, 1766.

The college was the eighth founded in the colonies and it had the humble origins typical of such institutions. Early efforts by the Rev. Theodore Frelinghuysen and his associates to found a college had met with disappointments and conflict.

Frelinghuysen, a minister of the Reformed Church, had crusaded in Amsterdam as early as 1759 for help in establishing a Dutch institution in the colonies, but his efforts were frustrated by the determined opposition of members of the church in the Netherlands.

Even after the charter was granted in 1766, five years were to elapse before the work of the college began.

A second charter, under which the college work actually got under way, was issued by Governor Franklin in 1770. It gave the institution the name of Queen's College in honor of Charlotte of Mecklenburg, the Royal Consort.

There is no known copy of the first charter in existence, but it seems certain that the charter of 1770 was very substantially the same. Under it, the Dutch settlers—both from New Jersey and from the Dutch settlements in the Hudson valley—who founded Rutgers were charged with the "education of youth in the learned languages, liberal and useful arts and sciences . . ."

First Classes in a Tavern

Classes first opened in 1771 in a tavern in New Brunswick, "The Sign of the Red Lion." The first and for some time only tutor at Queen's College was Frederick Frelinghuysen, a nephew of Theodore, the clergyman-pioneer. Young Frederick, only 18 or 19 when he accepted the teaching assignment, had just received his Bachelor of Arts degree at Princeton, then known as the College of New Jersey.

The College's first commencement was held on Oct. 12, 1774. The Rev. Jacob Rutsen Hardenbergh, who was later to become president of the institution, presided at this graduation ceremony and delivered an eloquent address on the proposition "that men of learning are of absolute necessity and extensive advantages to society." There was a single graduate at that first commencement, Matthew Leydt, who was 19 years old. Leydt was the son of a trustee, John, who was a clergyman in New Brunswick and one of the founders of the tiny college.

Not much is known about the younger Leydt beyond the facts that he was ordained a minister in the Dutch Reformed Church and held pastorates in Pennsylvania and New Jersey before his death in 1783. He was elected to the college's Board of Trustees in the year of his death and was the first graduate named to that body.

Early Struggles

The Revolutionary War almost ended the history of the infant Queen's College shortly after it began. A number of its students took up arms against the British and the actual location of the college was shifted several times as General Howe's army pursued Washington through New Jersey.

The first building built for the College was completed in 1791. It stood near the present Monument Square in downtown New Brunswick. It was not until 1809, however, that work began on Rutgers' oldest college structure, Queens. Original estimates called for the expenditure on it of $12,000, but when the building was finished, the cost was closer to $30,000, a not inconsiderable sum in those times.

When the handsome three-story brownstone building was completed, it housed professors and their families, classrooms, a library and chapel. It is now the administrative center of Rutgers and is a symbol of the university for students, faculty, alumni and friends of the institution throughout the world.

The completion of Old Queens by no means ended the financial problems of the young College, and twice during this period it continued to exist only through the Grammar School, forerunner of Rutgers Preparatory School.

There were to be other financial crises in the years ahead, but matters improved in 1825 after the trustees had renamed the institution Rutgers in honor of Colonel Henry Rutgers. A New York philanthropist and Revolutionary War soldier, he gave the college modest financial assistance and the bell which still hangs in the cupola of Old Queens.

Land-Grant and a New Role

During its early years, Rutgers, like most other colleges of the period, was almost exclusively a classical or liberal arts institution. In 1864, however, the Rutgers Scientific School, which soon included departments of agriculture, engineering, and chemistry, was organized and Rutgers was designated by the State Legislature as the Land-Grant College of New Jersey.

This major and decisive change in the fundamental character and work of Rutgers College was given even greater importance in 1880 when the State of New Jersey established the New Jersey Agricultural Experiment Station on the Rutgers campus.

Development of the College picked up speed after the beginning of the twentieth century. A ceramics department was organized, the Agricultural Experiment Station began its first formal program of extension work—soon to be organized as the nation-wide Cooperative Extension Service in Agriculture and Home Economics—and it held its first summer session.

Douglass College, now the coordinate women's college of the University, was established as the New Jersey College for Women in New Brunswick in 1918. It was renamed in 1955 in honor of its first dean, the late Mable Smith Douglass, and has since become one of the largest women's colleges in the nation.

Other divisions were soon added, including the School of Education (now Graduate School of Education) in 1923, an Extension Division in 1925, a College of Pharmacy (the New Jersey College of Pharmacy) in 1927, and University College, the degree-granting evening division, in 1934.

University—State University

Rutgers College assumed university status in 1924, and in 1945, after an association with the State reaching back to 1864, all of the University's divisions were designated as the State University of New Jersey.

When New Jersey decided to extend the designation of "State University" to all the units of Rutgers University, it was a comparatively small institution with a fraction of its present enrollment.

By 1945, however, it had become clear to many in positions of leadership in the State that there was an urgent demand for greatly expanded public higher education facilities in New Jersey.

On March 26, 1945, the State Legislature moved toward a solution of the problem when it approved an act which extended the designation of State University, previously given to the College of Agriculture, College of Engineering, Douglass College, and the College of Pharmacy, to all divisions to be "utilized as an instrumentality of the State for providing higher education and thereby to increase the efficiency of the public school system in the state."

Under this act, the New Jersey Agricultural Experiment Station became a part of the State University. Prior to this legislation, it had been located on the Rutgers campus in New Brunswick, but had not been a part of the University.

Campuses in Newark and Camden

During this period, the growing State University took two steps which were to give it major campuses in Newark and Camden. In 1946 the former University of Newark was incorporated into the University and Rutgers acquired a College of Arts and Sciences, a Law School, a College of Nursing and a School of Business (now the Graduate School of Business Administration). These together with the College of Pharmacy make up the Rutgers Colleges in Newark, institutions which now enroll about 3,600 students, including nearly 2,600 undergraduates and about 1,000 in professional and graduate courses.

Four years later, the College of South Jersey at Camden, consisting of a two-year college and a law school, was merged with the State University. The College, now expanded to a full four-year program, has almost 900 students and the law school about 130.

In both Newark and Camden the State University has participated in urban redevelopment programs which have removed old and dilapidated buildings to make way for modern university structures. In Newark, a fine law building has been opened for use as the first of the new structures to be erected on the campus there. In Camden, Rutgers is already using a new science building and a new student center and is soon to start construction on a classroom-office building.

A library had been built earlier on the Camden campus as the start of the new facilities for that college.

Board of Governors Created

The relationship between Rutgers and the State was carried a step further in 1956 when the Legislature, on the proposal of the Rutgers Board of Trustees, created a Board of Governors to serve as the governing body of the University. The name of the institution was also changed under this act to Rutgers – The State University.

The Board of Governors thus created is composed of 11 voting members, six appointed by the Governor of New Jersey with the advice and consent of the New Jersey Senate, and five elected by and from the Board of Trustees. This gave the State the majority voice in the control of the University. There are also two ex officio members, the State Commissioner of Education and the President of the University.

Since 1956 the State University has grown rapidly in enrollment, in physical facilities and in the variety and depth of its educational and research programs, particularly in the graduate and professional schools. In the fall of 1965 it enrolled more than 25,000 degree students in 16 colleges, including about 12,000 full-time undergraduates, 6,0000 graduate and professional students and more than 7,000 part-time students. Almost another 25,000 persons benefit each year from the University's educational offerings through extension programs, short courses and summer sessions.

While the undergraduate student body has grown tremendously in this period, growth of the graduate and professional student body has been even more spectacular. At the 1965 commencement, the State University awarded 137 Doctor of Philosophy degrees and 1,130 other advanced degrees. In addition to its Graduate School for advanced work in the liberal arts and sciences, the University has specialized graduate schools in education, business, social work and library service, and conducts law schools in Newark and Camden. A two-year medical school has been under development for several years and will admit its first class in the fall of the Bicentennial Year.

Recent Growth

Two college bond issues, approved by the voters of the State in 1959 and 1964, provided $29,850,000 and $10,069,000, respectively, for the State University. The bond issues were the base funds which, augmented by borrowing, federal funds, foundation grants and gifts, have financed a building program of more than $133,375,000 for residence halls, classrooms, laboratories, student centers and libraries on the principal campuses in New Brunswick, Newark, and Camden.

But while it has grown rapidly in recent years, Rutgers is still unable to accommodate all the qualified young people seeking admission. A committee of New Jersey citizens, including leaders in industry, business and education and headed by Dr. Robert F. Goheen, president of Princeton University, has warned that deficiencies in provision for higher education is one of the State's major problems and has advocated major expansion of the public colleges to meet the need.

The State University has formulated its own plans for future development to provide for a doubling of enrollment by 1975. This program, based on a study made for the University by the Cleveland management consulting firm, Robert Heller Associates, would provide physical facilities at New Brunswick, Newark and Camden to increase full-time undergraduate day-time enrollment from about 12,000 to 27,000 and increase full-time graduate enrollment from 2,700 to 6,600. It calls for the completion of two new colleges on the Kilmer Area campus and for the expansion of the two-year Rutgers Medical School to a full four-year school with teaching hospital.

Implementation of this program, which has a price tag of more than $288,000,000, depends on appropriation of State funds as the basic financing, but the total cost would also be met by borrowing, by federal grants, foundation aid and gifts to the University.

THE COMPLEX RELATIONSHIP
BETWEEN UNIVERSITY AND STATE

Rutgers – The State University is the capstone of the New Jersey public education system. An instrumentality of the State, it is charged with and dedicated to providing higher education in New Jersey and is governed by a Board of Governors whose majority is appointed by the Governor of the State with the advice and consent of the State Senate.

The present relationship between Rutgers and the State is a complex one which began more than a century ago. Historically Rutgers and the State of New Jersey (and its predecessor, the Province of New Jersey) have shared mutual interest since the original charter was granted by King George III of England. That document provided that the Governor of the Province should be president of the Board of Trustees and preside at the meetings he attended. This was amended through the years, but the Governor of the State continued to hold membership on the Board until the reorganization of the University under an act of the Legislature in 1956.

This act, under which the University is now governed, renamed it Rutgers – The State University, and a Board of Governors was established to manage and administer it.

The act of 1956 provided among other things that: "The Board of Governors shall have general supervision over and be vested with the conduct of the University: It shall have the authority and responsibility to:

1. Determine policies for the organization, administration, and development of the University;

2. Study the educational and financial needs of the University, annually acquaint the Governor and the Legislature with the condition of the University, and prepare and jointly with the State Board of Education, present the annual budget to the Governor and Legislature, in accordance with law."

The Board of Trustees continued in an advisory and trustee capacity, including review of the use of those properties—funds, real estate, other gifts to the University—which it had held prior to the reorganization.

The actual working relationship between Rutgers and the State began on March 21, 1863, when the New Jersey Legislature accepted the grant of land provided under the first Morrill Act. On April 4, 1864, the Legislature voted to pay the interest from the proceeds of the land grant to Rutgers College on a semiannual basis and further provided that the trustees of the college "shall devote such interest wholly and exclusively to the maintenance in that Department of Rutgers College known as Rutgers Scientific School, of such courses of instruction . . . as shall carry out the intent of said Act of Congress in the manner specifically described." From that act until the present, the ties between Rutgers and the State have steadily grown stronger.

On March 10, 1880, the State established the New Jersey Agricultural Experiment Station "for the benefit of practical and scientific agriculture, and for the development of our unimproved lands." This station was located on the experimental farm which the trustees of Rutgers College had purchased to meet their responsibilities under the legislative act of 1864. During the years which followed there developed at Rutgers one of the outstanding agricultural experiment stations in the nation.

Subsequent acts of the New Jersey Legislature designated the Agricultural Experiment Station and the "State College for the Benefit of Agriculture and Mechanic Arts of Rutgers College" as the recipient of various federal grants and programs for the purpose of increasing agricultural production.

In 1904 a court decision, upheld by the State's highest court one year later, ruled that it was constitutional to provide funds for Rutgers from the State's general funds. This was a significant ruling and stemmed from a suit by Rutgers to secure funds due the College under the Scholarship Act of 1890, which committed the State to make payments for 60 tuition scholarships a year at Rutgers.

On March 15, 1917, the Legislature named the Rutgers Scientific School, which included the College of Agriculture and the College of Engineering, as the State University of New Jersey. One year later the Trustees of Rutgers established the New Jersey College for Women (now Douglass College) as a coordinate college of Rutgers. In 1927 the former New Jersey College of Pharmacy became a part of Rutgers University, as the colleges had collectively become known in 1924.

By the end of World War II it had become increasingly clear that New Jersey would have to do something to meet the needs of its young people for public higher education and the State was ready to take another step in developing this relationship.

On March 26, 1945, the State Legislature approved an act which designated all units of Rutgers University as the State University of New Jersey to "be utilized as an instrumentality of the State for providing public higher education and thereby increase the efficiency of the public school system of the State." Under this act the New Jersey Agricultural Experiment Station, which, though located on the campus, had not been a part of Rutgers, also became an integral part of the State University.

Rutgers by this act became in its entirety the State University of New Jersey. The present relationship between New Jersey and Rutgers – The State University were clarified and formalized eleven years later under the act of 1956.

THE SPECIALIZED DIVISIONS
SERVE PARTICULAR AREAS

A large, modern university is a multidimensional institution. This is especially so in the case of a state university faced with the responsibility of providing the many services required in a complex, highly urbanized society. Among the particularly noteworthy divisions in the State University created in large part to meet these demands are the following:

Institute of Microbiology

The Institute of Microbiology, located on the University Heights campus, treats microbiology as a fundamental science. The Institute, founded in 1954, grew out of the work of the Nobel laureate, Dr. Selman

A. Waksman, in the discovery of streptomycin, the antibiotic that played a major role in the conquest of tuberculosis and the development of other antibiotic miracles. The Institute's scientific program investigates microorganisms from the standpoint of occurrence and classification, physiology, genetics, biochemistry, and the relationship between microbes and the higher forms of life, such as man and domesticated animals and plants.

Center of Alcohol Studies

The Rutgers Center of Alcohol Studies was developed at Yale University and moved to the University Heights campus in 1962 with the help of a grant from the National Institute of Mental Health.

It is an interdisciplinary center which operates as a department of the Graduate School and draws upon scholars with relevant skills throughout the University.

Eagleton Institute of Politics

The Eagleton Institute of Politics was established on the Douglass College campus to advance learning in the fields of practical political affairs and government. Its work is based on the belief that the two-party system is vital to the conduct of American public affairs. The Institute offers courses accepted by the Graduate School toward the Master of Arts degree and it sponsors programs designed to encourage undergraduate interest in practical politics. The Institute extends its work throughout New Jersey in a variety of ways—by serving as the New Jersey affiliate of the National Center for Education in Politics, under which it directs programs in politics for students at 17 New Jersey colleges and universities; by developing filmed courses and textbooks for use in the 12th grade of high school, by sponsoring research in politics through a grant-in-aid program to individual scholars; and by publishing a series of case studies which can be used as instructional material in college classrooms. The Institute is named for the late Dr. and Mrs. Wells P. Eagleton. A bequest from Mrs. Eagleton established the Institute and provides its major support.

Urban Studies Center

The Urban Studies Center was established in New Brunswick in 1959 under a Ford Foundation grant to marshal the resources of the University to assist public and private agencies in solving social, economic, and political problems facing urban communities. With the most urban state in the nation as a laboratory, the Center is developing a program of research, education, and extension, built in part on the University's experience with agricultural extension and its historic role as New Jersey's land-grant college.

Bureau of Community Services

In 1965 Rutgers established a Bureau of Community Services which is closely associated with the Urban Studies Center. The Bureau provides educational programs for citizens at large and for professionals in community affairs.

Institute of Management and Labor Relations

The State authorized the establishment of the Institute of Management and Labor Relations in 1947. In 1959 a private fund campaign was begun for the construction of a home for the Institute, with the building to be paid for by labor and management. The labor unit was dedicated on the Douglass College campus in 1962.

Institute of Animal Behavior

The Institute of Animal Behavior in Newark began work in 1959 and provides training and research in the psychological and physiological mechanisms of animal behavior.

Center for Information Processing

The Center for Information Processing on the College Avenue campus in downtown New Brunswick provides computational facilities for research and for classroom instruction, gives advice on methods of processing, and engages in research and instruction in the information processing sciences.

Bureau of Economic Research

The Bureau of Economic Research on the Rutgers College campus conducts research on both basic and applied aspects of economic life in New Jersey and the nation. It has published a number of studies and issues a monthly periodical, *Economic Indicators,* jointly with the New Jersey Department of Labor and Industry.

Statistics Center

The Rutgers Statistics Center also is located on the Rutgers College campus and is assigned administratively to the Graduate School but functions as an all-University department, including service assignments in five undergraduate colleges of the University.

Established in 1959, the Center conducts programs for graduates and undergraduates, is a consultative service to faculty and graduate students in designing experiments, and makes surveys in the analysis and interpretation of data.

University Extension Division

The University Extension Division has several units under its jurisdiction. These include the Stonier Graduate School of Banking, the Institute for Continuing Legal Education, the Bureaus of Conferences, Special Services, Community Services, Social Work, and Management Services, the Reading Center, the Summer School of Alcohol Studies, and the Government Services Training Program.

Other Research Bureaus

The Bureau of Biological Research, Bureau of Government Research, and Bureau of Mineral Research are organized for pure and applied research and function under the College of Arts and Sciences.

Division of Field Studies and Research

The Division of Field Studies and Research of the Graduate School of Education makes studies for school districts and institutions of higher education on problems of school building needs, district organization, administration, salary, curriculum development, and financing, among other areas.

New Jersey School Development Council

A cooperative organization of public school systems joined together for research and mutual benefit, the New Jersey School Development Council is concerned with the study of problems common to New Jersey school systems and the advancement of public education in New Jersey.

Bureau of Engineering Research

The Bureau of Engineering Research fosters and coordinates research activities and ensures integration with instruction. It coordinates research programs of the New Jersey Ceramic Research Station; the departments of chemical, civil, electrical, and mechanical engineering, mechanics; and the Rutgers University Planning Service.

Agricultural Extension Service

The Cooperative Extension Service in Agriculture and Home Economics provides educational services to farmers, the agribusiness structure, homemakers, and the young people of the State. A cooperative of federal, state, and county enterprises centered and directed at Rutgers, it carries to the people the results of federal and state research, for use in their daily lives.

Pharmaceutical Extension Service

The Pharmaceutical Extension Service, a personal consultant service for pharmacy in New Jersey, utilizes individual faculty efforts in solution of pharmaceutical problems.

Radiation Sciences Center

The Radiation Sciences Center is located on the University Heights campus. It engages in instruction, service, and interdisciplinary research in radiation science. The Center offers a one-year program in radiological health leading to a Master of Science degree, provides individual courses and cooperates in teaching others throughout the University.

Interdisciplinary Research Center

The Interdisciplinary Research Center in New Brunswick studies human behavior problems requiring the collaboration of two or more professions or scientific disciplines. The full-time staff includes psychiatrists, psychologists, and social workers. Other professions and disciplines which have been required by the work of the Center include biochemistry, psychiatric nursing, internal medicine, and mathematical statistics.

Bureau of Conservation and Environmental Science

The Bureau of Conservation and Environmental Science was established in 1962 as part of the College of Agriculture and Environmental Science. The Bureau was organized to provide Rutgers scientists the opportunity to work on conservation and environmental problems that are becoming more serious as the result of population growth and the resulting abuse of natural resources.

Water Resources Research Institute

In 1964 a Water Resources Research Institute was organized, with federal financial aid, to bring together the best-qualified people in New Jersey and the University for intensive research on and comprehensive study of the over-all water resources of New Jersey.

Bureau of Information Sciences Research

In June of 1965 the University announced the establishment of a Bureau of Information Sciences Research. The Bureau is part of the Graduate School of Library Service and will conduct certain of its teaching and research activities in conjunction with the University of Hawaii. The new Bureau is designed to study "how man communicates with himself and society." It will embrace such disciplines as computer science, library science, operations research, and cybernetics.

THE LIBRARY SYSTEM

The library system is the heart of a great university. At Rutgers, the University libraries contain over 1,200,000 volumes, 200,000 pamphlets and maps, and some 500,000 manuscripts housed in 21 libraries in various parts of the University. They include items ranging from sixteenth-century tracts on agriculture to the first newspaper published in New Jersey.

Annual accessions to the Rutgers library system total about 70,000 volumes.

The State University library is different from most university libraries in that it is unusually complex because of the large number of divisional and special libraries scattered throughout the campuses of Rutgers.

Keystone to the Rutgers library system is the central library in New Brunswick. The card catalogue contains a record of the holdings at all the libraries within the system, enabling a user of the library to tell at a glance where he can find the material he desires.

The central library was completed in 1956 at a cost of $4,000,000 and contains six floors of stacks with a capacity of 1,500,000 volumes. It is designed to accommodate 1,200 readers. Besides the main reading room, the library houses a reference department, periodical department, special col-

Lawn, a large former residence, was willed to the University by James Neilson in 1937. It now houses the Eagleton Institute of Politics.

A former bluing factory and a one-time Civilian Conservation Corps camp were acquired by the College of Agriculture in this period. The former factory now houses the Departments of Entomology, Economic Zoology, and Environmental Science, and the Department of Agricultural Communications. The former CCC structures are now occupied by the Department of Agricultural Engineering, its laboratories and equipment, and an agricultural museum.

Post-World War II growth has been rapid and continuous. An aircraft assembly plant which was to have been shipped to the Soviet Union was acquired and used as a "Commons," or dining hall, until 1964. This has since been converted for the University Registrar, Alumni Records, Scheduling Office, and the Center for Information Processing. The building also houses a central heating plant for the campus and a field house.

When the University of Newark was merged with Rutgers in 1946 the 40 Rector Street building, a former brewery, was the major structure in use by the University in Newark.

In the next few years several former residences along Washington Street and the former Eagle Insurance Company building at 18 Washington Place were acquired for the Colleges in Newark.

In 1950 the merger of the College of South Jersey and its law school brought a number of former residences and a law building into the University physical plant inventory. A year later a library was built with State funds.

Lipman Hall, which houses the Department of Soils and Crops, Soil Microbiology and Agricultural Biochemistry, was erected on the agriculture campus with State funds.

At this period a campaign among alumni provided assistance for construction of Demarest Hall, a dormitory on the Rutgers campus, and a student center at Douglass.

Significant development of University Heights began with construction of Wright Chemistry Laboratories in 1952 and Waksman Hall of the Institute of Microbiology in 1954.

The year 1956 saw completion of the University Library, built with State funds; the opening of Frelinghuysen, Hardenbergh, and Livingston dormitories, the Ledge, which is a student center, all on the College Avenue campus, and acquisition of the former YWCA at 53 Washington Street, Newark. The latter projects were financed with University funds and loans. The Newark building housed the gymnasium and School of Law until the School of Law in 1965 moved into the newly erected law center, Ackerson Hall, which also houses the law library.

Rutgers has been engaged in a massive construction program in recent years to meet the increased demands for student places in classrooms, laboratories, libraries, dormitories, and dining halls.

lections department, government documents department, and a photoduplication department.

The photoduplication department is equipped to make copies of virtually any printed material by several duplicating processes. The department also restores and preserves the library's rare manuscripts and other valuable items.

Many of these items are contained in the New Jersey Collection, devoted to New Jersey history and the largest of the library's special collections. The New Jersey Collection contains books, pamphlets, and a substantial portion of the library's manuscripts. Original letters, diaries, accounts, and other records of New Jersey citizens go back to colonial times.

Also prominent in the New Jersey Collection is a file of newspapers, some going back as far as the eighteenth century. There is a complete file, part of it on microfilm, of New Jersey's oldest surviving newspaper, the Elizabeth *Journal*, established in 1779. Also notable is a file of first issues of the State's first printed newspaper, founded in Burlington in 1778.

The Special Collections Department also maintains collections of old paper money, book plates, stocks and bonds, lottery tickets, and early American advertising art.

Three branch libraries in Newark are located at the College of Arts and Sciences, the School of Law, and the College of Pharmacy. In Camden branches are located at the School of Law and the College of South Jersey.

In addition to these libraries, the main library in New Brunswick is supplemented by branches at the College of Agriculture and Environmental Science, Douglass College, the Institute of Management and Labor Relations, the Bureau of Biological Research, and the Institute of Microbiology. The School of Chemistry and the departments of biology, ceramics, and physics, the Eagleton Institute, the Alcohol Studies Center, and the Bureau of Government Research also maintain small special libraries.

Funds for a new library of science and medicine to serve especially the new Rutgers Medical School and the science departments at University Heights have been provided by the 1964 College Bond Issue and a grant from the federal government and designs for the building are now on the drawing board.

FROM RENTAL QUARTERS TO A SEVEN-CAMPUS MULTIMILLION-DOLLAR PLANT

Rutgers' original facilities consisted of classroom space in a tavern, 'The Sign of the Red Lion,' in what is now downtown New Brunswick. Today the Rutgers physical plant is valued in excess of $132,000,000. Its 560 buildings are located on nearly 4,700 acres. Of this total, 2,720 are in New Brunswick and adjoining townships, 1,353 are at the dairy research farm in Sussex, 450 are at the crop and fruit research farms in Monmouth County, and the balance is in relatively small parcels in downtown Newark and Camden.

Rutgers has seven campuses, five in New Brunswick, one in Camden, and one in Newark. The five major areas of Rutgers in New Brunswick are: the central or College Avenue campus; University Heights, the Kilmer Area; the College of Agriculture and Environmental Science, and Douglass College.

Old Queens, the University's oldest permanent building, was erected on the central campus in 1809.

Considered an outstanding example of Federal period architecture, it housed the entire college when it was built, and today contains the principal administrative offices of the University.

Many of the buildings on the Queens campus were erected during the late nineteenth century. Van Nest was constructed as the College's first classroom building in 1845 and is now used by the Admissions and Publications offices and for a few classrooms. Schanck Observatory for the study of astronomy came in 1865. Geological Hall, home of science studies, went up in 1872. It now houses the Rutgers Geological Museum and the Bureau of Mineral Research as well as the Department of Geology. Kirkpatrick Chapel was built on Queens campus one year later.

The State of New Jersey made its first capital investment in the Rutgers building program in 1889 when it appropriated $40,000 for New Jersey Hall as quarters for the Agricultural Experiment Station. This building later housed instruction in the ·biological sciences until it was converted to modern classrooms and offices in 1962. The conversion was a major architectural and engineering undertaking, with the interior of the building being completely modernized while the exterior was left largely unchanged.

The first dormitory, Winants, built in 1890, now serves as an office building.

Ballantine, which now houses classrooms and a hydraulics laboratory, was opened as a gymnasium in 1894. It was badly damaged by fire in 1930 and later rebuilt for its present uses.

Voorhees Library was erected in 1903. It was converted to office use on completion of the new library and is being reconverted for the Department of Art and the University Art Gallery.

In 1909 the University constructed the Engineering Building (now Murray Hall) and a year later the Chemistry Building (now Milledoler Hall) on the downtown campus.

Murray Hall continues to house some departments in engineering although most of the College has been moved to its new Center on University Heights. Milledoler Hall was renovated in 1964-65 for the Dean of the College of Arts and Sciences and the School of Journalism.

The need for additional student housing a half century ago was met when the college built Ford Hall in 1915.

While these developments were taking place on the campus, the College of Agriculture and Environmental Sc ing to the south.

The first permanent agricultural facility, the Short was constructed with State funds in 1906.

An administrative building in 1914 and horticulture, p buildings in the early twenties continued expansion of the pus.

State aid to Rutgers growth was not limited to agri In 1920 a State appropriation was made for construction Building facing George Street. When the ceramics depa the Engineering Center at University Heights in 1963, converted for use by the Graduate School of Social Work.

Establishment of Douglass College in 1918 led to acqu Hall and Cooper Hall, former residences, in an area adja culture campus.

A year later the "old gymnasium" was constructed o crates, built to ship Liberty aircraft engines to France du I. The building is still in use as a gymnasium.

The first facility built exclusively for educational p lass, Federation Hall, was opened in 1922. It was financc raised by the State Federation of Women's Clubs.

In the mid twenties, State funds provided for Douglas tion, and Botany buildings.

Voorhees Chapel, financed through a bequest by the beth Rodman Voorhees of Clinton, New Jersey, was be same year the Little Theater was completed. The Music 1928, largely financed through contributions of the Sta Women's Clubs.

Residence facilities on Corwin, Gibbons, and James came available in 1922, 1926, and 1928, respectively.

On the Rutgers campus, too, new dormitories came o late twenties when the "Quad"—Hegeman, Wessels, Leup —was built.

Van Dyck Hall, a physics facility financed by State f in 1927 on Queens campus. The same year, through merg Jersey College of Pharmacy, a large building in North quired.

With the onset of the depression, acquisition of build only major construction in the 1930's provided an athlet nasium was completed in 1932 to replace Ballantine Gym and Rutgers Stadium at University Heights, across the R: the College Avenue campus, was opened in 1938. The 2 was built with the assistance of the Works Progress Admin

The campus to the south also had additions at th

Since 1958 a total of more than $133,375,000 has been committed to capital improvements on all campuses. A major part, about half, of the funds for the capital improvements program has come from two College Bond Issues approved by the voters of New Jersey in 1959 and 1964, from which Rutgers received $29,850,000 and $19,069,000, respectively. Most of the remainder was obtained through borrowing, federal grants, and gifts to the University.

The building program has brought about profound changes on all campuses.

Among the new facilities on the College Avenue campus in downtown New Brunswick are a 2,000-seat dining hall, graduate dormitory, a 1,000-man dormitory complex, an extensive classroom building, and a Graduate School of Education building. A new student union near the gymnasium is in the advanced planning stage.

A new library, dining hall, dormitories, a classroom-laboratory building, and a gymnasium have become landmarks at Douglass.

The Labor Wing of the Institute of Management and Labor Relations, a Mosquito Control Laboratory, and a Turkey Research building are among the new buildings at the College of Agriculture and Environmental Science.

The largest single development in the University has taken place at University Heights in Piscataway Township, across the Raritan River from the New Brunswick campus. A Science Center is growing swiftly at the Heights in an area which as late as 1950 was made up of farms, playing fields, and a golf course.

Study of the physical and natural sciences at New Brunswick is being centered where Wright Chemistry and the Institute of Microbiology were built in the early 1950's.

The third permanent structure at the Center was Nelson Biological Laboratories, which opened in 1960. One unit of this houses the Bureau of Biological Research.

The College of Engineering building, which cost approximately $5,600,000, opened in 1963. It contains several departments of the College and the Bureau of Engineering Research.

Rutgers, in collaboration with Bell Telephone Laboratories, Inc., in 1964 erected a 15-million-electron-volt tandem Van de Graaff accelerator. This came shortly after two physics buildings opened in 1963. The three structures together cost $5,500,000.

The University Medical School, established in June of 1961 with the aid of a $1,072,000 grant from the Kellogg Foundation of Michigan, will be located on the University Heights campus among the University's rapidly expanding science facilities. Abundant land is available here for construction of the building for the two-year medical school program, the science and medical library and its eventual expansion into a major medical center. This will include a four-year medical school, university hospital, and facilities for training individuals in the health-related sciences. The Rutgers Board of Governors in November, 1965, voted to investigate the possibility of establishing a four-year medical school. The College of Pharmacy has been authorized to move from Newark to the same area.

A new project on the University Heights campus will bring to 200 the additions in 1966 to the apartments in the married students' housing development and bring the total to 501. The married students' housing development on University Heights was started in 1946 with the erection of 301 units.

In Newark and Camden the University's construction is making major contributions to the urban renewal programs of those cities.

The campus being constructed at Newark is the first in the country to be built entirely on urban renewal land. It will contain, in its initial development, a School of Law, classroom, laboratory, library, science, and student center buildings. The law school building, Ackerson Hall, was completed in the fall of 1965. It houses the law library.

These six buildings will be the first structures designed for college use to be occupied by the University in downtown Newark. The first stage of the Newark construction is estimated to cost $11,500,000. It is being built on six city blocks totalling about 20 acres.

At Camden a $1,840,000 science building and a $1,084,000 student center went into operation in the fall of 1964.

Here, too, University construction replaces old buildings. Eventual development of the College of South Jersey campus projects a 16-acre campus area. A $3,000,000 classroom, faculty offices, and administration facilities building is in the planning stages.

Plans for the development of the Kilmer Area, a 540-acre portion of the former Camp Kilmer granted to the University by the federal government, are under way. The tract is adjacent to the University Heights campus in Piscataway Township.

The land is being used for the construction of an entirely new campus to provide for the anticipated vast increase in the demand for Rutgers educational services in the years immediately ahead.

This will be a particularly significant development because three modest-sized colleges are planned in the Kilmer Area as a possible answer to the problems of mass education which have arisen in some of the larger universities. Educators and others interested in the development of higher education in the face of increasing enrollments everywhere are certain to watch the development in the Kilmer Area.

Livingston College, named in honor of the first governor of the State of New Jersey, will be the first of three colleges of about 3,000 resident students each which the State University has planned in the Kilmer Area.

Now on the architects' drawing boards are buildings to accommodate half the eventual student population of Livingston College. These buildings, which will provide for 1,500 resident students and several hundred additional commuters, will cost more than $18,000,000. Two major units of the first phase of the new college, a classroom-laboratory building and a residence hall-food service complex, will cost $4,031,000 and $12,351,500, respectively. Of the total $9,900,000 will be provided from the College Bond Issue approved by the voters in November of 1964. The remainder will be borrowed or provided through federal funds.

CULTURAL EVENTS

Rutgers each year presents a number of cultural and intellectual events outside its academic program.

Late in 1965 the Rockefeller Foundation announced a $265,000 three-year grant to Rutgers and the Committee for International Composers Concerts, Ltd., to promote the playing and composing of contemporary music. It established the Contemporary Chamber Ensemble, a noted avant-garde chamber music group, as a State University residence group. A series of concerts will be played, both for the public and for students. The ensemble will also play other concerts in New York City and on college and university campuses throughout the nation.

Many of the events planned for the Bicentennial Year are offered directly by the University's Department of Concerts and Lectures which also assists other departments in arranging special programs. The oldest and most popular concert offering is the "Gymnasium Series" in New Brunswick, now in its 50th consecutive season.

For the Bicentennial Year, the University Choir was invited to sing with the Philadelphia Orchestra and the London Symphony. Membership in the University Choir, formed in 1950, is open to all undergraduates from all campuses as well as to a limited number of alumni and University staff members.

Working cooperatively with the Rutgers Music Department, the Department of Concerts and Lectures presents the annual "Naumburg Memorial Series" in Kirkpatrick Chapel. This program of four events usually concentrates on less frequently heard repertoire, particularly music of the Renaissance, Baroque, and Contemporary periods.

The Douglass College Music Department offers a variety of student and faculty recitals in Voorhees Chapel throughout the academic year. Similar concerts are given in Newark and Camden.

In addition, there are a number of student-sponsored concerts. The Rutgers Chapter of Carnegie Hall—Jeunesses Musicales which presents gifted young professional soloists from throughout the world as well as recitals, lectures, and demonstrations by students and faculty, is the principal student-sponsored group.

Drama offerings are given in New Brunswick by the Queens Theater Guild, in Newark by the Mummers, and in Camden by the Masqueteers. Dance performances are brought to various campuses, usually under the auspices of the various departments of physical education.

Lectures constitute a highly diversified and very extensive segment of intellectual life on all Rutgers campuses. Most University divisions sponsor lectures and symposiums by authorities in their fields. In addition, the Department of Concerts and Lectures brings to the campus distinguished personalities in the arts, sciences, and public affairs.

The Rutgers art collection includes over 3,000 pieces of painting, sculpture, drawings, and engravings which range from fourteenth-century Italian to European and American contemporary.

Exhibition of items in the fine arts collection has been hampered by lack of suitable space. However, the University is converting Voorhees Hall, on the New Brunswick campus, to include a gallery which will permit hanging of 80 to 90 paintings.

Formal art exhibitions at Rutgers are now confined to those by graduate students and faculty members at Douglass College in a small gallery there and to occasional exhibitions at the Colleges in Newark and Camden.

RESEARCH AND SCHOLARSHIP

At the State University research and scholarship range over a broad spectrum of the humanities, natural and social sciences, and professional fields. A recent University publication listed more than 3,500 different subjects under investigation by Rutgers scholars. Every department of every college is concerned with research in its own field.

The Research Council of Rutgers University is the administrator and coordinator of the great bulk of research conducted at the University. The Council advises individual members of the faculty on matters connected with research opportunities and funds and assists in some of the larger proposals that have gone from the University to the federal and other major granting agencies.

During 1964-65 $13,810,000 was committed to project research. This included grants from individuals, foundations, local, state, and federal government units.

This sum, however, does not fully indicate the dimensions of Rutgers scholarly and research activity since it includes only sponsored research, as opposed to projects undertaken without special financing.

Much research and scholarship at the State University is pursued without regard to specific application. It is motivated simply by the wish of the scholar or scientist to know more. Some of it, however, is committed to helping governmental, industrial, and other agencies in solving practical problems of many kinds in agriculture, urban studies, politics and education.

Many units of the University have research as their primary responsibility. They include the Agricultural Experiment Station, the Bureaus of Biological, Government, Engineering, Economic, Information Sciences, and Mineral Research, Community Sciences, and Conservation and Environmental Science; the Centers of Alcohol Studies, Information Processing, Interdisciplinary Research, Radiation Science, and Urban Studies; the Institutes of Animal Behavior, Water Resources Research, Management and Labor Relations, and Microbiology; and the Graduate School of Education's Division of Field Studies.

The outlook for increased research and scholarship at Rutgers in the Bicentennial Year is particularly bright. Its quality is reflected in the growth of research sponsorship by a variety of industrial organizations, governmental units, societies, and individuals. Investment in research at Rutgers has increased from a wartime low of under $159,000 in 1944 to $13,810,000 by 1965.

Facilities for research and scholarship, office space, laboratories, libraries, and the assistants, equipment, and books which go with them, have increased. These financial and physical indications of research development at Rutgers reflect the University's deep commitment to the necessarily close alliance of research and teaching.

The Rutgers Medical School is an outstanding example of the forward look at the State University and it seems particularly fitting that it should open its doors to its first class in the Bicentennial Year. Although the school will not accept its first students until the fall of 1966, an active program of research is under way. Its staff began assembling in the first months of 1964 and research began immediately in the departments of medicine, microbiology and psychiatry.

Research and scholarship in the humanities recently completed or in progress include the editing of texts, writing of biography, history and historiography, criticism of literary works, and the tracing of the history of ideas.

Studies range from antiquity to the present and from New Jersey to the Antipodes. They are only some of the means by which the humanistic scholar keeps alive the inheritance from the past.

Faculty members are also writing fiction and poetry, working in creative arts and studio programs in oils, water colors, sculpture, and graphics.

In the natural sciences a very small sampling of research at Rutgers would include: the control of fear by the sympathetic nervous system, the role of genetic and environmental variables upon the behavior of mice, work in bacterial metabolism, cancer chemotherapy and serology, abstract developments in mathematics, and the use of a 15-million-volt tandem electrostatic accelerator in physics research.

Social science research includes econometrics of world trade, population redistribution and economic growth, foreign trade studies, property tax variations in New Jersey, a history of agriculture in the United States, and the problem of political restoration.

All of the professional schools and special institutes at Rutgers are intensely concerned with research. Much of this research is on practical problems of immediate concern. The College of Agriculture and Environmental Science is focusing much of its attention on planned environmental studies and both it and the College of Engineering have conducted investigations into aspects of soil, air, and water for many years.

Studies are under way at the New Jersey Agricultural Experiment Station in New Brunswick on air pollution, ground and surface water pollution, characterization and treatment of solid and liquid wastes, factors affecting the state's fisheries, and the fate of pesticides.

A significant new enterprise at Rutgers, the Water Resources Research Institute, began operations in the summer of 1965 and is seeking possible solutions of the water shortage in the Northeast.

In the field of education, the Graduate School of Education uses the Division of Field Studies and Research and the New Jersey School Development Council to conduct special research projects. Studies range from theoretical projects such as investigation of existential educational philosophy to statistical analysis comparing the effects of different kinds of secondary school physics courses on the achievement in first-year college physics.

Research on the action of frost on soil has led to development of techniques of soil description and to an engineering characteristics soil map of New Jersey, the first such map in the country.

These maps and soil comparison investigations result annually in savings to the New Jersey Highway Department which are greater than the yearly cost of operating the College of Engineering.

Research by members of the law faculty at Newark and Camden have resulted in the adoption of a new uniform commercial code by the State of New Jersey. Research by the law faculty ranges from a study of sales laws under the uniform commercial code to an English translation of the Swedish Code of Civil and Criminal Procedure. They also include research on applying electronic data processing systems to retrieval of legal data, decision theory in law and science, and expropriation in underdeveloped countries.

Similarly impressive research is being conducted by the Graduate School of Library Service, the College of Pharmacy, and the Graduate School of Social Work. A checklist of American imprints from 1820 to 1825 and a study of statistical techniques applied to the inventory of library holdings are under investigation at the School of Library Service.

The College of Pharmacy is emphasizing research in analytical pharmacy, physical pharmacy, pharmaceutical administration, pharmaceutical chemistry, pharmacognosy, pharmacology, pharmaceutical microbiology, and public health.

The Graduate School of Social Work is particularly concerned with gathering information on various methods of social work and its practical application.

Opportunity for undergraduate research and scholarship is provided in most Rutgers divisions. At Rutgers College of Arts and Sciences, the

Henry Rutgers Scholar plan permits outstanding seniors to enter a special program freeing them from conventional work and permitting individual study, research and creative activity.

Other liberal arts and professional colleges of the University list honors programs or special courses which encourage scholarship and original research by superior students in areas not included in formal course organization.

THE ADVISORY BOARD

The Advisory Board for Research and Graduate Education, composed of distinguished persons in many fields, is appointed by the President of Rutgers University. The Board visits the University, studies particular areas of research and graduate education, and makes recommendations to the President.

Members of the Board for 1965-66 are:

Henry E. Ackerson, Jr., Keyport, New Jersey

Carl F. Bayerschmidt, Professor, Department of Germanic Languages, Columbia University

Charles H. Brower, Batten, Barton, Durstine & Osborn, Inc.

A. Paul Burton, W. B. Saunders Company

Robert R. Bush, Professor, Department of Psychology, University of Pennsylvania

Carl C. Chambers, Vice President for Engineering Affairs, University of Pennsylvania

Edward T. Cone, Professor, Department of Music, Princeton University

Harry L. Derby, Montclair

Sidney Goldmann, Judge, Superior Court of New Jersey

Moses Hadas, Professor, Department of Greek and Latin, Columbia University

Asger F. Langlykke, Vice President for Research and Development, E. R. Squibb & Sons

Richard H. Logsdon, Director of Libraries, Butler Library, Columbia University

William H. Lycan, Director of Research, Johnson & Johnson

V. D. Mattia, Hoffman LaRoche, Inc., Nutley

Deane Montgomery, School of Mathematics, The Institute for Advanced Study

Geoffrey H. Moore, Director of Research, National Bureau of Economic Research

Roy Earl Morse, Vice President for Technical Research, Thomas J. Lipton

Roy F. Nichols, Dean, Graduate School, University of Pennsylvania

William T. Pecora, Director, Geological Survey, U.S. Department of Interior

Gordon N. Ray, President, John Simon Guggenheim Memorial Foundation

Norman Reitman, M.D., New Brunswick

George T. Reynolds, Professor, Department of Physics, Palmer Physical
    Laboratory, Princeton University

Richard Schlatter, *ex officio*, Vice President and Provost, Rutgers
    University

Irwin W. Sizer, Chairman, Department of Biology, Massachusetts Institute
    of Technology

Lloyd B. Wescott, President, Board of Control, New Jersey Department of
    Institutions and Agencies

Monroe Wheeler, Director of Exhibitions and Publications, Museum of
    Modern Art

Benjamin Wolfson, Pennsauken

THE RUTGERS UNIVERSITY PRESS

The Rutgers University Press plans to publish two books directly concerned with the Rutgers Bicentennial during 1966. Dr. Richard P. McCormick, professor of history and University historian, is writing a formal
history of Rutgers which will be published by the University Press.
"Aloud to Alma Mater," edited by George J. Lukac, will be an anthology
of Rutgers stories and an attempt to capture in an informal way what
Rutgers has been like over the past 200 years. The title of the anthology is
from a Rutgers song.

The Rutgers University Press, founded in 1936, publishes about 35
books a year. Final publication selections are made by a 12-member council
composed of University officials, scholars, and persons with various publishing backgrounds. The Press issues scholarly non-fiction and regional
titles which cover a wide variety of subjects and are distributed throughout the world. The Press maintains its own sales and distribution facilities
but the books are produced through contracts with printers.

This June it played host in New Brunswick to the annual convention
of the American Association of University Presses.

In addition to books published by the University Press, there are a
number of scholarly, professional, and technical publications which
emanate from the University. Several divisions publish journals which have
a national or international reputation.

Among them are the *Quarterly Journal* of Studies on Alcohol, Rutgers
Law Review, Soil Science, Journal of the Friends of Rutgers Library, and
the Serological Museum Bulletin.

One of the oldest and best known of American literary and critical
magazines, the *Partisan Review,* has been published at Rutgers since 1963.
Its editor, William Phillips, is a professor of English in Rutgers College.
The managing editor of the *American Historical Review* is a professor of
history at Rutgers, Dr. Henry R. Winkler.

UNIVERSITY INCOME . . . AND EXPENSE

The income of Rutgers – The State University is derived from many sources. Principal categories are the annual State appropriation for operations, student fees, including tuition, outright gifts such as alumni contributions, corporate donations for scholarships or other purposes, grants and contracts for research, federal appropriations, and the income from endowments and auxiliary services. Included among the auxiliary services are the dormitories, the dining halls, and the University bookstores.

A breakdown of the University's income for the year 1966-67 totaling $70,638,557, follows below. It presents both the dollar amount of income by major categories and the percentage of the total. For example, the State's appropriation to the State University during 1966-67 was $28,952,950, or 40.99 percent of the total.

The accompanying breakdown of University expenses during the same period presents expenditures by total amounts and percentages for the major categories.

	1966-67	
Income	*Actual*	*Percentage*
State of New Jersey Appropriations	28,952,950	40.99
Student Fees	10,239,517	14.50
Federal Appropriations	1,458,270	2.06
Endowment Income & Miscellaneous	2,710,168	3.84
Gifts and Grants applied	2,740,058	3.88
Organized Activities relating to Educ. Depts.	255,595	0.36
Auxiliary Enterprises	11,297,401	15.99
Student Aid	1,362,868	1.93
Contract Research and Services rendered	11,618,207	16.45
Appropriation from University Funds	–	–
	70,635,034	100.00
Expenditures		
Administration and General Expenses	6,470,563	10.28
Instruction and Departmental Research	21,924,935	31.04
Organized Research	4,271,631	6.05
Extension and Public Services	4,518,758	6.40
Libraries	1,771,299	2.51
Operation and Maintenance of Physical Plant	5,010,707	7.09
Auxiliary Enterprises	10,938,687	15.48
Student Aid	2,134,303	3.02
Contract Research and Services	11,618,207	16.45
University Appropriations for Capital purposes	1,190,268	1.68
	70,638,557	100.00

STUDENT ACTIVITIES OUTSIDE THE CLASSROOM

The Office of the Dean of Student Affairs is responsible for all nonacademic activities on all campuses of the University. Specific programs of the several student personnel offices vary from campus to campus, but they all give careful attention to the individual student in personal problems, adjustment to university life, and attainment of his educational objectives.

The student personnel departments also supervise extracurricular activities, including social functions, and are responsible for student discipline, for the guidance and development of spiritual life on the campuses, and for the assistance of students with emotional or financial problems.

The Department of Student Affairs includes the Office of Financial Aids, Student Health Service, University Placement Services, Office of the University Chaplain, and the Psychological Service Center.

The functions and duties of these services are self-evident, but it should be noted that the University Placement Services and its divisions throughout the University provide a personal, confidential placement service to undergraduates, seniors, and alumni. All offices make available vocational libraries and extensive programs to assist registrants in obtaining positions. A separate office services candidates on all levels in the field of education.

Rutgers has maintained a concern for the "moral and spiritual" life of its students since it was founded in 1766. There are advisers to the major religious sects and student organizations of a number of faiths meet regularly on all campuses.

The Psychological Service Center offers counseling and guidance to students through use of psychological tests and clinical interviewing techniques.

All Rutgers colleges have extensive programs of extracurricular activities, including student newspapers, literary magazines, yearbooks, student governments, honor societies, debating, music, and curricular clubs.

Fraternities and sororities operate on all campuses except Douglass, where small residence units allow for self-government, stimulating friendships, and other group values.

A particularly noteworthy activity on the Rutgers College campus is WRSU, the student radio station serving Rutgers and Douglass.

International Weekend, which brings foreign students studying at colleges throughout the Northeast to Douglass for a weekend of discussion, is an important event in student life. Greek Week, when students dress in classical Greek costumes and hold special events, is a tradition at the College of South Jersey.

Students in several professional colleges publish special journals in their fields.

Varsity and intramural athletics play a large role in the lives of students at the State University. At Rutgers College athletes may participate in 16 varsity sports and an extensive intramural program in 10 sports provides opportunity for all students to engage in athletics. Freshmen and sophomores in most undergraduate colleges take part in physical education classes, where the emphasis is on activities which may be continued after graduation.

In Newark and Camden, the athletic programs are planned for the commuter student. They also include intramurals. At Douglass, in addition to the required physical education courses, several intercollegiate teams represent the women's college.

The Rutgers College intercollegiate program consists of football, lightweight football, soccer, and cross country in the fall; basketball, wrestling, fencing, swimming, and indoor track in the winter; and baseball, track, lacrosse, tennis, golf, crew, and lightweight crew in the spring.

Rutgers Newark fields varsity teams in basketball, bowling, fencing, wrestling in the winter, and baseball, tennis, and golf in the spring. There is a woman's fencing team at Newark. Rutgers College of South Jersey schedules soccer, basketball, baseball, golf, and tennis on the intercollegiate level.

RUTGERS INTERNATIONAL

Today the work of a major university is truly international in scope and Rutgers is no exception. Rutgers is celebrating both the Bicentennial of the founding of Rutgers and the Centennial of the arrival of the first foreign students on its campus.

It was just a hundred years ago that some of the first Japanese students ever to come to the United States enrolled at Rutgers, where they were tutored by an undergraduate, William Elliot Griffis. Many of these students later assumed positions of importance in their own country and Griffis himself became a professor in Japan.

In the present academic year there are 355 foreign students on campus, representing 60 nations on six continents. Last summer the Eleanor Roosevelt Memorial Workshop in International Human Relations brought 24 foreign nationals to the Douglass campus.

An equal number of teachers from Bulgaria, Denmark, Finland, Italy, Sweden, Brazil, Chile, and Japan in the fall of 1965 enrolled in a 13-week program in American civilization.

The Rutgers program is part of a cultural exchange project of the Department of State in which the State University has participated five times previously.

Rutgers and Tucumán University in Argentina plan to begin an exchange of graduate students and professors in the fall. The exchange will assist Tucumán, and ultimately other Argentine universities, in advanced areas of engineering and will also make Argentine education and research facilities available to American universities.

Other examples of University cooperation with foreign student programs can be seen in its participation in the Foreign Student Leadership project, a U.S. National Student Association program, which brings students here to observe United States student government, and in the African Scholarship Program of American universities.

The University Board of Governors has approved a proposal for qualifying students at Rutgers and Douglass to spend a junior year abroad at the University of Orléans, France, the program to start in 1967. The University already has a working arrangement for students to attend summer sessions at the University of Strasbourg, France.

A summer internship with the International Labour Organization office in Geneva, Switzerland, exchange programs with Alexander Universitat in Erlangen, Germany, and with San Andrés University, La Paz, Bolivia, are among other projects currently going on or completed.

Rutgers also is aiding developing nations throughout the world. Some of the advisory projects conducted in the past ten years are: development of the Royal Technical College of Kenya; assistance to schools and colleges in educational and psychological testing in West, South, and East Africa; aid to the University Law Library at Addis Ababa, Ethiopia; assistance in revision of Burmese law and legal education; help with the industrial relations program in Thailand; study of Paraguay's educational system; and statistical quality control assistance to India.

The increasing participation by Rutgers faculty and students in programs of international studies led to the establishment of a University Committee on International Education in 1963 to advise the President of the University on programs in the field.

Rutgers believes the benefits of an international contingent at the University are many. Foreign students and faculty members return to their home countries with a better understanding of American culture; the added awareness of international affairs and other cultures which their presence inspires in the American students and scholars is in return equally important to the total educational process at the University.

Among the larger foreign student delegations at Rutgers are the 58 from the Republic of China, 41 from India, 23 from Canada, 16 from the United Kingdom, 13 from Japan, and 11 from the Philippines.

RUTGERS ON RADIO AND TELEVISION

Rutgers maintains an extensive and growing program of information and education on radio and television.

The State University has three radio programs broadcast each week on more than forty New Jersey stations. The Rutgers Forum, on which newsmen interview a prominent New Jersey personality in public affairs, is the oldest continuous public interest program on New Jersey radio. During the Bicentennial Year the Rutgers Forum passed the one thousandth consecutive week in which it has been on the air.

Other regular Rutgers radio programs are Report from Rutgers and Rutgers Report on World Affairs. Report on World Affairs is an analysis of world events by Rutgers specialists in a wide variety of fields. Report from Rutgers presents University news and interviews with faculty members, staff, and students on developments at the University.

Rutgers radio programs also are heard throughout the country through distribution by the National Association of Educational Broadcasters.

Rutgers, too, has individual programs on public affairs topics and series on subject matter fields on metropolitan radio and television stations, including Channel 13, the educational channel in Newark. Programs of a more occasional nature are also carried on major commercial television channels in New York City and Philadelphia.

These occasional programs are of growing importance in the University's total program of information and education on radio and television. During the fall and early winter of 1965, for example, Dr. Gerald M. Pomper, an associate professor of political science, lectured on WABC-TV on presidential politics, Professor Moshe Mosston, chairman of the Teacher Training Division of the Department of Physical Education, presented a series of programs for children on WCBS-TV. Max Kirkland of the College of Agriculture and Environmental Science was host on the Challenge to Better Living program on WHYY-TV, Philadelphia, and Dr. Charles O. Richardson, assistant professor of history at Rutgers College of South Jersey, appeared on University of the Air, carried on WFIL-TV, Philadelphia.

THE GRADUATES OF RUTGERS

Rutgers is particularly proud of its alumni. The State University's alumni body is relatively young—about half the total has been graduated in the past twenty years—but they have been one of the University's greatest sources of strength.

They include architects and engineers, prominent medical scientists and instructors in medicine, editors, prize-winning journalists, internationally known broadcasters, writers and artists, notable historians and social scientists, attorneys and judges, college and university presidents, athletes, advertising and insurance executives, scientists (including a Nobel laureate), entertainers, men of affairs in the industrial and business world, and ranking public servants.

Through the years they have supported their Alma Mater loyally, and they support Rutgers more generously and faithfully than the national average for all colleges and universities.

In 1965, for example, almost 23 percent of the Rutgers alumni body contributed to the annual Rutgers Fund. The average for all universities and colleges, public and private, in the country was just over 22 percent. The backing among Rutgers alumni of their university takes on increased significance when it is realized that the national average for public universities in 1962-63 was only about 15 percent.

Douglass, the State University's women's college, maintains a separate Alumnae Fund in addition to the General Rutgers Fund. According to a survey of fund giving conducted by the American Alumni Council, Douglass was first among public women's colleges in participation during the College's 40th anniversary year.

In 1964-65 participation was almost 43 percent.

Moreover, alumni support of the University has been growing in recent years. Since the Rutgers Fund began in 1934, alumni have given the University more than $2,300,000 through this agency. In the 1965 campaign they contributed a record total of $311,270.

More than 8,000 individual gifts were made through the Fund in the campaign. The amount raised was equivalent to the interest at 4 percent on an endowment of $7,800,000.

The Douglass Alumnae Fund has secured contributions totaling $707,226 since its inception in 1931. The 1964-65 Fund received $66,243.

These funds are in addition to many other special gifts such as works of art, educational equipment, books, and bequests from graduates.

In addition, alumni have banded together four times in the past to provide major gifts through specially organized campaigns. During celebrations of the University's 100th and 150th anniversaries they raised $500,000.

A conservative estimate is that about one third of the University's $181,000,000 in assets (buildings, endowment, equipment, and grounds) is traceable to alumni gifts or to grants stimulated by alumni.

Alumni support is also reflected in other ways. The Rutgers Alumni Committee for the Support of Public Higher Education was effective in working for passage of the 1959 and 1964 College Bond Issues.

The total number of alumnae and alumni of the 16 degree-granting divisions of Rutgers is about 46,000. Almost 32,000 of them reside in New Jersey.

However, Rutgers alumni clubs operate throughout the country from New England to Florida to California. These organizations serve to maintain a link between alumni and their Alma Mater.

Rutgers Alumni Residing in New Jersey Counties
(Includes graduates through June, 1964)

Atlantic	312
Bergen	3,027
Burlington	549
Camden	1,239
Cape May	99
Cumberland	211
Essex	6,358
Gloucester	320

Hudson	1,475
Hunterdon	272
Mercer	1,183
Middlesex	4,356
Monmouth	819
Morris	1,375
Ocean	458
Passaic	1,723
Salem	96
Somerset	1,522
Sussex	232
Union	4,352
Warren	158
TOTAL	31,739

Information About Rutgers

The Rutgers Speakers Bureau is of particular importance during the Bicentennial Year. The Bureau maintains offices on the University campuses in Newark, New Brunswick, and Camden, and lists some 400 faculty and staff speakers and thousands of subjects. Among the subjects of particular interest this year are the University Bicentennial and plans for the future of the University.

General information about the State University may be obtained by writing to: Department of Public Relations, Rutgers – The State University, Old Queens, New Brunswick, New Jersey.

Inquiries concerning admission should be directed to the admissions office of the college concerned.

Persons desiring information about agricultural publications should write to: Bulletin Clerk, College of Agriculture and Environmental Science, Rutgers – The State University, New Brunswick, New Jersey.

Index

Aaron, Jeff, 175
Abernethy, Rev. Bradford S., 27, 101, 123, 141
Abernethy, Robert, 27-28, 28
Abrutyn, Elliot, 231
Ackerson, Henry E., Jr., 237, 273
Adams, Mary Elizabeth Goslin, 216
Adams, Ruth Marie, 38-39, 50
Adourian, John C., 215
Afflect, James, 84
Agricultural Experiment Station, 254, 257, 270, 272
Agricultural Extension Service, 261
Agriculture and Environmental Science, College of, 36, 57, 59, 70, 167, 176, 186, 246, 250, 262, 263, 265, 267, 270, 271-272
Alampi, Phillip, 59
Alcohol Studies, Center of, 163, 259, 263, 271
Alexander, Archibald S., 23, 24, 39, 229, 236, 237
Alexander Meiklejohn Award, 113, 159
Allen, Constance J., 231
Alumni, 279-280
  events, 33, 183, 185, 213-218
  tributes by, 143-148, 143, 144, 145, 147, 152-156, 154, 155, 156, 183, 222-226
Amioka, Shiro, 92
Anderson, Bill, 175

Anderson, Catherine McElligott, 216
Anderson, John F., 233
Anderson, Joyce Houghtaling, 214
Anderson, Rosemary Honecker, 215
Anfinsen, C. B., 65
Angle, Paul M., 55, 187, 190
Animal Behavior, Institute of, 260, 271
Anthologist, The, 192
Applegate, Robert E., 216
Armitage, Arthur E., 213
Art collection, 270
Astin, Jan K., 213
Atchley, Dana W., 237
Athletic activities, 30, 276-277 see also Football season (1966)
Atwood, Will G., Jr., 215
Ayers, Maurice T., 234

Balinky, Alexander S., 52, 53
Ballantine, Catherine Palmer, 213
Banking, Stonier Graduate School of, 260
Barker, Elizabeth Jones, 213
Barnes, William O., 233, 237
Barrow, Thomas, 83
Baskin, Robert, 231
Basler, Roy, 186
Bateman, John F., 214
Battaglia, Felice, 126
Battis, Emery S., 83

Baxendale, John R., 231
Bayerschmidt, Carl F., 273
Bayer, Mrs. John H., 237
Beal, Orville E., 237
Bear, Firman E., 57, 126
Beck, Msgr. Henry C. J., 184, 190
Beddoe, Sally Jo, 231
Begle, Edward S., 62, 63
Behrend, John A., 213
Benjamin, Curtis G., 55
Benjamin, Larry, 231
Bennett, David E., Jr., 217
Bennett, Raymond M., 217
Bergson, Abram, 52, 53
Berson, Harriet Winarsky, 214
Best, Jill M., 231
Bicentennial:
    Commission, vi, vii, viii
    committees, 231-233
    gifts to University, 105, 124, 125,
        139-141, 140
    official history, 155
    proclamation, 4-7, 171-172, 183,
        239
    tributes, 125, 126-129, 141-148, 143,
        145, 147, 152-156, 154, 155, 156,
        185, 198-205
Bicentennial Convocation, 93-123,
    95, 96, 97, 98, 99, 125, 184
Bicknell, Lucille De Angelis, 215
Biel, Dr. Erwin R., 233
Bixby, Frederick L., 39-40
Blackwood, Charles E., 139
Bliss, Sir Arthur, 16, 17
Bloch, Konrad, 65
Bloom, Julius, 20, 233
Blough, Roger M., 26, 27
Bluestone, Robert J., 231
Boehm, Werner W., 250
Bolger, Matthew J., 214
Bond issues, 160, 256, 280
Bonynge, Mrs. Winfield, vi, vii
Boocock, Philip M. B., 40, 215
Bor, Frank, Jr., 217
Borchers, John F., 214

Bowers, Roy A., 218, 250
Boyd, Elizabeth, 233
Boyd, Hugh N., vi, vii
Bragg, Floyd H., 233, 237
Braly, Donald W., 214
Brennan, E. Gaynor, 216
Brennan, Associate Justice
    William J., 66, 67
Brenner, Ardis Guice, 215
Brewster, Kingman, Jr., 127
Brohm, Hsin-min W., 217
Bronk, Detlev W., 98
Brower, Charles H., 40-41, 66, 98,
    100, 147, 216, 229, 236, 237, 273
Brown, Harry A., 213
Brown, Richard M., 83
Bryson, Vernon, 64
Burks, Ardath W., 89
Burlington, Craig, 231
Burton, A. Paul, 213, 233, 237, 273
Bush, Robert R., 273
Business Administration, Graduate
    School of, 37, 166, 178, 236, 246,
    250, 255
Busse, Robert G., 215

Cameron, Donald F., 54, 186, 232
Canfield, William, 31
Canter, Susan, 231
Cap, Mrs. Alma G., 233
Cap and Skull, 185
Carlozzo, Susan E., 231
Cartmell, Peter, 213, 237
Caruso, Elena M., 231
Case, Clifford P., 25-26, 147, 216
Cass, F. Richard, 218
Castle, Mrs. J. Manderson, 183
Castle, Mrs. William, 5
Ceramics Building, 265
Chamberlain, Basil Hall, 91
Chambers, Carl C., 273
Chapman, L. Bernice, 85, 250
Charanis, Peter, 231
Charter Day, 151, 152
Chesnutt, Evelyn Rauch, 215

Choir, 12, 47, 269
Christenson, Thomas G., Jr., 173
Ciardi, John, 55
Clark, Walter W., 213
Clevenger, Doris Johnson, 216
Clifford, Earle W., Jr., 25, 139, 234
Clothier, Robert, 187
Coffey, Katherine F., 41
Cohen, S. S., 65
College Hall, 265
Colleges *see* specific name of college
　or field of study
Collins, Basil E., 217
Collinson, D. W., 84
Comfort, W. W., 61
Commencement exercises (1966),
　35-50, 184
Community Affairs, Bureau of, 168,
　259-260
Comstock, Robert R., 213
Cone, Edward T., 273
Conferences, viii, 52-53, 57, 59,
　59-61, 61-64, 64-65, 69-83, 84,
　86-88, 88-92, 183, 184, 185
Connelly, Maureen F., 231
Conover, Bonnie A., 213
Conover, Brevoort C., 214
Conservation and Environmental
　Service, Bureau of, 262, 270
Contemporary Chamber Ensemble,
　19-21, 167, 269
Cook, Albert Stanburrough, 127
Cooper, Rev. Jacob, 127
Cooper Hall, 265
Cost, Dorothy Q., 233
Countess, Richard J., 231
Cowan, Thomas A., 218
Cox, Archibald, 28-29, 29
Cox, Judith Ann, 214
Crabiel, Edward J., vi
Crawford, Norman P., 186
Creager, Paul S., 216
Crochet, Evelyne, 20
Cross, John M., 232
Crystal, Herman, 233

Cubberley, Edward E., 214
Cultural events, 269-270
Cunningham, John, 190

Dagnall, Marie Lou Lindemann, 216
Dauber, Edward J., 22, 231
Davies, Rees E., 215
Davis, C. Malcolm, 87-88
Dechowitz, Fred L., 215
Dederbeck, Frank W., 218
Degrees awarded (1966), 245-247,
　250
Demarest, G. Stuart, 250
Denker, David D., 234
De Podwin, Horace J., 250
Derby, Harry L., 237, 273
De Witt, Simeon, 207
Dickerson, Donald M., 237
Dickinson, Merv, 175
Dickinson, William A., IV, 173
Dietz, Robert S., 84
Dillon, Douglas, 237
Dorian, Edith McEwen, 215
Dormitories, 264, 265, 266
Douglass, Mable Smith, 254
Douglass College, 29, 30, 36, 38, 50,
　139, 177, 183, 184, 188, 192, 213,
　235, 245, 247, 250, 254, 263, 265,
　276, 277, 278, 280
　programs of study, 241-242
Drake, Charles, 84
Drama Festival, 183
Drinkwater, David, 20
Dubos, Rene, 69, 75-78
Dukas, Paul, 18
Dulin, Jim, 33
Dunn, Richard S., 83
Dunne, Liam, 37
Durand, James B., 232
Durham, Elizabeth, vi, 36, 146
Durufle, Maurice and Marie-
　Madeleine, 20
Dvorin, James R., 231

Eagleton, Dr. and Mrs. Wells P., 259

Eagleton Institute of Politics, 120, 167, 235, 259, 263, 266
Easton, Elmer C., 87, 250
Eckert, Fred, 33
Economic Research, Bureau of, 260, 270
Edmonds, Donald R., 216
Education, Graduate School of, 36, 177, 235, 246, 250, 254, 261, 271, 272
Ekstrom, J. Fredrik, 232
Ellis, Albert, 184
Ellis, Mrs. Geraldine, 85
Ellison, Ralph W., 41-42
Emmer, Jack, 33, 34
Engineering, College of, 36, 87, 176, 184, 235, 246, 250, 267
Engineering Building, 163, 264
Engineering Research, Bureau of, 261, 270
Ennis, Lois Brown, 215
Ennis, Roger N., 215
Epstein, Jerome R., 216
Epstein, Miriam Feinsod, 216
"Et Occidentem Illustra" (choral work), 9, 10-12, 185
Ewing, Mrs. Marian G., 233
Extension Division, University, 186, 235, 250, 254, 260

Faculty statistics, 251-252
Falkin, Gary L., 21-22, 22, 231
Fantini, Mario, 88
Farrier, Robert M., 85
Fasmer, Hendrik, 16
Federation Hall, 265
Fehl, Noah E., 128
Feltman, Michael, 231
Ferguson, Clarence Clyde, Jr., 42
Finardi, Eloise Degenring, 217
Finifter, Stuart B., 231
Fischelis, Robert P., 218
Fisk, Barbara L., 231
Fjeldstad, Oivin, 15
Flanagan, Theodore R., 216

Flershem, Robert G., 90
Football season (1966), 21, 31, 32-34, 239
Ford Hall, 264
Forman, Phillip, 237
Fortas, Associate Justice Abe, 66, 67
Francis, David W., 215
Frankel, N. Ralph, 214
Franklin, Mary d'Evelin, 5
Franklin, William, 5, 7, 151, 183, 239, 252
Franklin Conklin Hall, 165
Frase, Robert W., 55
Frelinghuysen, Frederick, 219, 252
Frelinghuysen, Theodore, 10, 11, 105, 205, 252
French, J. Milton, 190
Friedlander, Jerome M., 216
Friedman, Marvin, 136
Friendly, Judge Henry J., 66
Fritzsche, Stephen J., 231

Galbraith, Robert E., 217
Gardner, Ernest T., 232, 233
Gardner, Richard N., 183
Gaskill, William J., 237
Gaver, Mary V., 55, 193
Gawarecki, Carolyn Grosse, 214
Geisler, Thomas M., 137, 233, 237
Genovese, Eugene D., 110, 158, 226-231
Geological Hall, 264
Giffen, Sue, 216
Gilliland, William N., 84, 250
Gilluly, James, 84
Gimson, Douglas E., 228
Gleason, Andrew M., 62, 63
Glee Club, 9, 47, 184
  European tour, 13, 172-176
Glick, Sara Holtzman, 216
Godlewski, Stanley P., 237
Goheen, Robert F., 148-151, 151, 160, 218-222, 256
Goldmann, Judge Sidney, 273
Goldsmith, Janice L., 232

Goodman, Paul, 66
Goodwin, Robert, 215
Gordon, Allen I., 216
Gordon, John F., 213
Gordon, Julia Weber, 42-43
Gorlin, Joan F., 232
Governors, Board of, 23, 226-230,
    236-237, 255, 257, 268, 278
Graduate Education Advisory
    Board for Research and,
    273-274
Graduate School, The, 36, 177, 235,
    250
Graduate schools *see* specific name
    of school or field of study
Granstrom, Marvin L., 233
Greenberg, Marvin W., 232
Greenberg, William, 67
Greenbaum, Margo S., 232
Griffis, William Elliot, 88, 89, 90, 91,
    92, 277
Grobman, Arnold B., 250
Gross, Mrs. Mason, 233
Gross, Mason W., 15, 16, 17, 18, 20,
    23, 24, 58, 69, 94, 98, 100, 118,
    124, 139, 147, 148, 161, 185, 190,
    216, 218, 234, 237, 238
    commencement address, 48-49,
    178-182
    Holland Society award, 133-134,
    148, 205-213
    Newcomen Society award, 133-134
    other addresses, 81-83, 101-105
    Salmagundi Club award, 129-133,
    130, 183
Gruninger, Frederick E., 147, 215
"Gymnasium Series," 269

Haber, David, 67
Hackett, John D., 215
Hadas, Moses, 273
Hall, Justice Frederick, vii, viii
Hall, Michael G., 83
Hall, W. Layton, 232, 250
Hallahan, Charles J., Jr., 232

Halsey, Carole A., 232
Hamond, John, 19
Handler, Philip, 65
Hanpole, Martin S., 217
Hardenbergh, Jacob Rutsen, 48, 105,
    253
Hardies, Ted, 232
Harding, Bruce, 216
Hardy, David W., 173
Harlow, Neal, 250
Harris, Sheldon, 19
Harris, Sidney L., 214
Harris, Wilma M., 232
Hasbrouck, Abraham Bruyn, 127
Hatfield, C. Lyman, 215
Hauptman, Harvey J., 214
Hazard, John, 52, 53
Hazel, Homer, 33
Hearn, Edward R., 232
Heckel, C. Willard, 66, 250
Heezen, Bruce, 84
Heller, Harold, 214
Henry E. Ackerson Hall, 52, 65-68,
    266
Henry Rutgers bell, 4, 182
Heranney, David L., 173
Herkness, Walter W., Jr., 213
Heschel, Rabbi Abraham Joseph, 185
Hess, Harry, 84
Hess, William H., 233
Hewlett, Gregory, 237
Higgins, Marion West, vii, viii
Hill, Bessie Nelms, 229, 237
Hitchner, Wilbert B., 213
Hoffman, Barnett E., 216
Hoffman, Diane Brod, 216
Hoffman, Robert P., 216
Hollingsworth, Helen Platt, 215
Holopigian, Lynn A., 232
Holsten, George H., Jr., 232, 233,
    234
Holstrom, Lt. Col. F. M. G., 60
Holt, Richard D., 214
Honorary degrees (1966), 38-50, 67,
    109-110

Hook, Sidney, 66
Hopkins, L. Nelson, Jr., 215
Horowitz, Vladimir, 9, 13-15, 239
Houghtaling, Earle, 216
Hughes, Richard J., viii, 4-7, 6, 66,
    95, 98, 100, 103, 107-109, 108,
    110, 118, 158, 171-172, 183, 239
Hulst, A. R., 95, 105-107
Humphrey, Hubert H., 94, 95, 98,
    100, 109-110, 111, 113, 118
    Bicentennial convocation address,
    112-123
Hurdle, Kenneth B., 232
Hurst, Victor, 216
Hutchens, John K., 56, 188
Hutchins, Robert M., 66

Illig, Rudolph F., 216
Information Processing, Center for,
    260, 271
Information Sciences Research,
    Bureau of, 262
Ingham, Van Wie, vi, 36, 146, 233
Institute of Continuing Legal
    Education, 42, 260
Intercollegiate student conference,
    21, 22, 25-29, 183
Interdisciplinary Research Center,
    261-262, 271
Irwin, Joseph C., 213
Irwin, Muriel De Rose, 213
Isbell, J. R., 62
Ishizuki, Prof. Minoru, 91

Jackson, Francis, 20
Jacobs, Andrew, 232
Jacobson, Joel R., 229, 237
Jaffer, Naomi Stern, 215
Jahnke, Otto C., 214
James, Alan, 187
Jamison, Rev. Wallace C., 141
Jansak, Paul J., 216
Japan-Rutgers Conference, viii,
    88-92
Jazz concerts, 18-19

Jazz Studies, Institute of, 18-19, 167
Jessen, Elizabeth, 233
Joffe, Jacob S., 186
John Cotton Dana Library, 165
Johnson, Franklyn A., 214
Johnson, Helgi, 84
Johnston, James A., 232
Jones, Hazel J., 90, 91
Jones, Walter H., vi, vii
Judson, Margaret A., 250
Jurgensen, Charles A., 229, 237

Kagan, Benjamin, 232
Kahn, Milton, 237
Kamin, Arthur Z., 213
Kammen, Michael G., 83
Kanai, Madoka, 92
Kandle, Roscoe, P., 59
Kandravy, George, 232
Kaneko, Tadashi, 91
Kaplan, Robert, 233
Katz, Stanley, 83
Katzenbach, Mrs. Edward L., 237
Kempf, Carl L., 216
Kennan, George F., 43
Kepner, M. Donald, 232
Kerr, Chester, 55
King, Philip, 84
Kingsbury, William F., 217
Kirk, Grayson, 127
Kirkland, Max, 279
Kirkpatrick Chapel, 5, 20, 83, 141,
    183, 264, 269
Kline, Eugene M., 19
Klinger, Edmond, 232
Knies, Lt. Col. Arthur S., 217
Knight, Robert L., 216
Knopoff, Leon, 84
Knox, Patricia Mate, 213
Kramer, George A., 234, 240
Kramer, Col. Vincent, 153, 222, 233
Kreeger, David L., 214
Kreyns, Stephen M., 214
Kriendler, I. Robert, 216, 237
Kughler, Francis V., 129, 130

Kunishima, Kokichi, 217
Kusakabe, Taro, 91-92
Kwast, Wobbina, 172

Lacy, Dan, 55
Lampen, Dr. J. Oliver, 64
Langlykke, Asger F., 273
Laraja, Ann Priory, 216
Lasswell, Harold, 66
Law, School of (Camden), 167, 250, 255, 263, 272
Law, School of (Newark), 36, 52, 165, 177, 184, 236, 250, 255, 263, 268, 272
Lectures, 183, 184, 185, 270
Lefever, David P., 232
Lehrman, Daniel S., 166
Leinsdorf, Erich, 10, 12, 185
Leis, Henry J., 232
Lenkey, John III, 152-155, 222-226
Lentz, L. James, 232
Letson, Stanley W., 215
Le Veck, John G., 231
Levin, Philip J., 237, 238
Levine, William, 218, 233, 238
Levis, Richard, 137, 233
Lewis, Willard D., 43-44
Leydt, Matthew, 35, 36, 253
Library Service, Graduate School of, 37, 178, 185, 235, 250, 262, 272
Library system, 235, 262-263
Liefeld, Grace M., 233
Linder, Robert, 214
Lindquist, Doris Libby, 215
Lipman, Jacob, 126
Lipman Hall, 266
Lipmann, Fritz, 65
Liston, Edward, 232
Little, Ernest E., 218
Livingston, John Henry, 50, 105, 106, 127
Livingston, Sir Richard, 219-220
Livingston College, 164-165, 164, 165, 250, 268-269

Loftus, Martin J., 218
Logan, William, Jr., 217
Logsdon, Richard H., 273
Lombardy, Jay, 214
Loree, Leonor F., 133
Lowenstein, Richard A., 215
Lozier, G. Gregory, 173
Lukac, George J., 146, 233, 274
Lukowsky, Jeffrey D., 232
Lundberg, Harold G., 137
Lusardi, Robert G., 233
Luthman, Rev. Carl A., 214
Luthman, Susan Gahs, 214
Lycan, William H., 273
Lynch, John A., vii, viii
Lynen, Feodor, 65
Lynton, Ernest A., 250
Lyons, Paul, 84

Mace, ceremonial, 139-141, 140
Madden, Thomas A., 213
Main, Charles F., Jr., 233
Management and Labor Relations, Institute of, 260, 263, 271
March, Stanley R., 216
Martin, Albina, 215
Masciuli, Leo, 232
Mason, Marilyn, 232
Masqueteers, 30, 269
Massel, Mark S., 66
Matsu, Arthur A., 214
Matsumoto, Shigeharu, 44
Matthes, Richard W., 173
Mattia, V. D., 238, 273
Maxwell, John C., 84
McAuley, Louis F., 61
McBride, Robert H., 214
McCarty, Harry J., 154
McCormick, Richard P., 6, 83, 139, 155-156, 156, 207, 231, 233, 274
McCulloch, Samuel C., 214
McDermott, Keith E., 232
McDonald, John F., 233
McDonall, Leslie G., 233
McDougal, Myres S., 66

McIntyre, William G., 213
McMahon, Ernest E., 186, 218, 233, 250
McMillen, Wheeler, 69, 70-73, 77
Meder, Albert E., Jr., 62, 98, 99, 233, 234
Medical School, Rutgers, 37, 85, 161-163, 162, 178, 185, 189, 235, 250, 263, 267, 271
Meetings, 184
Menard, H. W., 84
Mendrey, Francis G., 213
Menker, Stanley, 232
Merrill, Leland G., Jr., 250
Metzger, Karl E., 232, 234, 237, 238
Meury, John N., 216
Meyer, Frank S., 29
Microbiology, Institute of, 64, 184, 235, 258-259, 263, 267, 271
Miers, Earl Schenck, 54, 55, 186, 187, 193, 233
Migdal, Joel, 232
Millard, Donald A., 215, 238
Milledoler Hall, 264
Miller, Randolph J., 232
Miller, Samuel J., 185
Miller, William Christian, 44-45, 238
Millett, Barry M., 172, 173
Mitchell. Alan G., 213, 238
Mitchell, Mrs. William A., 238
Moevs, Robert, 9, 10, 11, 12, 96, 185
Montgomery, Deane, 273
Moon, Ridgeway V. C., 214
Moore, Geoffrey H., 273
Moreland, Wallace S., Jr., 215
Morgan, Gladstone W., 217
Morrill Act, 257
Morris, Richard B., 83
Morse, Roy Earl, 273
Mosston, Moshe, 279
Motoyama, Yukihiko, 90
Moxon, Rosamond Sawyer, 213, 229, 237, 238
Muccilli, Philip C., 230, 237, 238
Munger, Harold, 187

Murray, David, 91
Murray Hall, 264
Musical events, 9-20, 29, 30, 96, 167, 239, 269-270
Musto, William V., 228

Nagel, Gerald J., 217
Nagle, Claire W., 238
Nannes, Caspar Harold, 45, 214
National Football Hall of Fame, 32
Neidhart, Helen Stratton, 214
Nelson Biological Laboratories, 163, 267
New Jersey College for Women (later Douglass College), 254, 258
New Jersey School Development Council, 261, 272
Newark, University of, (later Rutgers-Newark), 255
Newark-Rutgers College of Arts and Sciences, 29, 30, 36, 139, 165, 166, 177, 183, 184, 189, 236, 246, 250, 261, 263, 268, 277
Newcomen Society award, 133-134
Newman, Howard, 213
Nichols, Roy F., 230, 232, 237, 238, 273
Northrop, F. S. C., 131
Nursing, College of, 85, 178, 185, 236, 246, 247, 250, 255
Nusbaum, Sidney G., 232

Olson, Alison, 83
O'Neill, John J., 250
Orlick, Joseph E., 215
Owen, Robert I., 217
Ozzard, William E., viii

Palmieri, Thomas M., 232
Pane, Remigio U., 233
Parke, John R., 173
Pawa, Irving, 232, 234
Peckar, Robert, 232
Pecora, William T., 84, 273

Periale, James G., 215
Peterson, Houston, 213, 233
Pfister, Frederick W., 238
Pharmaceutical Extension Service, 261
Pharmacy, College of, 36, 177, 185, 236, 250, 254, 255, 263, 268, 272
Philbrick, Herbert A., 185
Phillips, William, 274
Pickering, Sir George, 93, 94, 95
Pittendrigh, Colin S., 69, 78-80, 81
Plager, A. L., 214
Plumb, J. H., 83
Polacsik, Mary, 232
Pomper, Gerald M., 279
Poole, Robert F., 216
Powell, Agnes T., 216
Powell, Richard A., 217
Price, J. Russell, 140
Publications, 57, 138, 188, 190, 191, 274

Queen's Building, 3, 4, 182, 264
Queen's College (later Rutgers), 5, 7, 36, 37, 83, 127, 136, 137, 141, 151, 171, 176, 178, 189, 206, 207, 218, 219, 252, 253
Queens Theater Guild, 269

Racker, Efraim, 65
Radiation Sciences Center, 235, 261, 271
Radio and television activities, 278-279
Raitano, Marilyn, 214
Rand, Ayn, 24, 25
Raubinger, Frederick M., 237, 238
Ray, Gordon N., 273
Reager, Richard C., 186
Records Hall, 83
Reilly, Hilda Christine, 45-46
Reitman, Norman, 238, 274
Renne, Roland R., 58
Repp, Robert N., 217

Research and Graduate Education, Advisory Board for, 273-274
Research Council, 54, 270
Reuther, Walter P., 26, 27
Reynolds, George T., 274
Ricciardi, Amalia S., 218
Rich, Alexander, 65
Richardson, Charles O., 279
Richardson, Roy M. D., 230, 237, 238
Riche, Frances E., 233
Ridgeway, James, 184
Riedel, Eric R., 173, 175
Roach, Anne E., 232
Roberts, R. B., 65
Robinson, Dorothy, 232
Robinson, Frank S., 213
Robinson, James A., 66
Roe, Robert A., 59
Rogers, Diane Daly, 213
Rogosin, Israel, 46
Romano, Michael T., 69, 80-81
Ropke, Edgar L., 233
Rose, Leon, 215
Rosen, Gene, 232
Rosenberg, Joel, 232
Ross, Anne Schnepel, 215
Ross, Kenneth, 214
Rotgun, Lawrence M., 232
Rothen, Marshall G., 214
Rovner, Louise, 214
Rose, Thomas D., 218
Rubinstein, Prof. Aldin Z., 185
Rudestam, Rolf, 22-23, 232
Rutgers, Colonel Henry, 3, 8, 33, 37, 190, 253
Rutgers—From the Inside (film), 148
Rutgers Alumni Monthly, 146
Rutgers Athletic News, 31
Rutgers College of Arts and Sciences, 30, 36, 176, 183, 184, 189, 192, 218, 234, 241, 246, 247, 250, 272, 278
Rutgers Medal award, 150, 151

"Rutgers Night Around the World"
143-148, 143, 144, 145, 147, 185,
213-218, 223
Rutgers Preparatory School, 40, 253
Rutgers University,
admissions, 240-241
Board of Governors, 23, 39, 226-
230, 236-237, 255, 257, 268, 278
Board of Trustees, 44, 237-238,
257, 258
capital expenditures, 267-269
charter, 7, 83, 252
coat of arms, 37, 98, 99
component units, 234-236, 250
degrees awarded, 245-247
documentary film on, 148
Dutch heritage, 106-107, 173, 218
early presidents, 127
education costs, 247-249
faculty statistics, 251-252
foundation grants, 19, 20, 259,
269
founding of, 3, 7, 37
gonfalons of, 36-37, 98, 176-178
history, 252-256
income and expenditure (1966),
275
land-grant college, 8, 37, 133, 190,
253-254, 257
Motto, 10, 141, 173, 176, 234
New Jersey State University, 159,
161, 171, 190, 254, 255, 256-258
officers, 234
operating budget, 190
plans for expansion, 161-169
physical plant, 263-269
programs of study, 241-243
research and scholarship, 270-273
seals of, 31, 141, 234
specialized divisions, 258-262
student enrollment, 243-245, 250,
255-256
see also names of colleges and
fields of study
Rutgers University Press, 53, 274

anniversary convention, 54-56,
184, 186-188, 188-193
publications, 188, 190, 191, 274
Rutgers University Wind
Ensemble, 96

Sagotsky, Barry J., 232
Sahloff, Willard A., 238
Sakata, Yoshio, 91
Savidge, Edgar T., 238
Schanck Observatory, 264
Scheffer, H. M. J., 13, 174
Scheidegger, A. E., 84
Scherer, Everett, vii, viii
Schlatter, Richard, 85, 86-87, 97, 187,
192, 232, 233, 234, 274
Schlesinger, R. W., 65
Schlotfeldt, Rozella M., 85
Schnefel, Susan E., 232
Scholarships, 247, 248, 249, 273
Schreiber, David C., 138
Schreihofer, Capt. Alan G., 217
Schurmann, Carl W. A., 95
Schwartz, Edwin J., 214
Scott, Austin, 127
Scott Hall, 142
Sedita, Salvatore J., 215
Seeley, Robert D., 215
Seminars *see* Conferences; Lectures
Seth Boyden Hall, 165
Shangold, Mark, 174
Shapley, Harlow, 184
Shilling, Abbott, 214
Short Course Building, 265
Shugg, Roger W., 187
Shulman, Mark D., 59
Sibley, Walter C., 233
Siegel, Julian A., 214
Sills, Arthur J., 46-47
Silvers, Earl Reed, 54, 186
Simon, Morton S., 232
Simpkins, Charles F., 232
Sinclair, Donald A., 233
Sitzmann, Thomas G., 232
Sizer, Irwin W., 238, 274

Slade, James J., 216
Slater, Terry, 232
Sloane, William, 54, 55, 186-188, 190, 191, 233
Smith, Barbara, 233
Smith, Frederic W., 238
Smith, W. Douglas, 217
Smith, Judge William F., 218
Social Work, Graduate School of, 36, 178, 235, 250, 265, 272
Soil Science, 57, 274
Soleri, Paolo, 69, 74
Sorkin, Stanley, 232
South Jersey, College of, 29, 30, 139, 167, 178, 183, 184, 185, 189, 213, 236, 243, 246, 250, 255, 263, 268, 276, 277
Spear, Peter D., 232
Spencer, Dickson, 232
St. Lawrence, J., 60
Stark, Harry F., 233
Starnes, Ordway, 143, 217
Statistics Center, 260
Stearns, Marshall W., 19
Steinberg, William, 17
Steinbock, Jose A., 233
Stern, Barrie S., 232
Stetten, DeWitt, Jr., 85, 163, 250
Stevens, Donald E., 233
Stevens, Edwin L., 186
Stevens, Norman D., 234
Stewart, Helen, 190
Stonier Graduate School of Banking, 260
Student,
    Bicentennial participation, 21-34, 232-233
    employment, 248-249
    enrollment, 243-245, 250, 255-256
    exchange program, 277-278
    newspaper, 228
    organizations, 21, 22, 31, 67, 276-277
    services, 276-277
Student Bar Association, 67

Student Council, 21, 22, 31
Sullivan, Fred R., viii
Sutton, Prof. Robert B., 216
Sweoka, Dr. Noborw, 65
Swift, Arthur C., 213
Swink, John L., 232, 234, 237, 238
Symposia (Bicentennial Year), 52-92
    see also Conferences; Lectures
Szasz, Gus, 139

Talbott, Malcolm D., 85, 86, 213, 232, 234
Tanaka, Hisako, 92
Tanzman, Norman, viii
Targum, 228
Tate, Herbert H., 238
Taub, Rita Farrer, 214
Taylor, Donald J., 214
Taylor, George V., 216
Taylor, Ralph L., 232
Taylor, Mrs. S. Herbert, 238
Tedrow, John C. F., 152
Temple, Samuel B., 215
Terango, Bernadette, 217
Thayer, Theodore, 83
Thomann, Robert V., 58
Thomas, C. A., 65
Thomas, Donald, 214
Thomas, Norman, 29
Torrey, Henry C., 250
Travisano, Frank P., 213
Tretheway, Bruce T., 213
Tributes, Bicentennial,
    by alumni, 143-148, 143, 144, 145, 147, 152-156, 154, 155, 156
    by educational institutions, 125, 126-129, 141-142, 142, 198-205
    by learned societies, 129-136, 198-205
    by others, 137-138, 185
Trinka, Frank G., 217
Trokan, Josef, 129
Trustees, Board of, 237-238, 257, 258
Tuckwell, Barry, 15
Twitchell, Albert W., 147, 215

Tyson, Cyril, 88

Umetani, Noboru, 90
Underhill, A. Heaton, 58
Underwood, George B., 238
Unger, Leslie H., 147, 215
University College, 30, 177, 183, 235, 243, 247, 250, 254
University Extension Division, 186, 235, 250, 254, 260
Urban Studies, Center of, 120, 167, 235, 259, 271

Van Dyck Hall, 265
Van Heuvelen, Allen, 215
Van Iderstine, Mary Lou Farry, 214
Van Nest Building, 264
Venables, Thomas G., 232
Vhugen, Harold F., 216
Vogel, Helen Eldridge, 214
Vogel, Henry J., 64
Voorhees, Elizabeth Rodman, 265
Voorhees, Tracy S., 238
Voorhees Hall, 168, 169, 264, 265, 269, 270

Wagner, Aubrey J., 69, 73-74
Wagner, Rev. C. Peter, 217
Wagner, Mrs. Douglas G., viii
Wagner, Margaret Denton, 213
Waksman, Selman A., 64, 69, 125, 259
Waksman Hall, 64, 266, 268
Walter, F. Austin, 12, 47, 50, 172, 173, 174, 175, 185, 233
Walton, Grant F., 152
Ward, Chester, 216
Warren, Chief Justice Earl, 52, 65, 67, 193-198
Wasserman, David R., 232
Water Resources Research Institute, 58, 167, 262, 271, 272
Webber, Neil S., 232
Weber, Thomas, 233

Weiker, Walter F., 29
Weinrich, Carl, 20
Weintraub, Joseph, Chief Justice, N.J., 66
Weisenfeld, Allan, 47
Welsh, James W., 232
Went, Fritz W., 60-61
Werblin, David A., 216, 238
Wescott, Lloyd B., 274
Wettstein, Elizabeth Smedley, 213
Wheeler, Monroe, 274
Whipple, Brig. Gen. William, Jr., 58
Wigner, Eugene P., 61
Wiles, Peter, 52, 53
Williams, David Alan, 83
Wilson, Billy Ray, 70
Wilson, J. Tuzo, 84
Windeler, Robert R., 215
Winkler, Henry R., 231, 274
Winter, Daniel T., 215
Winterling, Grace M., 238
Wolf, Dale E., 214
Wolfson, Benjamin, 238, 274
Woloszyn, John J., 232
Woodbury, Brig. Gen. Jarry G., Jr., 58
Woodward, Herbert P., 213, 232
World's Fair salute, 23, 31, 139
Wright, Barbara E., 232
Wright, Paul M. G., 151, 218
Wright Chemistry Laboratory, 163, 266, 267
Wurtzel, Ruth Mann, 216

Yanitelli, Rev. Victor Robert, S.J., 48
Ylvisaker, Paul N., 87
Yung, C. T., 128

Zagoria, Samuel, 214
Zaldivar, Javier, 217
Ziegler, Frederick O., 213, 238
Zimmerman, Ernest R., 233